Democracy by Force
US Military Intervention in the Post-Cold War World

Since the end of the Cold War the international community, and the USA in particular, has intervened in a series of civil conflicts around the world. In a number of cases, where actions such as economic sanctions or diplomatic pressures have failed, military interventions have been undertaken. This book examines four US-sponsored interventions (Panama, Somalia, Haiti, and Bosnia), focusing on efforts to reconstruct the state which have followed military action. Such nation-building is vital if conflict is not to recur. In each of the four cases, Karin von Hippel considers the factors which led the USA to intervene, the path of military intervention, and the nation-building efforts which followed. The book seeks to provide a greater understanding of the successes and failures of US policy, to improve strategies for reconstruction, and to provide some insight into the conditions under which intervention and nation-building are likely to succeed.

KARIN VON HIPPEL is Political Advisor to the Representative of the UN Secretary-General for Somalia. She was a MacArthur Post-Doctoral Associate at King's College London in 1995–6, and Project Manager for the Complex Emergencies Unit at the Centre for Defence Studies, King's College London. She is the author of several journal articles, book chapters, and reports for the European Commission.

Democracy by Force

US Military Intervention in the Post-Cold War World

Karin von Hippel

CAMBRIDGE
UNIVERSITY PRESS

PUBLISHED BY THE PRESS SYNDICATE OF THE UNIVERSITY OF CAMBRIDGE
The Pitt Building, Trumpington Street, Cambridge, United Kingdom

CAMBRIDGE UNIVERSITY PRESS
The Edinburgh Building, Cambridge CB2 2RU, UK
http://www.cup.cam.ac.uk.
40 West 20th Street, New York, NY 10011-4211, USA   http://www.cup.org
10 Stamford Road, Oakleigh, Melbourne 3166, Australia

First published 2000

Printed in the United Kingdom at the University Press, Cambridge

Typeset in Monotype Plantin 10/12 pt. [wv]

A catalogue record for this book is available from the British Library

Library of Congress Cataloguing-in-Publication Data
von Hippel, Karin.
Democrary by Force: US military intervention in the Post-Cold War World
Karin von Hippel
        p.   cm.
Includes bibliographical references (p.).
ISBN 0 521 65051 8. ISBN 0 521 65955 8 (pbk.)
1. United States–Foreign relations–1989–2. Intervention (International law)
I. Title.   E840.V63 1999   327.73–dc21   99-12838   CIP

ISBN 0 521 65051 8 hardback
ISBN 0 521 65955 8 paperback

Table of Contents

Maps

Acknowledgements

This research has been conducted under the auspices of the project, Regional Security in a Global Context, in the Department of War Studies, King's College London (KCL), with funding provided by the John D. and Catherine T. MacArthur Foundation. Special thanks go to a number of individuals for their assistance on different sections of this book. For Panama, US Ambassador William Crowe, Dr Roy Licklider (Rutgers University), and Professor Eli Lauterpacht (Cambridge University); for Somalia, Sagal M. Abshir, Dr Babafemi Badejo (UNPOS), Matt Bryden (WSP), Professor Walter Clarke (Army War College), Kyla Evans, Dr Bernhard Helander (Uppsala University), Professor Jeffrey Herbst (Princeton University), Sigurd Illing (EC Special Envoy), Professor Kenneth Menkhaus (Davidson College), David Stephen (RSG, UNPOS), and Dr Alexandros Yannis; for Haiti, Dr Mats Berdal (Oxford University), Anne Bonifanti (UNMIH), Lakhdar Brahimi (SRSG, UNMIH), Tom Carothers (Carnegie Endowment for International Peace), Colonel Doug Daniels and members of the 445th Civil Affairs Battalion (UNMIH), DPKO in New York, Dave Eckerson (USAID), Eric Falt (UNMIH), Nicole Lannegrace (UNMIH), Tayeb Merchoug (UNMIH), Neil Pouliot (UNMIH), General Sir David Ramsbotham, and other civilian and military personnel at UNMIH for their assistance and generosity; for Bosnia, Dr Richard Caplan (Oxford University), Dr James Gow (KCL), Dr Amir Pasic (Brown University), and Jane M.O. Sharp (CDS).

General thanks go to Dr Charles Alao (KCL), Marc Arnold, Dr Chris Bellamy for titular assistance (Shrivenham), Dr Jarat Chopra (Brown University), Professor Christopher Dandeker (KCL), Dr Mark Duffield (Birmingham), Paris Foot, Nolan Frederick, Professor Lawrence Freedman (KCL), Pedro Gonzalez, Judy Graham, Dr Malory Greene (OECD), Don Hawkins, Steven Hellman, Graham Horder, Dr Hela Husek, Jeanne Irwin, Dr Peter Viggo Jakobsen (University of Copenhagen), Dr Randolph Kent (CDS), Lars and Carol Kørschen (Peponi), Lisa Ann Kurbiel (OLS-UNICEF), Vinca LaFleur, Dr Roy

Licklider (again), Dr John Mackinlay (KCL), Professor James Mayall (Cambridge University), Dr Jaime Medal, Professor Brendan O'Leary (LSE), Dr 'Funmi Olonisakin (KCL), Fiona Paton, Bill Reinking, Dr Chris Smith (CDS), Jen Smith (CDS), Dr Mike Smith (KCL), Carol Spagg, Dr Joanna Spear (KCL), Dr Claire Spencer (CDS), Jerry Vittoria, Susy and Tarik Wildman, Lt. Col. Phil Wilkinson (MOD), Sue Willets, Vittore Zanardi, Dr Alexandros Yannis (again), and my family – the Drs von Hippel.

A final and very special thanks to Professor Michael Clarke, Executive Director of the Centre for Defence Studies (CDS), for his support during the final stages of completion of this book, and John Haslam, Nicole Webster and Carol Fellingham Webb of Cambridge University Press. As always, I take full responsibility for the views expressed here.

Abbreviations

CA	Civil Affairs
CIA	Central Intelligence Agency
CIMIC	Civil-Military Co-ordination
CINC	Commander-in-Chief
CIVPOL	UN Civilian Police training unit
CMOC	Civil-Military Operations Center
CMOTF	Civil-Military Operations Task Force
CSCE	Conference on Security and Cooperation in Europe
DEA	Drug Enforcement Agency
DOD	Department of Defense
DPKO	Department of Peacekeeping Operations
EC	European Commission
ECOMOG	ECOWAS Monitoring Group
ECOWAS	Economic Community of West African States
EU	European Union
FRY	Federal Republic of Yugoslavia
GOH	Government of Haiti
GOP	Government of Panama
HDR	Human Development Report
HNP	Haitian National Police
ICFY	International Conference on the Former Yugoslavia
ICITAP	International Criminal Investigative Training Assistance Program
IDP	Internally Displace Person
IFOR	Implementation Force
IGAD	Inter-Governmental Authority on Development
IPSF	Interim Public Security Force (Haiti)
IPTF	International Police Task Force (Bosnia)
JAP	Joint Action Programme
JNA	Yugoslav People's Army
LSE	London School of Economics and Political Science
MAD	Mutually Assured Destruction

MICIVIH	International Civilian Mission in Haiti
MIPONUH	UN Civilian Police Mission in Haiti
MNF	Multi-National Force
MOOTW	Military Operations Other Than War
MSG	Military Support Group
NATO	North Atlantic Treaty Organisation
NGO	Non-Governmental Organisation
OAS	Organization of American States
OAU	Organization of African Unity
OECD	Organisation for Economic Cooperation and Development
OIC	Organisation of the Islamic Conference
OSCE	Organization for Security and Cooperation in Europe
PDF	Panamanian Defense Forces
PRD	Democratic Revolutionary Party (Panama)
PSYOPS	Psychological Operations
P5	Permanent members of the Security Council (China, France, Russia, the United Kingdom and the United States)
QUANGO	Quasi-NGO
SACB	Somalia Aid Coordination Body
SFOR	Stabilization Force
SRSG	Special Representative of the Secretary-General
TNC	Transitional National Council
UNCRO	UN Confidence Restoration Operation
UNDP	UN Development Programme
UNHCR	UN High Commission for Refugees
UNITAF	Unified Task Force
UNMIH	UN Mission in Haiti
UNOSOM	UN Operation in Somalia
UNPROFOR	UN Protection Force
UNSMIH	UN Support Mission in Haiti
UNTAES	UN Transitional Authority in Eastern Slavonia, Baranja and Western Sirmium
UNTMIH	UN Transition Mission in Haiti
USAID	US Agency for International Development
WEU	Western European Union
WTO	World Trade Organisation

1   Introduction: dangerous hubris

It is a dangerous hubris to believe we can build other nations. But where our own interests are engaged, we can help nations build themselves – and give them time to make a start at it.[1]

This remark, by former US National Security Adviser Anthony Lake, aptly depicts the policy of cautious engagement embraced by the US administration since the botched Somalia intervention. When US marines landed on the beaches of Mogadishu in December 1992, international euphoria about building a 'new world order', led by the lone Superpower, was at its peak due to the demise of communism and the defeat of Saddam Hussein. However much the Somalia debacle may have altered the US approach to nation-building, as Vietnam did to the generation before, it in no way aborted it. The US administration and military have been involved in nation-building[2] and promoting democracy since the middle of the nineteenth century and 'Manifest Destiny'.[3] Another failed intervention could not reverse over one hundred years of American experience.

---

[1] Anthony Lake, Assistant to the President for National Security Affairs, Remarks at George Washington University, 'Defining Missions, Setting Deadlines: Meeting New Security Challenges in the Post-Cold War World', 6 March 1996.

[2] The term 'nation' in fact signifies what is known as a 'state', but in the United States, the term 'state' gets confused with the fifty states that comprise the USA. Although the term 'nation-building' incorrectly depicts what the US government is attempting to do, as it rarely strives to create a nation, inhabited by peoples of the same collective identity, this term has become synonymous with state-building. For example, when the US government and the UN attempted to rebuild Somalia, they did not try to reunite all Somalis living in Djibouti, Kenya, and Ethiopia with Somalis in the former Somali Republic, which would have indeed created a Somali nation, but rather they focused on rebuilding the former Somali Republic.

[3] 'Manifest Destiny' originally meant westward expansionism, but later evolved into a campaign bent on spreading democracy to foreign cultures.

Nation-building has indeed evolved from the Cold War days, when it was primarily an American- (or Soviet-) controlled endeavour, to today's occupation jointly run by any combination of the US government, the United Nations, and some member states.[4] The campaign has also progressed, albeit incrementally, due to lessons learned from previous experiences. In order to assess what in fact has changed since 1989, this book analyses the developments in nation-building following US-sponsored military intervention through an examination of the four post-Cold War cases in which both took place: Panama, Somalia, Haiti, and Bosnia.

Somalia obliged the US government and the UN to re-evaluate their roles in international crises and was responsible for a retrenchment in activity abroad, yet the sharp increase in domestic conflicts since 1989 has simultaneously compelled both to consider better conflict prevention, management and resolution techniques – no matter how unpopular involvement might be. The very notion of an international system based on supposedly equal, sovereign states, as envisaged in the UN Charter, has in fact deteriorated over the past decade because of the inability to respond consistently when states implode and/or systematically abuse their citizens' rights.[5] During the same period when membership of the UN shot up by 16 per cent, primarily due to the dissolution of the Soviet Empire, over one-third of the total number of states in Africa alone have collapsed or are at risk,[6] the global count of internally displaced persons (IDPs) has been steadily rising,[7] and the number of 'civil' wars (one of the supreme oxymorons in political science) outpaces all other types of conflicts. Between 1990 and 1996, the world

---

[4] Soviet attempts at spreading communism could also be referred to as nation-building, although this book considers US-led efforts.

[5] See, for example, Jarat Chopra and Thomas G. Weiss, 'Sovereignty is no Longer Sacrosanct: Codifying Humanitarian Intervention', *Ethics and International Affairs*, Vol. 6, 1992, pp. 95–117; or Stanley Hoffman, 'The Politics and Ethics of Military Intervention', *Survival*, 37, 4, Winter 1995–96, pp. 29–51. For a historical overview of the concept of self-determination, see Karin von Hippel, 'The Resurgence of Nationalism and Its International Implications', in Brad Roberts, ed., *Order and Disorder After the Cold War*, Cambridge, MA, CSIS, MIT Press, 1995, pp. 101–16 (previously published in *The Washington Quarterly*, 17, 4, Autumn 1994, pp. 185–200).

[6] See chapter 6, which draws on Karin von Hippel, 'The Proliferation of Collapsed States in the Post-Cold War World', in Michael Clarke, ed., *Brassey's Defence Yearbook 1997*, London, Centre for Defence Studies, 1997, pp. 193–209.

[7] See, for example, UNHCR, *The State of the World's Refugees*, Oxford, Oxford University Press, 1995–1998.

witnessed a total of ninety-eight armed conflicts; of these, only seven were between states, the rest were domestic.[8]

This rapid upsurge in civil conflicts and the subsequent international media spotlight that now homes in on the concomitant misery in real time, along with other factors that directly affect developed states (such as refugee flows), have caused the international community – particularly the United States – to respond to some, but significantly not all, situations that would have been overlooked during the Cold War. When mounting diplomatic pressure and economic sanctions do not mitigate the conflict, the ultimate response is undertaken: military intervention. Yet after a military operation, the intervening parties are then forced to concentrate on how to rebuild the state so that a similar crisis will not recur. This book's emphasis on nation-building *after* military intervention – democracy by force – therefore, considers issues of serious concern to the US government, the UN, and other major powers, as intervention and nation-building will continue to take place, irrespective of the desire to eschew such activity.

Military intervention and nation-building: an historical overview

An analysis of these post-Cold War cases would not be complete, however, without a discussion of the evolution in military intervention (and the non-interventionary norm) and nation-building since World War II, as these changes have informed the recent operations. For clarity of argument, 'military intervention' is defined as a coercive tactic used to manipulate a country into taking a certain path that would not otherwise have been chosen. In strict terms, it consists of military involvement or the encouragement of the use of force by an outside power in a domestic conflict. This differs from peacekeeping that is the result of an invitation, usually by both parties in a dispute, such as in the Western Sahara or Cyprus. Richard Haass noted, 'Armed interventions entail the introduction or deployment of new or additional combat forces to an area for specific purposes that go beyond ordinary training or scheduled expressions of support for national interests.'[9]

---

[8] Dan Smith, 'Europe's Suspended Conflicts', *War Report*, February–March 1998, p. 11.
[9] Richard N. Haass, *Intervention: the Use of American Military Force in the Post-Cold War World*, Washington, DC, Carnegie Endowment for International Peace, 1994, pp. 19–20.

The evolution of the non-interventionary norm

The principle of *non-intervention* in the domestic affairs of other states has largely been upheld in international law since the Treaty of Westphalia in 1648 – the original formula stated *cuius regio eius religio* (to each prince his own religion). An updated version was legally enshrined in the UN Charter, Article 2 (7), and its precise meaning appears to be definitive: 'Nothing contained in the present Charter shall authorize the United Nations to intervene in matters which are essentially the domestic jurisdiction of any state.' Yet an appeal to Chapter VII of the UN Charter is permitted – the Security Council can advocate military intervention in the interest of international peace and security.

The sudden disappearance of Superpower competition and the consequent threat of the Security Council veto, along with the increase in civil conflicts, have allowed (or compelled) the US government and the UN to put humanitarian concerns high on the agenda, effectively ignoring state sovereignty when so desired by labelling the crises threats to international peace and security. This is not to say that during the Cold War both Superpowers complied with the non-interventionary norm, which they also ignored at whim. Rather, interventionary policy was based on the policy of containment, the prism through which most foreign policy decisions were measured.

Between 1969 and 1973, the Superpowers had come to several agreements whereby they tacitly regulated the arms race and tried to avoid conflict in sensitive areas, such as the Middle East and Berlin. The end result was that both sides engaged in more interventions in smaller conflicts precisely because such crises normally did not threaten to bring about nuclear war.[10] In these areas, the Soviet Union intervened to spread communist ideology (and/or counter US advances), while the Americans did the same, ostensibly to spread democracy (and/or contain communism). Hence the Vietnam War, the invasion of Grenada, and the covert activity in Central America.

Since the end of the Cold War, US foreign policy no longer has the luxury of subsuming all decisions under one sweeping campaign, but rather it must encompass a range of issues. Particularly since April 1991, when safe-havens for the Kurds were established after the Gulf War due to their unforeseen flight to the mountains in large numbers, and with the Reagan Doctrine no longer applicable, Chapter VII has been applied to cases that would have been considered distinctly domestic during the

---

[10] Philip Windsor, 'Superpower Intervention,' in Hedley Bull, ed., *Intervention in World Politics*, Oxford, Clarendon Press, 1985, p. 47–8.

Cold War – without significant international opposition.[11] As Thomas Weiss explained,

access to civilians has become a recognized basis for intervention, building logically on precedents established by the actions of developing countries themselves against white minority governments in Rhodesia and South Africa, where violations of human rights were considered not just an affront to civilization but also a threat to international peace and security.[12]

This humanitarian concern is also based on a drastic increase in civilian casualties in conflicts since World War II, when 90 per cent of deaths were military and the rest civilian. Today, the statistics are the exact reverse.[13]

A comparison of the response to two African interventions illustrates the significant change in the non-interventionary norm. When Tanzania invaded Uganda to remove Idi Amin in 1979, there was an international outcry against Tanzania and the Organization of African Unity (OAU) condemned the invasion, even though most observers agreed that Amin was one of the most brutal dictators of the twentieth century. Yet, after Nigerian troops intervened in Sierra Leone in early June 1997, ironically to restore the democratically elected government that had been overthrown in a coup, the international response was muted, and this time the OAU gave its nod of approval after the event.

Approximately 900 Nigerian troops were already in Sierra Leone as part of the West African-sponsored ECOMOG peacekeeping force, under an ECOWAS mandate.[14] These troops, however, did not have a mandate to reverse the coup (nor, correspondingly, has Nigeria much experience in democracy). *Operation Alba*, the Italian-sponsored intervention in Albania initiated in March 1997 under the auspices of the Organization for Security and Co-operation in Europe (OSCE), also proceeded without any serious objections by the international community.

[11] See James Mayall, 'Nationalism and International Security After the Cold War', *Survival*, Spring 1992, pp. 19–35.

[12] Thomas G. Weiss, 'Collective Spinelessness: UN Actions in the Former Yugoslavia', in Richard H. Ullman, ed., *The World and Yugoslavia's Wars*, New York, the Council on Foreign Relations, 1996, p. 62.

[13] This statistic comes from a number of sources; see, for example, the International Federation of the Red Cross on the Web (www.ifrc.org), or Dan Smith, 'Towards Understanding the Causes of War', in Ketil Volden and Dan Smith, eds., *Causes of Conflict in the Third World*, Oslo, North/South Coalition and International Peace Research Institute, 1997, pp. 9–10.

[14] ECOWAS stands for the Economic Community of West African States, while ECOMOG stands for the ECOWAS Monitoring Group.

The cases examined in this book start with Panama, which may have appeared a typical Cold War intervention because it took place without UN approval, but it also did not fall under the Reagan Doctrine because the Soviet Empire had already collapsed, and anyway there was no communist threat in Panama. Even though the Security Council deemed the post-Panama cases 'unique, complex and extraordinary', the non-interventionary norm again evolved because these civil conflicts were described as threats to international peace and security – threats that would not have been considered as such during the Cold War. By the time the USA intervened in Haiti, the reversal of democratic elections, initiated after western pressure, was one such threat.

In Panama, however, this rationale was not yet sanctioned, although it was given as one justification by the Bush administration. In fact, five days before the invasion, on 15 December 1989, the General Assembly passed a resolution entitled, 'Respect for the principles of national sovereignty and non-interference in the internal affairs of States in their electoral processes'. The resolution 'Affirm[ed] that it is the concern solely of peoples to determine methods and to establish institutions regarding the electoral process, as well as to determine the ways for its implementation according to their constitution and national legislation'.[15] Just five years later, the democracy excuse was approved in the Security Council, albeit the democratic entitlement was not considered a universal right. Here, the motives behind military intervention and nation-building would finally merge.

The significant change in policy with respect to the democracy rationale and the non-interventionary norm can also be illustrated by the current widespread use of external observers to validate domestic elections. States now invite international observers to monitor their *national* elections, and the approval of these observers endows the newly elected government with the sought-after mandate to direct *domestic* affairs. Similarly, the Somalia and Bosnia interventions also broke new ground as a result of their humanitarian pretext, although, as with the democracy excuse, this would not be applied universally.

The international legal obstacles for all these cases have been overcome by the UN granting a member state a lead role in the intervention, but only with the participation of other member states, to uphold Article 2 (4) of the UN Charter, which prohibits state-to-state interference. This is now referred to as 'subcontracting', i.e., a UN-authorised, multinational intervention carried out under the leadership of one country,

[15] General Assembly Resolution A/RES/44/147, 82nd plenary meeting, 15 December 1989.

such as France in Rwanda, the US government in Kuwait, Somalia, and Haiti, Russia in Georgia, and Italy in Albania, with the lead country supposedly paying the bulk of the intervention costs and undertaking the command and control of the operation. After the military intervention takes place, responsibility is often transferred to a peace support operation, as in Somalia, Haiti, and Bosnia.

American allowances

Just as the legality of armed intervention in domestic conflicts has evolved at the UN since the demise of the Soviet Empire, so too have these rationales become more acceptable to the US government, although at the same time, American enthusiasm to right the world's wrongs has abated considerably. Before committing itself to intervene, the US government now tends to adhere to a mixture of guidelines set out by John M. Shalikashvili, former Chairman of the Joint Chiefs of Staff, Warren Christopher, former Secretary of State, and Anthony Lake, former National Security Adviser. The three men have also correspondingly represented the different foreign policy communities within the US government: defence, state, and intelligence.

Shalikashvili described the instances when the military would be used to protect US national interests:

1   First in priority are our vital interests – those of broad, overriding importance to the survival, security, and territorial integrity of the United States. At the direction of the NCA, the Armed Forces are prepared to use decisive and overwhelming force, unilaterally if necessary, to defend America's vital interests.
2   Second are important interests – those that do not affect our national survival but do affect our national well-being and the character of the world in which we live. The use of our Armed Forces may be appropriate to protect those interests.
3   Third, armed forces can also assist with the pursuit of humanitarian interests when conditions exist that compel our nation to act because our values demand US involvement. In all cases, the commitment of US forces must be based on the importance of the US interests involved, the potential risks to American troops, and the appropriateness of the military mission.[16]

---

[16] John M. Shalikashvili, Chairman of the Joint Chiefs of Staff, 'National Military Strategy, Shape, Respond, Prepare Now – A Military Strategy for a New Era', 1997. His strategy built on that of his predecessor, Colin Powell, who said that force would be used if we would definitively answer the following

Christopher's prerequisites include:

1   Clearly articulated objectives;
2   Probable success;
3   Likelihood of popular and congressional support; and
4   A clear exit strategy.[17]

Lake outlined the instances that could lead to the use of force by the United States (which, incidentally, are also after-the-fact justifications for interventions already undertaken):

1   To defend against direct attacks on the United States, its citizens, and its allies;
2   To counter aggression [e.g., Iraq's invasion of Kuwait];
3   To defend our key economic interests, which is where most Americans see their most immediate stake in our international engagement [e.g., Kuwait];
4   To preserve, promote and defend democracy, which enhances our security and the spread of our values [e.g., Panama and Haiti];
5   To prevent the spread of weapons of mass destruction, terrorism, international crime and drug trafficking [e.g., Panama for the last];
6   To maintain our reliability, because when our partnerships are strong and confidence in our leadership is high, it is easier to get others to work with us, and to share the burdens of leadership [e.g., Bosnia];
7   And for humanitarian purposes, to combat famines, natural disasters and gross abuses of human rights with, occasionally, our military forces [e.g., Somalia, Haiti, and Bosnia].

The three sets of guidelines are purposely rather vague – which gives the US government latitude in deciding whether to become engaged. As such, a new type of conflict could be subsumed under one of the above. At the same time, it would be legitimate to claim that these conditions did not apply universally. Anthony Lake explained,

Not one of these interests by itself – with the obvious exception of an attack on our nation, people and allies – should automatically lead to the use of force.

questions: 1. Is the political objective we seek to achieve important, clearly defined, and understood? 2. Have all other non-violent policy means failed? 3. Will military force achieve the objective? 4. At what cost? 5. Have the gains and risks been analysed? 6. How might the situation that we seek to alter, once it is altered by force, develop further and what might be the consequences? (Colin L. Powell, 'US Forces: Challenges Ahead', *Foreign Affairs*, 72, 5, Winter 1992–93, pp. 32–45.)
[17] From testimony before the Senate Committee on Foreign Relations in April 1993. Cited in Haass, Intervention, pp. 16–17.

But the greater the number and the weight of the interests in play, the greater the likelihood that we will use force – once all peaceful means have been tried and failed and once we have measured a mission's benefits against its costs, in both human and financial terms.[18]

Certainly it is impossible to ensure that any of the conditions elaborated by the three can be met throughout and, in some cases, such as in Somalia, they could change dramatically once the intervention is underway, which makes it very difficult – and often dangerous – to have a fixed exit strategy, for example. This only encourages war-lords and militias to regroup, rearm, and wait until foreign troops leave, while confidence-building measures are not taken seriously because there does not appear to be a public, long-term commitment to help rebuild the state. Despite such problems, it is important to spell out when the US government will consider military engagement for reasons of consistency and to provide an early warning signal to errant leaders. Even though many motives to intervene exist, less emphasis is placed on the aftermath of the intervention. It is to this subject, often termed 'nation-building', that we now turn.

Nation-building and democratisation defined

While UN and US government allowances for intervention have increased significantly since the end of the Cold War, with conventional notions of sovereignty effectively ignored in certain cases, the commitment to nation-building has also evolved, albeit in the opposite direction. For continued clarity, the terms 'democratisation' and 'nation-building' will be defined in the following manner.

The promotion or support of democracy, also known as 'democratisation', has developed in several stages since World War II, when it stood for demilitarisation, denazification, and re-education of an entire country's population, to Vietnam and later in Central America, when it was equated with the fight against communism. Then, attention was placed more on challenging communist advances than on actually implementing democratic reforms.[19]

Only since the end of the Cold War has the campaign once again

---

[18] Examples in brackets are author's inclusions. The conditions and quote come from Anthony Lake, Assistant to the President for National Security Affairs, Remarks at George Washington University, 'Defining Missions, Setting Deadlines: Meeting New Security Challenges in the Post-Cold War World', 6 March, 1996.

[19] For more information, see Thomas Carothers, *In the Name of Democracy: US Policy Towards Latin America in the Reagan Years*, Berkeley, University of California Press, 1991.

attempted to fulfil its stated purpose, with the ultimate aim now the enhancement of international peace and security. The promotion of democracy is based on the assumption that democracies rarely go to war with each other, and therefore an increase in the number of democratic states would imply, and indeed encourage, a more secure and peaceful world. Anthony Lake described this transition of US policy in the following way:

Throughout the Cold War, we contained a global threat to market democracies; now we should seek to enlarge their reach, particularly in places of special significance to us. The successor to a doctrine of containment must be a strategy of enlargement – enlargement of the world's free community of market democracies.[20]

Efforts to reinforce or establish democratic and transparent institutions are undertaken by a variety of organs, including parts of the US government, NGOs, QUANGOs, and multilateral institutions such as the UN, the OSCE, and the Organization of American States (OAS).[21] Activities include programmes that strengthen the rule of law, enhance respect for human rights, support international electoral observers, improve financial management and accountability, promote decentralisation, expand civilian control of the military, and improve electoral processes, the judicial system, the police, legislatures, political parties, the media, and education at all levels of society. Most of the organisations undertaking these programmes prefer to work with local and grassroots groups in host countries, and normally do not have a specific formula to implement, but rather a compendium of ideas and policies that are adapted on a case by case basis.

Nation-building, which really means state-building (see footnote 2), signifies an external effort to construct a government that may or may not be democratic but preferably is stable. The US-led ventures in Germany and Japan were intended to build democracies, while in Vietnam and most of Central America, the focus was on establishing anti-communist governments that did not necessarily have to be democratic. For the purpose of this book, however, nation-building as pursued by the US government since the end of the Cold War will imply an attempt to create a *democratic* and secure state.

Although it will no longer abet a dictator only because he is not communist, there are cases, such as in China, Saudi Arabia or Uganda, where the

---

[20] 'From Containment to Enlargement', Address at the School of Advanced International Studies, Johns Hopkins University, 21 September 1993.
[21] An NGO is a non-governmental organisation, while a QUANGO is a Quasi-NGO.

US government will provide support to a country, even though it may not be pursuing a democratic agenda, or at least reforms deemed satisfactory to the US government. Here, however, the USA is not involved in nation-building. In Panama, Somalia, Haiti, and Bosnia, however, it has attempted to assist in the establishment of at least rudimentary forms of democracy. Thus democratisation efforts are part of the larger and more comprehensive nation-building campaign, but democratisation can also occur in places where the state is relatively secure and does not need to be rebuilt, such as with electoral reform in Mexico.

The apex of nation-building: the Allied occupation of Germany and Japan

Even though promoting democracy and peace are major objectives of President Clinton's foreign policy, the actual resources – financial, time, and personnel – devoted to this have been down-graded significantly since the Allied occupation of Germany and Japan immediately after World War II. In neither the Cold War nor the post-Cold War period have democratisation and nation-building been as intense. The US government did spend vast sums trying to contain communism during the Cold War, especially in the western hemisphere and in Vietnam, but the actual focus on democratisation in nation-building efforts took a back-seat to the struggle against communism.

The US defeat in Vietnam particularly caused the nation-building process to be pared down significantly (which will be discussed after the efforts in Germany and Japan have been addressed). When Vietnam faded from memory after the euphoria that accompanied the fall of the Berlin Wall, the Somalia disaster once again put the brakes on the nation-building machine (see chapter 3). An analysis of the nation-building efforts in Germany and Japan after World War II thus provides an instructive point of departure for the cases examined in this book.

Germany and Japan: an overview

The following depiction of Germany just after the war illustrates the challenge that lay ahead for the Allies: 'The war had destroyed 33 per cent of [the country's] wealth, nearly 20 per cent of all productive buildings and machines, 40 per cent of the transportation facilities, and over 15 per cent of all houses.'[22] Moreover, it created at least 20 million

---

[22] Edward N. Peterson, *The American Occupation of Germany: Retreat to Victory*, Detroit, Wayne State University Press, 1977, p. 114.

refugees and IDPs, and was responsible for the loss of life of 20 per cent of the population.[23] The scale of destruction resembles that which has occurred in more recent civil conflicts, in Rwanda, Somalia, and Bosnia, for example. Yet today's thriving democracies in Germany and Japan attest to the success of externally sponsored nation-building efforts. Significantly, as Roy Licklider explained, 'the resulting governments are impressive testimony that it is possible for outsiders to establish relatively benign governments which locals will support for at least half a century'.[24]

There were, however, three significant factors that facilitated this process in Germany and Japan – factors that do not exist to nearly the same extent in the cases discussed in this book. One, the unconditional surrender after World War II gave the Allies *carte-blanche* to do what they wanted. Two, the level of development and education in both countries – Germany and Japan were (and still are) highly literate industrialised societies – favoured and facilitated change. And three, the serious commitment on behalf of the Allies to create democratic states in both countries was evident. Despite these differences, it is important to consider the Allied occupation in discussions of political reconstruction because these experiences shaped the way the US government – especially the US military establishment – has approached nation-building in less-developed countries. Further, the Allied occupation also demonstrates the breadth of US experience in democratisation, a point that isolationists in the United States and Europe often deliberately and conveniently overlook.

This discussion focuses primarily on US involvement in Germany and Japan, even though the Soviets, British, and French were also in charge of different sections of Germany, because this book concentrates on US-sponsored nation-building attempts.[25] The preoccupation of Britain and France with their own societal restructuring, much of it backed by

[23] Michael Ermarth, ed., *America and the Shaping of German Society, 1945–1955*, Oxford, Berg, 1993, pp. 4–5.
[24] Roy Licklider, 'State Building After Invasion: Somalia and Panama', Presented at the International Studies Association annual convention, San Diego, CA, April 1996. The relevance of the Allied Occupation to this book was inspired by Dr Licklider's paper. The author would like to thank him for developing this link.
[25] In Germany, the Allies and the Russians managed their own zones in distinct fashion. Stalin, in fact, had demanded large quantities of German machinery and several million Germans for the reconstruction of Russia. For more information, see Roy F. Willis, *The French in Germany, 1945–1949*, Stanford, Stanford University Press, 1962, and Ian D. Turner, ed., *Reconstruction in Post-War Germany: British Occupation Policy and the Western Zones, 1945–1955*, Oxford, Berg, 1989.

US financial support, also permitted US policy to take the lead overall.[26] Finally, the Soviet Union never intended to set up a democratic state.

In both Germany and Japan, the Americans initially expected the occupation to last a few months, which, of course, was completely unrealistic. In Germany, three of the occupation powers (Britain, France, and the United States) helped to establish a federal state by 1949, and the majority of foreign troops remained until 1955. In Japan, the effort was directed entirely by General Douglas MacArthur, and the bulk of US troops stayed until 1952. Germany and Japan are still home to US troops.[27]

Nation-building in Germany and Japan encompassed the development and reconstruction of the press, education (through a purge policy of re-educating the entire country), the economy, industry, legal institutions (including the establishment of a war crimes tribunal), reparations and restitutions, police retraining (another purge programme that removed those tainted with the previous regimes), and finally, sweeping disarmament, demobilisation and demilitarisation activities, which concluded successfully with no soldiers, no weapons and disarmed police forces. In both Germany and Japan, US government representatives also played a major role in the preparation of the new constitutions, which was anyhow the prerogative of the victor. Most of these activities would be integral components in the subsequent nation-building attempts discussed in this book, although once again, because of the difficulties experienced, they would not be carried out in such a thorough and organised manner.

Germany

The US military government in Germany was tasked to prevent 'Germany from ever again becoming a threat to the peace of the world . . . [and to prepare for] an eventual reconstruction of German political life on a democratic basis'.[28] Beyond destroying any future possibility of

[26] The US and British zones were united in an economic unit on 30 July 1946, with the aim of facilitating industrial and economic recovery, while the French were more preoccupied with security so did not join this bizonal area until the North Atlantic Pact united all these countries in common defence. All three did co-operate on major decisions, even though they may have conducted matters separately in their spheres.

[27] Approximately 45,000 US soldiers are stationed in Japan, while Germany is home to 75,000 troops. *The Military Balance*, London, International Institute of Strategic Studies, 1996/97.

[28] 'Documents on Germany 1944–1985', US Department of State, Office of the Historian, Bureau of Public Affairs (USDS), 1985, as cited in Richard L.

renewed German military capacity, this meant full-scale democratis-ation, which was implemented in co-operation with Germans. The Ger-mans adapted the above-mentioned components of democratisation to their own particular traditions, especially in developing the Basic Law, which later became the constitution.

Although US involvement was significant, as Edward Peterson stressed, 'The occupation worked when and where it allowed the Ger-mans to govern themselves.'[29] This devolution of power resulted from necessity due to the pressing need to feed 45 million Germans and keep them alive, without the US government footing the whole bill. The focus on ameliorating the widespread famine remained the priority through-out the first three years of the occupation.

Accordingly, the reduced emphasis on democratisation was a retreat from the more interventionist original plan. Even in the denazification programme, considered vital to the rehabilitation of Germany, it became expedient to let the estimated 10 per cent of the population who were proven anti-Nazis conduct this process themselves.[30] Practical exigen-cies thus tended to take precedence over theoretical ones. Nevertheless, the commitment remained enormous, and far greater than in the four main cases discussed in this book.

Working with the residents of the host country would normally have been integral to any democratisation plan, but because the entire pro-gramme was led by a US military governor, General Lucius Clay, after a horrific war in which it was believed that the majority of Germans had been brainwashed or were just plain evil, complete co-ownership of the process was just not possible. Moreover, it was estimated that most of the population needed to be re-educated – or *re-oriented* as many called it at the time. As described in the 1944 US Army Military Handbook (concerning the fact that Germans had been cut off from the 'truth' for so long and were therefore ignorant of what had been occurring in the world):

Where this state of affairs concerns you is in the irritation that will naturally arise in you when in the normal contact of occupation you try to tell the Ger-mans what the score is, and they reply with their parrot-like repetition of 'All lies. All Democratic propaganda.' Don't argue with them. Don't try to convince them. Don't get angry. Give them the – 'Okay-chum-you'll-find-out-soon-enough' treatment and walk away. By NOT trying to convince them, or to shout them down, by the assumption of a quiet demeanor you can help to create a

Merritt, *Democracy Imposed: US Occupation Policy and the German Public, 1945–1949*, New Haven, Yale University Press, 1995, p. 270.

[29] Peterson, *The American Occupation of Germany*, p. 10.

[30] Willis, *The French in Germany*, p. 155.

genuine longing and thirst for the truth and real news in the German people, and break down their resistance to it.[31]

The new Bonn constitution was prepared under the supervision of General Clay, although written primarily by Germans. The resulting federal constitution suited the Germans and the Allies: both believed that a democratic and decentralised state – the antithesis of the preceding government – could succeed where the fascistic and highly centralised state had failed. The Nazi government brought them only shame and ruin, not world domination as promised, while pre-Hitler Germany was essentially federal, enshrined in the Weimar constitution adopted in 1919.[32] The Allies also wanted to avoid a repeat of such a concentration of power, and thus supported the decentralised option, with a new army only to be used for defensive purposes. Finally, a federal option left open the possibility of a reunited Germany.[33]

Democratisation in Germany started at the grass-roots level and worked up in an orderly fashion to the top. For example, local council elections preceded regional elections, which were held before national elections. As General Clay explained, 'The restoration of responsible German government from the village to the state within the United States Zones was a systematic, planned, and to a large extent scheduled-in-advance program to carry out our objectives.'[34] Political party formation was also encouraged from November 1945, and again started locally and then expanded from the states to the occupied zones.

The path to democracy in Germany was not an entirely smooth transition, and troubles were encountered throughout the reconstruction period. This is hardly surprising as democratisation is by necessity experimental, and proceeds on a trial-and-error basis because

---

[31] *Information and Pocket Guide to Germany*, US Army Service Forces, 1944, p. 20.

[32] At least initially the Germans preferred this system. Polls in mid-1948 showed an increasing German interest in a more centralised state. For more information on these polls, see Merritt, *Democracy Imposed*, pp. 340–1.

[33] Interestingly, as described in greater detail in chapter 3, the project in which this author was involved from 1995 to 1997, which disseminated information on different types of decentralised governments that could be compatible with a future Somali state, was originally undertaken on a similar premise. Somalis believed that only a decentralised state could prevent another dictator usurping power at the centre as Siad Barre had done for far too long. Somalis also naturally conduct their affairs in a very decentralised fashion. Moreover, this project was conceived by a German, Sigurd Illing, who grew up during the occupation.

[34] Lucius D. Clay, *Decision in Germany*, New York, Doubleday, 1950, p. 393.

democratic reforms need to be adapted to the changing particularities of different cultures. Democracy also allows for open debate, which by definition creates controversy. As Alexander Hamilton commented in *The Federalist Papers,*

I never expect to see a perfect work from imperfect man. The result of the deliberations of all collective bodies must necessarily be a compound, as well of the errors and prejudices as of the good sense and wisdom of the individuals of whom they are composed. . . How can perfection spring from such materials?[35]

Add in the complication of outside interference from more than one state, and the result is bound to be even more diluted. At the same time, it is important to emphasise that externally influenced, US military-controlled, democratic reforms successfully permeated all segments of German society, to the point that most Germans today believe that their country is firmly democratic.[36]

Japan

As in Germany, democratic reforms in Japan were implemented in a relatively autocratic manner by the US military, in fact even more so because General Douglas MacArthur retained tight control of the entire operation. President Truman bestowed upon MacArthur the title of Supreme Commander for the Allied Powers (SCAP). As one political adviser to MacArthur later commented, 'This was heady authority. Never before in the history of the United States had such enormous and absolute power been placed in the hands of a single individual.'[37]

Presidential Policy, Part I described the goal of the US government:

The ultimate objectives of the United States in regard to Japan . . . are . . to bring about the eventual establishment of a peaceful and responsible government which will respect the rights of other states and will support the objectives of the United States as reflected in the ideals and principles of the Charter of the United Nations. The United States desires that this government should conform as closely as may be to principles of democratic self-government *but it*

---

[35] Alexander Hamilton, *The Federalist Papers*, edited by Isaac Kramnick, Harmondsworth, Penguin, 1987, p. 484.

[36] For more information on how Germans rebuilt trust and instituted safeguards in their constitution to avoid a repeat of a fascist government, see Merritt, *Democracy Imposed*, pp. 349–82.

[37] Cited in Toshio Nishi, *Unconditional Democracy: Education and Politics in Occupied Japan, 1945–1952*, Stanford, Hoover Institution Press, 1982, p. 34.

is not the responsibility of the Allied Powers to impose upon Japan any form of government not supported by the freely expressed will of the people.[38]

The overall intent was to change the economic and political institutions. In fact, MacArthur chose to work indirectly through existing government institutions, and did not overhaul them as occurred in Germany. Instead, the US government focused on an extensive re-education programme for the masses – and this programme proved to be highly successful because the Japanese hold a deep respect for education.[39] The emphasis on re-education would no longer be a priority in the post-Cold War cases, although here the problem was the lack of basic education in countries with high illiteracy rates.

Presidential Policy explained it this way: 'The Japanese people will be encouraged to develop a desire for individual liberties and respect for fundamental human rights, particularly the freedoms of religion, assembly, speech, and the press. They shall also be encouraged to form democratic and representative organizations.'[40] Land reforms also took place, which gave farmers ownership of the land they worked on, and removed it from absentee landlords. The Americans additionally encouraged the formation of political parties and labour unions, and separated Church and State.[41]

Another major component of US policy was to purge tainted Japanese from public life. Overall, between two and three hundred thousand Japanese were eventually removed, including military officers, government officials, party politicians, and business leaders. While over 80 per cent of military personnel were purged, the bureaucracy remained essentially the same, only 16 per cent of the pre-war Diet and 1 per cent of civil servants were replaced (many, however, committed suicide).[42]

Although the Japanese wrote the first draft of their constitution, this draft was heavily influenced by MacArthur and his staff, much more so than in Germany. After reading the draft, MacArthur was still unsatisfied and therefore decided to prepare a new one, which included the famous renunciation of future wars as well as the ban on the army, navy, and air force (the Japanese were eventually 'allowed' limited

---

[38] Cited in Edward M. Martin, *The Allied Occupation of Japan*, Westport, CT, Greenwood Press, 1972, p. 45. Emphasis added.

[39] See Nishi, *Unconditional Democracy*, for more information about the sweeping educational reforms.

[40] Cited in Martin, *The Allied Occupation of Japan*, p. 46.

[41] Nishi, *Unconditional Democracy*, p. 286.

[42] Paul J. Bailey, *Postwar Japan: 1945 to the Present*, Oxford, Blackwell, 1996, p. 34.

rearmament for self-defence purposes). MacArthur then forced his draft on the Japanese cabinet, the members of which made minor revisions and then adopted it, as did the Diet with no further changes. The new constitution went into effect in 1947.

As in Germany, the Japanese public desired a distinctly different government from the imperialistic and militaristic rulers who had brought them to defeat, although the emphasis was not on decentralisation as in Germany, but rather on general democratic reforms. Finally, hunger was also a major issue in Japan. And as in Germany, hunger forced the Japanese government to embrace democracy.

While the Allied success in democratising Germany and Japan was enhanced by public will, even more important were respect for education, high literacy rates, and high levels of industrialisation. Although local support for a change in government has been a factor in the cases discussed in this book, the last three factors have not been evident, barring Panama and Bosnia to a lesser degree in terms of moderately high literacy rates. Success in Germany and Japan was also achieved by a significant Allied commitment to policies that administered vast economic, political, and educational reforms affecting the entire population and most government institutions. Finally, these reforms were facilitated by the unconditional surrender, also not evident in the post-Cold War cases.

The nadir of nation-building: Vietnam

Despite the successes experienced in democratising and rebuilding Germany and Japan, and later in South Korea, the US government would significantly down-grade its democratisation and nation-building efforts after Vietnam. The most prominent US foreign policy disaster of the twentieth century and one that touched all Americans, the US defeat in Vietnam has subsequently had a profound impact on US foreign policy, not only in military terms, but also in democratisation and nation-building. Three million US troops served in Vietnam, and 58,000 were killed. Between 1965 and 1973 when the last combat soldier left Vietnam, the US government sunk over $120 billion into what it called a nation-building campaign, but what was in fact a war based on the erroneous assumption that the entire region would fall to communism without American intervention.[43]

President John F. Kennedy saw in South Vietnam his opportunity to

---

[43] See Stanley Karnow, *Vietnam: A History*, London, Century, 1983, p. 24, and entire book for a comprehensive account of the war.

test America's increasingly visible international role, and particularly the chance to build a democracy in another part of south-east Asia after China had 'fallen' to communism.[44] The quest to change Vietnam was in many ways nothing new: it abided with America's historic missionary zeal to 'enlighten' other societies, what Daniel Bell has referred to as America's perception of its own 'exceptionalism'.[45] The crusade to remould Vietnam also transpired when US confidence was at a peak: Americans believed they could rebuild the world in their image, and they sent out government experts to many developing countries to accomplish this task. As Stanley Karnow explained, the Americans did not think they were

imposing colonialism but, rather, [they were] helping the Vietnamese to perfect their institutions. They called it 'nation-building,' and they would have been arrogant had they not been utterly sincere in their naïve belief that they could really reconstruct Vietnamese society along Western lines.[46]

Nation-building in Vietnam, originally instigated by John Foster Dulles, US Secretary of State from 1953 to 1959, involved organisations that promoted democracy through various propaganda and aid channels. The International Rescue Committee, for example, described itself as a 'lighthouse of inspiration for those eager to preserve and broaden concepts of democratic culture'.[47] Between 1955 and 1961, the USA gave more than $1 billion in economic and military assistance to South Vietnam. By 1961, it was the fifth largest recipient of US foreign aid, with military assistance taking up the bulk (78 per cent).[48] Roads, bridges, railroads, and schools were built while development experts worked on agricultural projects. Teachers, civil servants, and police were trained in the 'American way'.[49] US advisers even helped draft a constitution, again western-style.

Despite the infusion of funds, experts, and enthusiasm imported from abroad, things did not go as planned in South Vietnam, especially after the war was fully underway, for two major reasons. First, there was no co-ordinating mechanism for US government departments working in Vietnam – the State Department, the US Agency for International Development (USAID), the United States Intelligence Agency, the

---

[44] As cited in Karnow, *Vietnam*, p. 247.
[45] As cited in Karnow, *Vietnam*, p. 11.
[46] Karnow, *Vietnam*, p. 255.
[47] As cited in George C. Herring, *America's Longest War: The United States and Vietnam, 1950–1975*, 2nd edition, New York, Alfred A. Knopf, 1986, p. 56.
[48] Herring, *America's Longest War*, p. 57.
[49] Herring, *America's Longest War*, p. 61.

Department of Defense, and the Central Intelligence Agency (CIA) – and consequently each operated fairly independently of the others, which inevitably meant overlap and agencies working at cross-purposes.[50] Brown pointed to another side-effect of the lack of co-ordination: six major western-promoted economic and political strategies operated simultaneously throughout the war.[51]

Second, unlike in Germany and Japan, democracy was not the priority in Vietnam. Halting the communist advance was more important, which is why the bulk of foreign assistance went on military spending. The greater emphasis on military aid meant less funding for sustainable development programmes, and a reduced effort to understand how democracy could be adapted to Vietnamese culture, or if indeed this was at all desired or possible. Additionally, many of the democratisation programmes were overly concentrated in the cities, even though 90 per cent of Vietnamese lived in rural areas.

The straightforward economic assistance also did not help establish a stable economy, but rather most of it artificially buffered the Vietnamese economy. As Herring explained, this aid only 'fostered dependency rather than laying the foundation for a genuinely independent nation . . . Vietnamese and Americans alike agreed that a cutback or termination of American assistance would bring economic and political collapse.'[52] Herring concluded, 'Lacking knowledge of Vietnamese history and culture, Americans seriously underestimated the difficulties of nation-building in an area with only the most fragile basis for nationhood. The ambitious programs developed in the 1950s merely papered over rather than corrected South Vietnam's problems'.[53] The same criticism would later be levelled against the US government after the ineffectual Somalia intervention, and also with the benefit of hindsight (even though most of the well-known expatriate experts on Somalia had been consulted throughout the operation). In South Vietnam, the Americans only made a feeble attempt to generate ownership of the democratic process, in

---

[50] T. Louise Brown, *War and Aftermath in Vietnam*, London, Routledge, 1991, p. 225.

[51] These were: social mobilisation and organisation building; improvement of local government and administrative reforms (UK-sponsored); the authoritarianism and power concentration practised by Diem and later by Thieu; the building of democratic institutions advocated by certain, more liberal Americans; the stability and economic development option; and the military occupation approach of the US Army. Brown, *War and Aftermath in Vietnam*, p. 236.

[52] Herring, *America's Longest War*, p. 63.

[53] Herring, *America's Longest War*, p. 72.

sharp contrast to the communist campaign emanating from North Vietnam, which was more responsive to the needs of the largely rural population. Indeed, it is always a challenge to compete with a home-grown insurgency movement.

As has occurred in other parts of the world, the danger of an external power promoting half-hearted reforms, while ignoring the undemocratic methods pursued by the US-backed leader (e.g., Ngo Dinh Diem), is that it often causes the population to revolt against that government. In Vietnam, the beneficiaries of this ill-conceived US policy were the communists. And once the revolution overtook South Vietnam, it was too late to do anything about it.

Interestingly, critics of the war argued that the nation-building component harmed the war effort, just as they would again after Somalia. Kennedy's general, Maxwell Taylor, later remarked, 'We should have learned from our frontier forebears that there is little use planting corn outside the stockade if there are still Indians around in the woods outside.'[54] (!) In 1966, Senator Fulbright ruminated about the ability of the US government 'to go into a small, alien, undeveloped Asian nation and create stability where there is chaos, the will to fight where there is defeatism, democracy where there is no tradition of it, and honest government where corruption is almost a way of life'.[55] One could replace the word 'Asian' and the question would be similarly apt for the cases examined in this book (except perhaps concerning the will to fight, which is no longer an aim of US policy). Earlier, in August 1954, US intelligence predicted that 'even with solid support from the United States, the chances of establishing a strong, stable government were "poor" '.[56]

Despite these negative views, the proponents won the day. Their spokesman was Henry Luce, who argued in his well-known essay entitled 'The American Century' that Americans had to 'accept whole-heartedly our duty and our opportunity as the most powerful and vital nation in the world and in consequence to exert upon the world the full impact of our influence, for such purposes as we see fit and by such means as we see fit'.[57] In Vietnam, not only did America have a moral duty to interfere, but South Vietnam was also seen as the 'linchpin' of

---

[54] As cited in William Appleman Williams, T. McCormick, L. Gardner, and W. LaFeber, eds., *America in Vietnam: a Documentary History*, New York, W.W. Norton, 1989, p. 144.

[55] Appleman Williams, et al., *America in Vietnam*, p. 233.

[56] Herring, *America's Longest War*, p. 47.

[57] As cited in Appleman Williams, et al., *America in Vietnam*, pp. 22–3.

the region, based on the Domino Theory.[58] Few parts of the world today are viewed in such a critical light. Perhaps the most recent manifestation would be the fear of creeping Islamic fundamentalism, the so-called 'Clash of Civilizations', as Samuel Huntington famously argued in *Foreign Affairs* in 1993.[59] Yet even this view is discounted by sufficient government policy makers to ensure that it does not dominate.

The US defeat in Vietnam damaged an American psyche that had become arrogant in its belief that it could change the world, embodying the dangerous hubris about which Anthony Lake warned. In reference to Henry Luce, Stanley Karnow remarked that the war represented,

the end of America's absolute confidence in its moral exclusivity, its military invincibility, its manifest destiny . . . the price, paid in blood and sorrow, for America's awakening to maturity, to the recognition of its limitations. With the young men who died in Vietnam died the dream of an 'American Century'.[60]

The after-shocks of Vietnam can be noted in a variety of ways, not only in terms of a pared-down nation-building mandate.[61] In the United States, this defeat also led to an increased isolationist stance and greater cynicism in the workings of government. LaFeber concluded, 'The United States tried to impose its values on Vietnam in such a way that it succeeded only in corrupting those values at home.'[62] The war caused inflation, it forced many young men to flee the United States as draft dodgers, it widened racial cleavages, and eventually led to Watergate and the first resignation of an American president. In Vietnam, the war destroyed much more: it ruined the fabric of society, and was responsible for massive civilian casualties – over a million dead – and refugees – one-third of the population of South Vietnam. The defeat therefore mostly erased from modern memory the success achieved by the US government in democratising Germany and Japan.

---

[58] Simply put, the theory alleged that if one country in the East Asian region fell to communism, all others would soon thereafter follow suit.

[59] See Samuel P. Huntington, 'The Clash of Civilizations?', *Foreign Affairs*, Summer 1993.

[60] Karnow, *Vietnam*, p. 9.

[61] Today, the senior ranks of the US military are primarily staffed by servicemen who served at least one tour in Vietnam, as if this experience was a rite of passage. This has had obvious effects on US military policy, which manifested itself in the execution of the Gulf War, but the gradual retirement of most of these men will pave the way for a different type of soldier to fill the ranks. There will be more women, and soldiers whose only combat experience may have been in the short Gulf War or in a peace support operation.

[62] Walter LaFeber, 'Introduction to Part IV: The Rise and Fall of American Power 1963–1975', in Appleman Williams, et al., *America in Vietnam*, p. 233.

Nation-building wanes in the new world order

Defeat forced change, and in the United States, change meant retreat. This did not imply a full retreat from engagements abroad – the communist threat was still perceived as the most important foreign policy challenge – but it meant instead more covert activity and the end of the draft, which in turn meant fewer body bags. 'Democratisation' carried on, albeit at a reduced level compared with Vietnam: the US government continued to prop up non-democratic regimes in Central America, the Middle East and Africa because they were anti-communist. Attempts at actually building democratic states, however, virtually stopped.

The demise of communism at the end of the 1980s, however, forced the US government to rethink its role because the demand for involvement in new humanitarian crises increased significantly. Although the pay-back for the financial commitment and time spent reviving the German and Japanese political economies has been substantial in the post-World War II period – most notably in terms of trade, security, and close political relations – the effects of Vietnam still linger, causing a reluctance to become fully engaged abroad. Particularly since the deaths of eighteen US Army Rangers in Somalia in 1993, the US government has attempted to reduce its financial, military, and political commitments abroad when there is no obvious strategic interest. And in the post-Cold War world, there has been little agreement as to what exactly constitutes an obvious US strategic interest.

While the US government has tried to limit its engagements abroad, the UN has also proceeded with caution in its involvement in nation-building efforts. As James Mayall explained,

Firstly, for historical reasons in Asia and Africa . . . .. there is no support for the creation of UN protectorates or the revival of UN trusteeship. If there were, this would give the Organisation an explicit interest in nation-building, and would involve its leading members in expensive and long-run commitments. Secondly, if the UN cannot reasonably be expected to act like an empire, it must find itself handicapped whenever it becomes deeply embroiled in attempts to preside over the transformation or reconstruction of a political system. . . Given the reluctance of the major powers to enter into open-ended commitments, it seems unlikely that the UN will be in a position to develop this kind of expertise in the future.[63]

[63] James Mayall, ed., *The New Interventionism, 1991–1994: United Nations Experience in Cambodia, former Yugoslavia and Somalia*, Cambridge, Cambridge University Press, 1996, p. 23.

The result is an unhealthy combination: both the US government and the UN have lengthy pedigrees in democratisation, and both would benefit enormously by an increase in democratic governments world-wide for political, economic, and security reasons to be discussed in this book, yet neither wishes to engage in it. What has developed instead for the US government and the UN, partly by default and also through lack of alternatives, is an uncomfortable middle path between trusteeship and complete withdrawal.

Issues addressed: why these case studies?

'Reconstruction' has recently been described by Bojicic, Kaldor, and Vejvoda as a 'strategy for achieving and sustaining a stable peace not a strategy to be initiated after peace has been achieved'.[64] Although it is not possible to have an overall strategy for all crises, as plans need to be tailored to the particularities of each case considered, certain patterns have emerged due to the evolution of policy with applications of lessons learned from previous operations. This book examines the changes in nation-building since the end of the Cold War in an attempt to clarify these patterns. Only with a greater understanding of the failures and successes can we hope to eliminate problems in future operations, improve general strategies for reconstruction, and possibly predict where intervention and nation-building are likely to succeed before beginning the undertaking.

Although there have been many 'lessons learned' assessments of the operations discussed in this book (which will be referred to throughout), there has been no comprehensive study of the major post-Cold War, US-sponsored interventions that were followed by nation-building efforts. This book, therefore, analyses the operations in Panama, Somalia, Haiti, and Bosnia before, during, and after the interventions in order to address this gap. Such an analysis, by necessity, considers the factors that put the US government on the path to military action in the first place, changes in peace-support operations, the relationship between civilian and military authorities within these operations, and the corresponding nation-building efforts.

The Gulf War – a fifth major US-sponsored military intervention that has taken place since the demise of the Soviet Empire (although the second sequentially) – is not included because nation-building was never

---

[64] Vesna Bojicic, Mary Kaldor, and Ivan Vejvoda, 'Post-War Reconstruction in the Balkans', Sussex European Institute Working Paper No. 14, November 1995, p. 3.

a main thrust of the intervention.[65] Additionally, the war conformed to the Cold War standards of intervention in that it was a response to aggression and territorial aggrandisement, which breached international law, in a region rich in a strategic natural resource. The factors that influenced the interventions in this book therefore differed from those at work in Kuwait and from those of the Cold War as the interventions with which we are concerned were largely undertaken on humanitarian premises. Rwanda and Albania also fall outside this study because the US government was not significantly involved, albeit there have been parallels, and certain lessons learned and applied that will be mentioned.[66]

Panama provides the appropriate starting point for a study of this kind because it straddles the Cold War and post-Cold War interventions: it was the first attempt to apply the democracy rationale without the corresponding threat of communism. US troops also used the post-World War II plans as their guide for the reconstruction of Panama. Somalia then served as a test case for a purely humanitarian crisis that did not affect the developed world. Its failure hindered any massive reaction in the next major humanitarian crisis in Africa, that in Rwanda. Events in Somalia did not stop the US government from intervening in Haiti, however, because of the latter's proximity to the United States and problems associated with the increase in refugee flows to Florida. Haiti then became the first case in which the aims of the military intervention and the nation-building attempt were the same: to establish a democratic state. The US government also considered Somalia when trying to eschew involvement in Bosnia, but eventually it was pressured into acting there as well, again on humanitarian grounds, although maintaining the credibility of NATO and US leadership in Europe was factored in as well.

Three of these interventions took place in the developing world and only one in Europe, yet the similarities between all four are considerable. In each, the US government increased diplomatic and economic pressure to try and force a change, either of government or to put an end to a civil war. In each, the decision to intervene was based on a combination of factors, including increased refugee flows that affected

[65] After the war, the US government did apply cursory pressure on the Kuwaiti government, which agreed to hold elections and liberalise the economy. Progress, however, has not been forthcoming, and correspondingly, neither has US pressure to adhere to these agreements.

[66] These cases have also been informed by many recent peacekeeping operations, such as in Angola, Mozambique, El Salvador, and Namibia, some of which experienced relative success in carrying out their mandates. Again, when relevant, comparisons will be drawn.

developed countries, the media spotlight that homed in on the massive suffering, continued defiance by nasty rulers, and increased sanctions. All these caused the 'Do Something Effect', and pushed the US government and other western countries into utilising the military option, which only then led to the inception and application of the nation-building component.

Building castles in the swamp

A significant issue raised in this study is whether or not democratisation can resolve or overcome the underlying problems that generate many of the current civil conflicts. In other words, should the United States and other western democracies continue to promote democracy as a development tool? Can significant decentralisation of power help to mitigate major problems typically associated with rogue states, as occurred in Germany?

Although the United States has made democratisation a priority for enhancing international peace and security, and multilateral organisations increasingly require it for full membership, most states will not be able to adopt American-style democracy and, instead, will require safeguards to protect minorities. Alternative democratic models, where deeply divided groups can work together in the same state, are being developed and tested in different parts of the world, yet it is far from clear whether they can provide the necessary security to prevent conflicts. Additionally, some states have maintained stability, and indeed, promoted economic growth, through distinctly non-democratic means, while also enjoying international support (e.g., Peru, Turkey, and Uganda). These states argue that democratic reforms implemented too early would only serve to *destabilise* the state.

As Hume once remarked,

> To balance a large state or society, whether monarchical or republican, on general laws, is a work of so great difficulty that no human genius, however comprehensive, is able, by the mere dint of reason and reflection, to effect it. The judgments of many must unite in the work; EXPERIENCE must guide their labor; TIME must bring it to perfection, and the FEELING of inconveniences must correct the mistakes which they inevitably fall into in their first trials and experiments.[67]

This description could also aptly encapsulate the changes in UN peace support operations and the US experiences in nation-building described in this book, which have necessarily been a trial-and-error process, as the subsequent cases attest.

---

[67] Hume's *Essays*, 'The Rise of Arts and Sciences', I, p. 128, as cited by Hamilton, in *The Federalist Papers*, p. 486.

Invasion or intervention? *Operation Just Cause*

Just one year into his presidency, George Bush ordered the invasion of Panama, a decision that would have far-reaching implications not just for Panamanians, but also for the US government as it assumed its lone Superpower role. In many respects, this action had more in common with the US invasion of Grenada in 1983 and other Central American incursions than the post-Cold War interventions. The Panama and Grenada operations were allegedly undertaken to restore democracy, yet in neither case were democratic reforms high on the agenda, nor was either sanctioned at the UN. Panama differs, however, from the entanglements in the western hemisphere during the Reagan era because US troops landed just one month after the fall of the Berlin Wall: the Soviet menace could no longer provide the pretext, and even if it could, there were no communists threatening to take over the canal. US policy was about to move in an altogether different direction.

Subsequent large-scale, US military interference in international crises would be labelled *interventions*, as opposed to another Panama-style *invasion*, but the mistakes made prior to this operation, during the invasion itself, and in the post-conflict period taught US policy makers valuable lessons, particularly for the reconstruction phase. Some of these lessons would be brought into practice without delay, others would not be applied until Haiti and Bosnia, while still others are yet to be realised. This chapter explores in greater detail the invasion of Panama by first discussing whether the cause was just through an examination of the period leading up to it, how the plans for the military component and the post-conflict political reconstruction were conceived and implemented, and finally, what mistakes were made and lessons learned.

In the run-up to invasion

A painfully close Panamanian–American relationship

The co-dependent relationship between Panama and the United States dates back to Panama's formal declaration of independence from

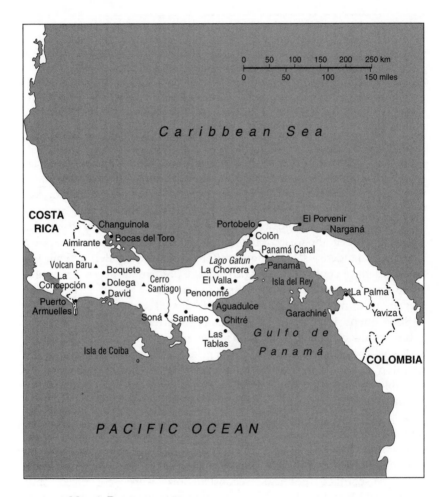

Map 1 Panama

Colombia in 1903, a move motivated by President Theodore Roosevelt's desire to build the canal. Completed in 1914, the canal extends for 52 miles and is sandwiched by two 5-mile zones, all placed under the charge of the United States 'in perpetuity'. The existence of the canal gave various US governments an excuse to interfere in matters normally considered exclusively domestic in Panama, and justified the significant US military presence in this strategic region.

Panamanian resentment of US control over the canal and, hence, over much of Panama's economy, gradually increased over the years, especially after World War II. Another thirty years would pass, however, before the Americans gave any real consideration to local sentiment, and even then, the decision to transfer ownership ultimately was based on US recognition that the canal no longer held such strategic importance. On 7 September 1977, US President Jimmy Carter and Colonel Omar Torrijos, the military leader of Panama, signed two canal treaties that would transfer full control of the canal to Panama by the year 2000. In return, Torrijos would prepare the country for a transition to democracy. Over the next few years, Torrijos fulfilled three promises he had made to Carter during the negotiations over the transfer: he allowed political exiles to return, the press to operate freely, and political parties to function legally. Yet these reforms were not to last: four years after signing the treaties with Carter, Torrijos was killed in a plane crash.

From 1981, internal power struggles dominated the political arena, until 1983 when General Manuel Antonio Noriega emerged as the new leader of the Panamanian Defense Forces (PDF). One year later, Noriega had consolidated his position as the *de facto* ruler of Panama. National elections that were to return the country to civilian rule were finally held on 6 May 1984. Amid rumours of electoral fraud, Noriega's hand-picked candidate was voted in by a slim margin, only to be replaced in 1987 by a more pliant candidate.

Meanwhile, the United States had been covertly propping up Noriega's regime. The US government had initiated relations with Noriega as far back as the 1950s, when he was a cadet at the Peruvian Military Academy, as part of a campaign to recruit candidates to help counter the growing communist threat. Noriega was hand-picked by US intelligence agents, who were well aware of his dubious reputation.[1] US agents trained him in intelligence gathering and guerrilla warfare, and warned him on occasion of impending threats to Panama.

Reagan continued to support Noriega – despite receiving evidence that he had rigged the 1984 elections, and was involved in illegal arms trading and drugs trafficking. Noriega generously returned the favour:

[1] For example, he had reputedly raped and beaten a prostitute.

he assisted Reagan in his war against the Sandanista regime in Nicaragua, provided security for US bases, permitted military operations in Panama that exceeded the mandate of the original canal treaty, and ironically, supplied the US Drug Enforcement Agency (DEA) with information. Frederick Kempe emphasised that Noriega's assistance to the DEA 'had DEA agents working in Panama impeding the work of DEA's Miami officials'.[2] Throughout this period, there was no substantial support for or interest in democratisation in Panama.

Drugs and diplomacy: just say no

Noriega's illicit activity and cosy relationship with the US administration could only be concealed for so long. In Washington, DC during the spring of 1986, rumours of Noriega's drug trafficking, arms dealing, and violation of the Cuban embargo encouraged several senators to push for congressional hearings. In June 1986, Seymour Hersh transformed these reports into national news by writing a front-page story in the *New York Times* entitled, 'Panama Strongman Said to Trade in Drugs, Arms and Illicit Money'. Just one year later, a former member of the PDF, Col. Roberto Diaz Herrera, publicly accused Noriega of drug trafficking and money laundering, causing domestic Panamanian opposition to mount. Peaceful demonstrations were harshly repressed by Noriega, and well covered by the foreign press.

US domestic and international political events sidelined these accusations for over a year until February 1988, when two federal grand juries in Miami and Tampa, acting independently of US foreign policy, indicted Noriega on twelve counts of drug trafficking, money laundering, and racketeering.[3] The drug charges included accusations of collaboration with the Colombian Medellin cartel to transport cocaine and marijuana to the United States in return for millions of dollars. After tolerating Noriega's drug dealing for many years – even during Nancy Reagan's much-publicised campaign against drugs – the negative publicity and the Florida indictments finally embarrassed the US

---

[2] Frederick Kempe, 'The Panama Debacle', in Eva Loser, ed., *Conflict Resolution and Democratization in Panama: Implications for US Policy*, Washington, DC, The Center for Strategic and International Studies, Significant Issues Series, XIV, No. 2, 1992, p. 19.

[3] Roy Licklider noted that this independent action by the federal prosecutors, at variance with Reagan's foreign policy, highlights a 'peculiarity' of the American system, 'which sometimes has an unusual impact on foreign policy', and an incident that most likely would not occur in other countries. From personal correspondence with the author.

administration into taking action to remove Noriega from power. The fight against drugs was, after all, a cornerstone of Reagan and Bush's policy toward Latin America.

Several opportunities to remove Noriega in a peaceful manner arose, but the US government reneged on them for fear that Noriega would not fulfil his part of the deal, and that anything short of trying Noriega for drug charges would be looked upon very unfavourably by the US public during George Bush's campaign to become US president. At the end of February 1988, Panamanian President Eric Arturo Delvalle tried to fire Noriega in a televised announcement, and instead was himself replaced by the Minister of Education, Manuel Solis Palma. The United States continued to recognise Delvalle and imposed stiffer economic sanctions (originally instituted in autumn 1987), which included freezing Panamanian assets in the United States, suspending canal payments to the government, revoking Panama's most-favoured-nation trade status, and banning all payments into the country from the United States.[4]

As in the subsequent interventions discussed in this book, sanctions only served to debilitate the domestic economy without achieving their aim: Noriega remained entrenched. Economists reckon that the economy in 1988 declined by 20–25 per cent, while unemployment rose by 20 per cent.[5] In addition to sanctions, in April 1988 a further 3,444 US troops were dispatched to Panama to augment the 9,589 soldiers already there. These troops participated in very public training exercises, but even these 'scare tactics' did not achieve the desired goal.

Count-down to the invasion

Because of significant US pressure, but also because he was confident of victory, Noriega finally agreed to hold elections on 7 May 1989, and even invited foreign observers. His over-blown self-assurance was primarily derived from his skill over the years at playing different departments of the US government off each other, and from his successive victories over the US administration as it vainly attempted to remove him from power.[6] The Panamanian opposition agreed to participate,

---

[4] Eytan Gilboa, 'The Panama Invasion Revisited: Lessons for the Use of Force in the Post Cold War Era', *Political Science Quarterly*, 110, 4, 1995–6, p. 550.

[5] *The May 7, 1989 Panamanian Elections*, Washington, DC, National Democratic Institute for International Affairs and National Republican Institute for International Affairs, 1989, p. 20.

[6] For more information, see Gilboa, 'The Panama Invasion Revisited', pp. 539–62.

because they believed that the presence of international observers and media would ensure fair elections. The observers (over 270 of them, from 21 countries) played a pivotal role throughout the process, and included dignitaries such as former US presidents Jimmy Carter and Gerald Ford.

Despite the foreign presence and the widespread participation by Panamanians in the elections, Noriega's 'Dignity-Battalions' attacked the opposition, while his PDF troops hampered the electoral process. Although the results of the elections gave the opposition an overwhelming victory, Noriega was not about to lose and nullified the elections three days later on 10 May, claiming foreign interference and insufficient documentation. The Church laity and opposition groups had conducted independent polling during the election, and denounced the fraud, which was anyway easily detectable. Jimmy Carter used information from the Church polls to publicise the fraudulent elections and tried unsuccessfully to arrange a meeting with Noriega. The NDI–IRI delegation held a press conference on 8 May to condemn Noriega's action, and the Organization of American States (OAS) followed suit.[7] Although the elections were stolen, the opposition did organise a successful campaign, and Panamanians voted in large numbers, expressing their desire for change. Moreover, international television coverage relayed images of the bloody beatings meted out to several members of the winning opposition team.

Now it was just a matter of time and sufficient provocation before the military option would be chosen, although the US administration did make a few last-ditch efforts to forestall the inevitable. Several times Bush called on the Panamanian people to overthrow Noriega: 'They ought to do everything they can to get Mr Noriega out of there,' he said.[8] As late as November 1989, Bush authorised the CIA to spend $3 million on a secret plan to recruit Panamanians to overthrow Noriega.[9] Despite such encouragement, these activities came to nought for a variety of reasons, primarily related to the disorganised nature of Bush's new government.

Finally, in October 1989, there was an attempted coup by a member of Noriega's clique. The wife of Moises Giroldi informed the US military that her husband was planning a coup and asked for assistance.

[7] NDI stands for National Democratic Institute for International Affairs while IRI stands for the International Republican Institute, representing the American Democratic and Republican QUANGOs that support democratisation.

[8] Cited in Bob Woodward, *The Commanders*, London, Simon and Schuster, 1991, p. 92.

[9] Woodward, *The Commanders*, p. 140.

The coup took place but it was only given partial assistance by the US military, who claimed that it was poorly organised. Bush's public solicitation for a coup implied to Panamanians that there would be full-scale support of any attempt, since it would rid Bush of the potential unpleasant side-effects of doing the job himself. Chaotic US policy, leaks to the press, and bureaucratic infighting in Washington only ensured that those who carried out the unsuccessful coup were brutally tortured and then murdered. Where was the resolve that Bush seemed to portray?

Admiral William Crowe, Chair of the Joint Chiefs of Staff until several months before the invasion, and well known for his reluctance to use force, predicted the outcome well in advance – to him it was a question of 'when' not 'if'.[10] And Noriega's errant behaviour ensured that it would occur sooner rather than later. Over the next few months, several incidents transpired, including the killing of one US citizen and the harassment of two others in Panama, that provided the US government with what it considered sufficient grounds for the invasion. On 15 December, just days before US troops launched the operation, Noriega was declared maximum leader and head of government, while the Chamber of Peoples Deputies passed a resolution declaring that 'a state of war existed in Panama because of the North American aggression'.[11]

Until the very end, administration officials denied that an invasion was being planned. Secretary of Defense Richard Cheney said that US troops would 'not be involved with deciding who governs Panama', although that is in fact exactly what transpired.[12] Noriega interpreted the policy waffle and u-turns as sufficient proof that he could continue his illicit and aggressive activity unhindered, and that he was being protected by his friends in the US government. It is also easy to understand why Noriega continually out-manoeuvred US attempts to remove him from power. There was no coherent policy, but rather bureaucratic squabbling between and within intelligence agencies, the Department of Defense, the Congress – even Reagan and Bush did not follow consistent approaches during their own presidencies.

On 17 December 1989, just seven months after the cancelled elections, President Bush ordered the commencement of *Operation Just Cause*, which required 48 hours minimum advance notice. Just after

[10] From an interview with Ambassador Crowe, US Embassy, London, UK, 9 September 1996.

[11] Cited in John T. Fishel, *The Fog of Peace: Planning and Executing the Restoration of Panama*, Carlisle, Pennsylvania, Strategic Studies Institute, US Army War College, 15 April 1992, p. 4.

[12] Cited in Gilboa, 'The Panama Invasion Revisited', p. 554.

midnight on 20 December 1989, 14,651 US troops landed in Panama, while thousands of other troops relocated from US bases within the country (a total of 27,684 troops were in Panama at the time of the invasion).[13] According to plan, the day before troops landed, the winners of the cancelled election, Guillermo Endara, Ricardo Arias Calderon, and Guillermo Ford (also known as the 'Big Three'), were sworn in as President and Vice-Presidents respectively at the US military base. On 7 February 1990, the US House of Representatives approved Bush's actions by a large margin (389 votes in favour, 26 against).

Officially, US troops invaded for four reasons: to save American lives and protect US property, to restore democracy, to preserve the integrity of the canal treaties, and to apprehend Noriega, who had, after all, declared a state of war against the United States and was acting accordingly. Bush also cited riots in 1987 and the brutal murder in 1985 of Hugo Spadafora, an eminent Panamanian political critic, who was tortured and then decapitated, probably by Noriega's PDF. Although these goals were laudable (and they will be examined later in this chapter), the more plausible rationale was that Bush was forced into action because he was embarrassed once Noriega's drug dealing was made public after the Miami indictment, and because of the continued humiliations experienced during the period when the administration had tried peacefully to remove him from office.

The general consensus from international experts as well as from prominent members of the Panamanian opposition was that the US intelligence community would have continued to support Noriega had the drug allegations *not* been made public in the United States during a period when a major focus was on the fight against drugs.[14] The Panama invasion followed two years of a failed policy of pressuring Noriega to leave, and over thirty years of a policy of supporting Noriega that was flawed from the start. The democracy excuse also rang hollow and was reminiscent of the Reagan years, when Reagan had used it to wrest more money from Democrats in Congress to fight his war in Nicaragua.

In Panama, where there was no leftist threat, there was no corresponding American pressure to democratise until after the invasion. In addition, the US administration, despite being fully apprised of the situation, had willingly overlooked the election fraud of May 1984 in which Noriega's candidate won. As Thomas Carothers concluded, 'The notion

---

[13] Information provided by Major J.G. Curtin, Public Affairs Officer, US Army South.

[14] See, for example, Thomas Carothers, *In the Name of Democracy: US Policy towards Latin America in the Reagan Years*, Berkeley, University of California Press, 1991.

that a burning desire to bring democracy to Panama pushed the Bush administration to military action is groundless. The US government managed to live with a nondemocratic government in Panama for decades before it turned against Noriega in 1988.'[15] Finally, President Bush had assumed the mantle of 'leader of the free world', and if he could be pushed around by a small-time thug in an even smaller country, any hoped-for new world order really was unattainable (Clinton would later adopt this same attitude in Haiti).

Plans conceived and completed

Planning an invasion

Just days before the coup attempt, General Colin Powell replaced Admiral Crowe as Chair of the Joint Chiefs of Staff. Powell was more willing than Crowe to use force, but he was also concerned that if force were to be used, a comprehensive plan had to be adopted to eradicate the entire regime. Detailed plans for a possible military intervention in Panama dated as far back as November 1987, with the main plan to counter the PDF drawn up in February 1988. In addition to the military operation, the US Army from as early as March 1988 had instructed several Civil Affairs (CA) units to prepare for the organisation of a future Panamanian government in the aftermath of a US invasion. The political reconstruction phase was then intended to endure for only one year past the intervention – as unrealistic a goal as that of the original Allied plans for Germany and Japan.[16]

Several scenarios were envisaged, beginning with *Operation Elaborate Maze*, which was later subsumed within *Operation Prayer Book* (see Figure 2.1). In *Prayer Book*, the intervention was divided into two phases: the military component followed by post-intervention reconstruction. The military phase was first called *Operation Blue Spoon*; later it became *Operation Just Cause*. The reconstruction side also changed names: *Operation Krystal Ball* (completed in August 1988), then *Blind Logic*, and finally, both were subsumed under *Promote Liberty*. *Liberty* was officially initiated on 20 December, and fell under the direction of US Southern Command's Directorate of Policy, Plans, and Strategy (SCJ-5).[17]

[15] Carothers, *In the Name of Democracy*, p. 182.

[16] 'Civil Affairs in *Operation Just Cause*', *Special Warfare*, 4, Winter 1991, p. 28.

[17] Richard H. Shultz, Jr., *In the Aftermath of War: US Support for Reconstruction and Nation-Building in Panama Following Just Cause*, Maxwell Air Force Base, AL, Air University Press, 1993, p. 16.

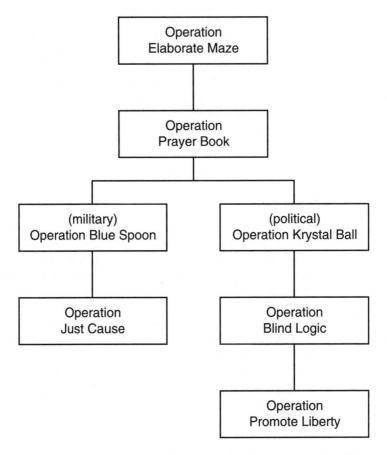

Figure 2.1 Political and military plans for the invasion of Panama, including all name changes.

When drafts were initially drawn up in 1988, most of the military planners were on 31-day assignments. This meant that several teams rotated through the planning cell, each altering and therefore complicating the designs. Eventually two plans were completed, one for the Commander in Chief (CINC), and the other for the agencies that would execute them.

As mentioned, CA planners used the post-World War II reconstruction plans as their guide. Included in an early version was a contingency for the overthrow of Noriega, with General Woerner, CINC US Southern Command, assuming he would be in control of the Panamanian government for a maximum of one month if the civilian government did not exist (this was the supposed alternative to the US Ambassador taking the helm).[18] His plan was not approved, and he was soon replaced by General Thurman. Woerner's removal caused some controversy,[19] though his strategy for reconstructing Panama proved to be too hands-on for a military that was supposed to be subservient to civilian control.[20]

Fortunately there was no need for a US general to run the Panamanian government because the elected team was in place, albeit not entirely in control. Because the Panamanian government effectively consisted of the three elected officials, however, the US Embassy and the US military were heavily involved in running the government for the first few months of the transition. In terms of the US end of the operation, the CINC was in charge, with a hand-over to the US Ambassador to occur at a later date. After Panama, military intervention would be followed by a peace support operation, and in this, the person directing civil–military operations would be a civilian, normally called the Special Representative of the Secretary-General (SRSG) or Special Envoy.

Even though political reconstruction plans existed, little time had been spent on their upkeep since most of the focus was on the military side of the invasion. In addition, the US military was not prepared for the political vacuum that was created after the troops landed, and thus they hastily reworked their drafts to execute *Blind Logic*. As Richard Shultz explained, 'the bifurcation of the planning process had serious, if unintended, consequences during implementation'.[21]

Operation Promote Liberty *and the military support group: after the invasion*

For public relations purposes, *Operation Blind Logic* became *Operation Promote Liberty* just after US troops secured Panama. The modest task assigned to the Civil-Military Operations Task Force (CMOTF), originally entrusted with administering *Liberty*, was to reconstitute the Panamanian government, even though the group lacked the necessary training, organisation, and personnel to accomplish such a herculean feat.

---

[18] Cited in Fishel, *The Fog of Peace*, p. 8.
[19] His removal had more to do with his reluctance, along with Crowe, to use force to replace Noriega, as opposed to their replacements, Thurman and Powell, who were more willing to use force, albeit under certain conditions.
[20] Ambassador Crowe reiterated that this close involvement was not the job of the military. Interview with Ambassador Crowe, 9 September 1996.
[21] Shultz, *In the Aftermath of War*, p. 16.

CMOTF personnel worked directly with the Panamanian ministers of Justice, Planning and Finance, Industry and Commerce, Foreign Relations, Treasury, Presidency, Labour, Agriculture, Health, Education, Housing, and Public Works in attempting to carry out this mandate.[22] The troops were also directed to initiate a 'ministerial rebuilding program that enhanced public well-being and encompassed the principles of a representative democracy as its basis'.[23] The immediate priorities outlined by the CMOTF were ordered in the following manner:

1   Medical, fire fighting, water, power, communications, postal service, sanitation, and return to work program;
2   Build a national police force, weapons turn-in, security for Government of Panama (GOP) officials;
3   Food distribution and warehouse security;
4   Neighbourhood night watch program;
5   Protection of property and security of GOP facilities;
6   City clean-up, GOP funding, GOP rebuild Panama, remove graffiti, register those killed in graves;
7   Publish Spanish newspaper;
8   Grass roots;
9   Counternarcotics, military flight requests, civil aviation, human rights, detainees;
10 Fuel.[24]

Supposedly by mid-January 1990, the core functions of the Panamanian government had been rebuilt and the police made functional. As the military report explained,

[CMOTF] established the government of Panama and restored essential government services. It moved from being the initiator of the actions of the Panamanian government (with government and Embassy approval) to being the advisor and facilitator of resources to the President, two Vice Presidents, and the Ministers as they were appointed.[25]

As will become apparent, this statement glossed over the fundamental problems encountered.

---

[22] DOD Memorandum for SCCS, Subject: History of Actions and Activities Preceding JUST CAUSE, Reference: Chief of Staff Memorandum, Control Number 291531May 90, 20 June 1990, Justification, para. 3.
[23] DOD Memorandum for SCCS, Subject: History of Actions and Activities Preceding JUST CAUSE, para.2.
[24] DOD Memorandum for SCCS, Subject: History of Actions and Activities Preceding JUST CAUSE, para. 5.
[25] In Fishel, *The Fog of Peace*, p. 42.

When *Just Cause* officially terminated in mid-January 1990, *Promote Liberty* launched the Military Support Group (MSG), which was to last for one year. The MSG's mandate was to 'conduct nation building operations to ensure that democracy, internationally recognized standards of justice, and professional public services are established and institutionalized in Panama'.[26] The MSG comprised Special Operations, Civil Affairs, Psychological Operations (or PYSOPS), and combat/combat service support.[27]

As would also occur in Haiti, Civil Affairs troops worked with local governments in planning and implementing projects; in some, Panamanians provided the funding and labour to build roads and bridges, and repair schools and hospitals, while US troops advised on their execution. The PYSOPS unit was shut down after five months because the US Ambassador was concerned about the implications of maintaining units that were engaged in activity directly in support of the Panamanian government.[28] To the Ambassador, this implied partisanship.

Though the rhetoric appears similar, the mission of the MSG differed from that of the CMOTF. As John Fishel explained, 'Where the mission of the [CMOTF] was to reestablish law and order and to support the establishment of a Panamanian government (and, informally, to function as that government while the various ministries were being organised), the MSG was to support a partially structured government and a rapidly growing US civilian governmental presence.'[29] In other words, the MSG was tasked to continue the operation initiated by the CMOTF. During both phases, meetings were held on a frequent basis – between Panamanian government ministers, US military planners and US Embassy personnel, including the US Ambassador – to evaluate progress. Other meetings between US military commanders and the 'Big Three' continued in this fashion even after the MSG was discontinued (in January 1991).[30]

[26] From the MSG document, 'US Military Support Group Panama: Envision the Future ... Then Make It Happen', Headquarters Southern Command (April 1990), cited in Shultz, *In the Aftermath of War*, p. 33.

[27] Shultz, *In the Aftermath of War*, p. 34.

[28] For example, they produced TV video clips for the government.

[29] Fishel, *The Fog of Peace*, p. 43.

[30] In Haiti, frequent meetings were also held with the government of Haiti, representatives from the UN Mission (civilian and military), and the US Ambassador, with the military playing a more subservient role, which will be discussed in chapter 4.

Policing the police

Prior to implementing democratic reforms and as a necessary step in upholding them, the state needs to re-establish a sufficient degree of security. Normally this is accomplished by reforming the police, the military, and the judicial system. In Panama, the new legislature abolished the military, and therefore police and judicial reforms became the focus of reform.

Corruption permeated all ranks of the Panamanian Defense Forces (PDF), which could nominally be called a police force. Officers routinely terrified civilians through extortion and torture, and subsequently never gained the confidence of the population. An entirely new police force was necessary, one that could ensure public safety, especially after the serious looting that took place in Panama during the first few days of the invasion. In addition, the US military considered it of utmost importance to have a working Panamanian presence on the streets so that the US troops would not be considered an occupying force.

Initially, US troops decentralised the force into three separate services: a Department of Justice (for criminal investigations), Department of Corrections (prison services), and a re-organised Presidential Guard, which would fall under the Office of the President. They also took a controversial decision to recruit some former PDF members due to the sense of urgency and the belief that it would take longer to train new officers than to retrain the old. This dilemma has surfaced in most peace support operations, including Haiti, Somalia, and Bosnia, and has not been fully resolved, though the method applied in Haiti appears to have garnered more domestic support (i.e., phasing out the old force in increments, while simultaneously recruiting and training new troops; see chapter 4 for more information). In Panama, only the extremely corrupt former PDF members were weeded out, and even then, it was difficult to gather intelligence on the worst offenders. All recruits did, however, go through an intensive 20-hour training course.

US law, however, prohibits its soldiers from training foreign police, and although the rules were relaxed in the immediate aftermath of the invasion, their involvement was considered a temporary, stop-gap measure. In February 1990, Congress prohibited further military training of police in Panama, not just because of US law and the fact that US troops had earlier trained many members of the corrupt PDF, but also because the duties to be performed by police officers differ from those of soldiers, even of military police. By the time of Somalia, Haiti, and Bosnia this lesson had been learned: police train other police.

Training was subsequently handed over to the largest civilian agency

involved in the reconstruction, ICITAP (International Criminal Investigative Training Assistance Program), supported by the US Department
of Justice, which developed a five-year, $60 million programme to
'equip, train and professionalize' the Panamanian police.[31] ICITAP programmes consisted of sessions led by retired FBI agents on subjects
such as criminal investigations and law enforcement, with a particular
focus on management and organisational techniques. Unfortunately,
ICITAP was in no way prepared for the enormity of the task assigned
to it, nor did the organisation have any experience in building a police
force completely from scratch. Moreover, their plans for restructuring
police were long-term ones, which did not prove helpful in Panama
where short-term exigencies ruled.

ICITAP instructors did, however, teach a transition course for former
PDF members to assist in curbing human rights abuses.[32] ICITAP staff
also distrusted the US military, and preferred to maintain separate
offices and programmes, despite offers for shared space and assistance.
Only from necessity, therefore, were US troops occasionally asked to
conduct joint patrols with the new Panamanian police force, with these
troops serving in a supporting capacity to ICITAP. US troops also
assisted in weeding out PDF members tainted by their close affiliation
to Noriega.

After eight months of the new force, there were still no non-PDF
recruits. It was also becoming increasingly apparent that the new officers
were not performing up to expectations, and many were behaving in as
corrupt a fashion as they had under Noriega.[33] The Panamanian public
soon lost faith in the programme. Additionally, operational funds were
inadequate; for instance, some police stations could not even provide
writing material to fill out reports, petrol for daily car patrols, or
monthly salary cheques.[34] The US government was not going to be
responsible for funding the Panamanian police, while the new Panamanian government resented the inclusion of former PDF members in the
force and therefore withheld funds.

Towards the end of its first year, there was a coup attempt from
within the new police force, which US soldiers had to put down, as the
Panamanian police were unable to do so. The MSG had been preparing

---

[31] USAID was involved in a similar initiative to rebuild the judiciary.
[32] For more information, see Shultz, *In the Aftermath of War*, pp. 45–55.
[33] Even by 1992, only 8 per cent of the new police force were not former PDF
personnel.
[34] John T. Fish and Richard D. Downie, 'Taking Responsibility for Our
Actions: Establishing Order and Stability in Panama', *Military Review*, April
1992, p. 75.

to wind down, but the coup attempt forced the US Ambassador to request that it remain active until the New Year (it finally was shut down on 17 January 1991, one year after it started). The humiliation of having US soldiers ward off a coup, coupled with an economy that had not received the jump-start necessary for adequate recovery after years of economic sanctions, further eroded Panamanian domestic support for the US effort. There were, however, some modest success stories in security sector reform. For instance, the weapons-for-cash exchange in Panama recovered 4,000 guns at a cost of $800,000.

In the aftermath of the aftermath

Not only were police reforms plagued with difficulties, but other parts of the reconstruction phase experienced major problems. With plans for reconstruction prepared well in advance, and different highly skilled teams of US soldiers assigned to carry out the job once the operation was underway, what went wrong in Panama? Six obstacles were encountered in Panama, many of which continue to plague peace support operations.[35]

1. *Poor understanding of what would happen in the immediate aftermath.* The massive looting and collapse of civilian agencies in Panama came as a complete surprise to US troops, although according to John Fishel, the military did anticipate some trouble and factored the reaction into earlier plans. Unfortunately these specific components were not included in the final version of *Blue Spoon*.[36] The looting lasted throughout the first week, and it was not just the shops that were ransacked, but also government offices.

In fact, much of the looting was carried out by those who knew they would have no job to go back to because of their close affiliation to the Noriega regime. Moreover, its occurrence gave the impression that US troops were not managing the situation they had created. The estimate for overall damage reached $1 billion. Since Panama, contingency planning for similar pillaging has been incorporated into military strategy.

2. *High-level security concerns prevented the inclusion of civilian agencies in the planning process.* Because the military wanted to catch Noriega and the PDF off guard, it was considered essential that only the minimum

---

[35] This section draws heavily on the following studies: Fishel, *The Fog of Peace*; Licklider, 'State Building After Invasion: Somalia and Panama'; and Shultz, *In the Aftermath of War*.

[36] Fishel, *The Fog of Peace*, pp. 13, 26. Fishel also explained that US troops were operating on the periphery of Panama City, thus leaving a power vacuum in the centre.

number should know that the invasion would occur. Even within the military, knowledge of plans for reconstruction was reserved for a select number of people. Civilian democratisation agencies with significant experience in Central America were thus not involved until after the invasion. The opposite took place in Haiti, when civilian agencies (as well as the general public) knew that the intervention was a distinct possibility, and subsequently had time to orchestrate their role for the post-military phase (as will be discussed in chapter 4).

Because of this secrecy, the involvement of the US military in the nation-building phase was extensive and resembled the Allied occupation of Germany and Japan, which made many in US military and civilian circles uncomfortable, including the US Ambassador to Panama, Deane Hinton.[37] As Shultz pointed out, 'US Army colonels are not supposed to become advisors to foreign heads of state and when it happened in Panama it disturbed the US Embassy – the MSG had crossed over into its territory.'[38] Since Panama, the US military no longer directs the political side of the reconstruction process, which the military prefers since it is difficult to train for this type of unpredictable, or 'grey', activity.

3. *The military and political reconstruction plans were disconnected.* Because both were prepared by soldiers, this ensured that more attention would be paid to the fighting than the reconstruction phase: most of the focus was on *Blue Spoon*, not on *Blind Logic*. As General Maxwell R. Thurman, US Commander in Chief of the Southern Command (USCINCSO), remarked, 'I did not even spend five minutes on *Blind Logic* during my briefing as the incoming CINC. . . the least of my problems at the time was *Blind Logic*. . . We put together the campaign plan for *Just Cause* and probably did not spend enough time on the restoration.'[39] Shultz added, 'restoration was generally of secondary importance throughout most of the 22 months leading up to 20 December 1989'.[40]

Crowe, who was the Chair of the Joint Chiefs of Staff until October 1989, did not remember any discussions about rebuilding Panama in the aftermath of an invasion – it just was not considered the job of the military.[41] This point aptly demonstrates how few people within

---

[37] See Shultz, *In the Aftermath of War*, pp. 40, 57–61, for more details. Ambassador Crowe also agreed that this task should not be entrusted to the military.

[38] Shultz, *In the Aftermath of War*, p. 62.

[39] Cited in Shultz, *In the Aftermath of War*, p. 16.

[40] Shultz, *In the Aftermath of War*, p. 16.

[41] From an interview conducted at the American Embassy, London, 9 September 1996.

the military were involved in the political reconstruction dimension of the invasion, or even were aware that such plans existed. In addition, because Civil Affairs units would carry out most of the reconstruction work, and the military establishment considers CA work to be peripheral to its main goal, the commitment to reconstruction was minimal.

Because this lack of interest in reconstruction emanated from the top, it quickly permeated the entire operation, which is the opposite of what occurred in Haiti, where the optimism and enthusiasm from above were contagious. In Panama, this low-priority sentiment was evident everywhere, e.g., there were few rehearsals of *Blind Logic* – even on a simulation basis – and little knowledge of available units.[42] In the months prior to the intervention, *Blue Spoon* was revised several times, but *Blind Logic* remained unchanged.

Staffing was irregular throughout the planning and execution phases, the majority of those involved worked on a voluntary basis, and the planning units therefore lacked the specialists and continuity required for the tasks. Finally, within the US Department of Defense (DOD), there was no approval for a reserve call-up, which also excluded participation by many specialists working in civilian agencies. In Panama, the discontinuity between the military and political tasks diminished the effectiveness of the operation. This formal separation would later impair the Somalia and Bosnia operations. The exception to this rule occurred in Haiti, when the political and military components were tightly integrated, and this ensured a smoother operation.

4. *There was an unclear chain of command in the reconstruction phase.* This confusion occurred because the unit that planned *Blind Logic* (SCJ-5) also executed it – not the norm for military operations. As Thurman explained, 'The J-5 is a staff agency, headed by a staff officer. It simply does not have the communication or transportation services, nor does it have the necessary organizational fabric. Thus, it is a bad plan when the J-5 ends up commanding anything.'[43] The message was simple: planners plan and implementers implement.

There were also too many different military units working on rebuilding Panama, and initially they did not have a clear picture of their place in the overall scheme. There was thus some overlap between and even within organisations. In addition, because the reserves participating in the mission did not come from the same Army units (since

---

[42] Shultz, *In the Aftermath of War*, p. 23.
[43] General Thurman interview in Shultz, *In the Aftermath of War*, p. 22.

they came as individuals on a voluntary basis), there was little cohesion within the groups, and difficulties agreeing upon the methods for running day-to-day tasks, even down to simple accounting procedures. This type of problem would become even more complicated in subsequent operations as foreign troops would be introduced into the equation, bringing with them their own distinct military cultures.

5. *Funding was inadequate.* The Bush administration promised $1 billion in aid for Panama after the invasion, yet originally only half that amount was transferred, and much of it came in the form of security assistance through the Urgent Assistance to Democracy in Panama Act (February 1990) that was not visible to the Panamanian public. Remaining funds were either cut back by DOD or by Congress, although some funds that had been withheld during the embargo were later released for additional security assistance, medical, and other emergency relief.

The financial commitment to reconstruction, and to peace support operations, will always be an obstacle to their smooth running, especially when the majority of it is supposed to come from the United States. Most Americans have an incredibly short political attention span. Thus in the immediate aftermath of an intervention, support is very high as Americans are still heady after watching their troops land in overwhelming numbers, feed the starving, and stop the killing. After a few months, when murders and rapes are less frequent, and troops are no longer parachuting in but are instead building bridges and repairing roads, public attention soon shifts to the next crisis, and funding that had previously been considered appropriate is then deemed too steep by the US Congress, and cut back accordingly.

6. *There was an unclear picture of what Panama would look like in the immediate, medium, and long term.* Missing in all the enthusiastic rhetoric was a practical understanding of what kind of democracy would be suitable for Panama, one that would be endorsed by the local population and suitable to their needs. The US military had not fully conceptualised what was achievable, nor did it recognise that Panama's lack of experience with democracy would be a significant factor in attempting to 'restore' any such thing: there were no democratic and civic traditions in Panama, and therefore no base on which democratic reforms could be rebuilt. Democracy needed to be installed, not restored; the context was misunderstood.

As Fishel noted, '*Blind Logic*'s major strategic weakness was that it failed to address the strategic issue of democracy. President Guillermo Endara's observation that the United States "didn't have a specific plan to help us in establishing democracy" is a telling confirmation of that weakness.'[44] This fault could also be attributed to the assumption on the part of the US military that there would be functioning Panamanian civilian agencies that could take responsibility once the 'bad guys' were removed. In fact, most analysts at the time did not predict that they would have to rebuild an entire government.

Initially it was hoped that responsibility for reconstruction could be transferred to the US Embassy after a short period, similar to the way military forces transfer responsibility to the UN in peace support operations. The Embassy would in turn prepare the Panamanian civilian agencies and politicians for the management of local affairs. The US Embassy in Panama, however, was understaffed due to the significant reductions that had occurred for security reasons in the months prior to the invasion. Even had the Embassy been fully staffed, they had been kept out of the planning process and so would have had difficulties taking the reins on such short notice. There was thus an uneasy, *ad hoc* working relationship between military and civilian personnel in subsequent democratisation efforts.

As Shultz concluded, 'The US did not have, at the time of *Operation Just Cause*, a policy for the period following the use of force.'[45] Fortunately *Blind Logic* was succeeded by the MSG and *Operation Promote Liberty*, which tried to rectify the mistakes made earlier. It is also true, however, that the 'democracy deficit' varies considerably between countries, and this accounts for many of the problems experienced in the cases discussed in this book (and in peace support operations in general). Indeed, few experienced democratisation organisations and advisers have a detailed picture of the democratic requirements for most countries, including their own.

Evolving international law

Just as the role of the US military in the aftermath of an intervention would be transformed due to the problems encountered in Panama, so too would international law. At the UN and the OAS, the US aggression was denounced on grounds justified under international law. The UN General Assembly voted 75 to 20 on 29 December 1989 to condemn the invasion and demanded a US withdrawal, while at the OAS, the count was 20 to 1 (US vote) against it. It must be pointed out, however, that while OAS members publicly opposed America's violation of

[44] Fishel, *The Fog of Peace*, p. vii.
[45] Shultz, *In the Aftermath of War*, p. 67

Panamanian sovereignty, many privately sanctioned the invasion because they were glad to be rid of Noriega.[46]

The US administration appealed to the self-defence provisions in Article 51 of the UN Charter and Article 21 of the OAS Charter, arguing that all peaceful means had been tried. Thomas Pickering, US Ambassador to the UN, argued that 'the survival of democratic nations [was] at stake'.[47] Beyond the absurdity of the self-defence application, which completely distorted the principle (necessity, proportionality, and immediacy), the still-intact Reagan Doctrine did not endorse military intervention in a situation where the Soviet Union was not supplying arms. Further, the US Senate had earlier accepted that intervention in Panama would *only* be permissible in the event of a breach in the canal's neutrality, and not as a result of domestic political events.[48]

As mentioned, Bush claimed four causes for the intervention: to save American lives, to restore democracy, to preserve the integrity of the canal treaties, and to apprehend Noriega. A closer examination of these four reveals that at the time of the invasion, the excuses were not legitimate, although they did pave the way for a change in international law in the direction advocated by Bush, which will become evident in subsequent chapters in this book.

1. *Protect Americans.* International law allows a state a limited right of intervention to safeguard its citizens. In Panama there was no threat.[49] Only one American had been killed prior to the intervention. This was the worst US–Panamanian incident in twenty-five years, despite the large US presence. This low incidence rate could be replicated in only a handful of very small American towns, and was completely out of kilter with most major American cities. The excuse was previously used in the Grenada intervention, and would again be used in Haiti.

2. *Restore Democracy.* Although this rationale was successfully applied in the Haiti intervention, at the time of the Panamanian invasion it was not considered legitimate under international law, as mentioned in chapter 1 with reference to the UN General Assembly resolution

---

[46] From interviews held at the offices of the Organization of American States, Washington, DC, 1994.

[47] Cited in David J. Scheffer, 'Use of Force After the Cold War: Panama, Iraq, and the New World Order', in Louis Henkin, et al., eds., *Right vs. Might: International Law and the Use of Force*, 2nd edition, New York, Council on Foreign Relations, 1991, p. 122.

[48] Scheffer, 'Use of Force After the Cold War', in Henkin, et al., eds., *Right vs. Might*, p. 113.

[49] See Giancarlo Soler Torrijos, *La Invasion a Panama: Estrategia y Tacticas para el Nuevo Orden Mundial*, Panama, CELA, 1993, p. 28.

entitled, 'Respect for the principles of national sovereignty and non-interference in the internal affairs of States in their electoral processes'.[50] According to Louis Henkin,

All the framers of the Charter purported to believe in democracy. They were hardly agreed as to what it meant, but they were agreed that force was not to be used against another state even to achieve democracy, however defined. Over forty years later states are still not agreed as to what democracy means, but they are still agreed that it is not to be achieved by force. The Charter would be meaningless if it were construed or rewritten to permit any state to use force to impose its own version of democracy. Such a view of the Charter would permit 'aggression for democracy' against any one of 100–150 states by any self-styled democratic champion.[51]

The opposing view was presented by Eli Lauterpacht, who argued the following:

the United States acted in support of the democratic process – a concept of internationally recognized relevance. The United States has replaced a leader who ruled without electoral support by one whose credentials for the position rest upon success at the ballot box – a success then forcibly frustrated by General Noriega. What matters in law is not the technical propriety of the United States action at its inception but whether the Government of Panama itself now regards that action as lawful. For this purpose the proper representatives of Panama are those who have been democratically elected.[52]

Bush followed a similar line when he explained that Endara, the legitimate president, publicly backed the intervention once it was underway. Further, the State Department claimed that it requested permission from Endara prior to the invasion, which he also supposedly granted. Neither of these points, however, has been substantiated in public documents.

In January 1990, however, the Panamanian Ambassador to the OAS concurred with the Lauterpacht reading when he said, 'We consider ourselves liberated by the United States of America – and this, gentlemen, whether many of you like it or not, is what the absolute majority of Panamanians believe.'[53] According to polls taken just after the event,

[50] General Assembly Resolution A/RES/44/147, 82nd plenary meeting, 15 December 1989.
[51] Louis Henkin, 'Use of Force: Law and US Policy', in Henkin, et al., eds., *Right vs. Might*, pp. 61–2.
[52] Eli Lauterpacht, Director, Research Centre for International Law, University of Cambridge, from a letter to *The Times*, 23 December 1989.
[53] 'Panamanian Envoy to OAS Criticizes Organization'. FBIS, Latin America, 12 January 1990.

the invasion was supported by 92 per cent of Panamanian citizens.[54] Likewise, President Endara said, 'The Panamanian people welcome the US soldiers as friends, not as invaders.'[55] Henkin wryly noted, 'People have welcomed conquering armies since the beginning of time, especially when the conquering army is still there.'[56]

3. *Preserve the integrity of the canal treaties.* There was no threat against the canal nor was the security of American forces under threat.

4. *Apprehend Noriega.* Even Hollywood screenwriters would be ridiculed for developing the following plot: US troops enter a foreign, sovereign state – uninvited – torment the leader of that country out of hiding in a monastery by playing very loud rock music (which he is known to hate), abduct the leader – who although not elected, controlled most of the country – and finally, transport him to a US jail where he is given a forty-year sentence for drugs trafficking and money laundering.[57] In fact, the US government is a signatory to several international treaties that proscribe intervention on the pretext that a dictator has breached the rule of law at home. Even when trying to apprehend known drug traffickers, a state needs to obtain permission from another state before crossing into its jurisdiction. It was also unclear whether the Panamanian constitution permitted the extradition of one of its citizens.

International law, however, is malleable, and based on precedent. Bush first changed US law (and the Reagan Doctrine), which would later affect international law, to include the right to arrest errant leaders who threaten US interests. As Scheffer concluded, 'Armed with the two legal memoranda of the Office of Legal Counsel in the Justice Department, which sanctioned nonconsensual arrests abroad by the FBI and by US armed forces, Bush swept aside the international legal impediments to a search-and-seize venture against Noriega.'[58] In future operations, Bush and Clinton would successfully utilise such changes in

---

[54] According to a CBS poll released on 5 January 1990, cited in Woodward, *The Commanders*, p. 194.

[55] 'Endara Speaks at Assembly Installation 1 Mar'. FBIS, Latin America, 2 March 1990.

[56] From the American Society of International Law, Proceedings of the 84th Annual Meeting, Washington, DC, 28–31 March 1990, pp. 251–2.

[57] On 4 March 1999, a federal judge reduced Noriega's prison sentence from forty years to thirty, which means that he could be released as early as 2000, according to his attorneys, but definitely by 2007. Associated Press, 4 March 1999.

[58] Scheffer, 'Use of Force After the Cold War', in Henkin, et al., eds., *Right vs. Might*, p. 121.

international law to their advantage by appealing to the United Nations for endorsement, which is how the right to support the electoral process in Haiti would later be validated by the Security Council.

Conclusions

Since the invasion, the US government has continued to apply pressure on the Panamanian government to proceed with democratic reforms, with a special emphasis on establishing multiparty processes and respect for human rights. Even though *Promote Liberty* officially ended in September 1994, democratisation continues under the auspices of USAID. In 1996, for example, the organisation expected to spend $4.5 million on economic development and democracy promotion in Panama, including programmes with regard to continuing police training, strengthening the rule of law, electoral processes, the executive branch, alternative opinion and information sources, civil society and political culture, political party development, and military conversion.[59] The MSG had earlier made a realistic prediction that the reconstruction would last until the end of this century, and made economic and political development, security concerns, and an anti-drugs campaign the top priorities.

Panama's population of approximately 2.5 million is mostly educated and literate, and the outlook for maintaining a democratic system is good. The country has the basic framework for upholding a democracy, including political parties from all points on the spectrum, a free press, and a free market. Indeed, the index of the 1997 UNDP Human Development Report (HDR) ranked Panama at number nine for developing countries, while the 1998 HDR put Panama at number forty-five, which was in the top two-thirds of the category called 'high human development'. The economy is largely based on the service sector, the canal, and Panama's position as an international banking centre. Further revenues come from the US military presence and subsidies for the canal.

Partly because of charges of corruption and partly because his government was installed by US force, Endara lost the 1994 elections. His task was daunting in any case since he took over a government in which corruption was endemic. Rooting it out would take more than one term, and he was obstructed by the lack of available funding – Noriega was responsible for incurring $6.2 billion worth of debt. In addition, infrastructure, especially in the countryside, was in

---

[59] See USAID information on Panama on the USAID home page on the Web (www.info.usaid.gov).

serious disrepair. On 8 May 1994 the Democratic Revolutionary Party (PRD), Noriega's party, was re-elected to office with only 33 per cent of the vote under the leadership of Ernesto 'El Toro' Perez Balladares. The PRD claimed to be affiliated to the western European Social Democratic club, disowned Noriega and asserted that it would continue the Torrijos reforms, such as expanding social justice and the economy.

The complete disappearance of the Panamanian army has placed overall Panamanian security in the hands of the new police force, which has limited powers. Corruption within the new force remains a problem, while minorities are largely excluded from participation. GDP remains lower than in pre-invasion days because economic sanctions imposed by the United States drastically affected the economy, although by 1994, debt had declined from 133 per cent to 81 percent of GDP.[60] Some still say that Panama is far from being an open democracy, and remains as corrupt as before, with accusations of drug trafficking and money laundering surfacing again in June 1996.[61]

Lessons learned

The list of blunders committed by the US government prior to and during the Panama invasion is weighty. Successive administrations had nurtured Noriega while ignoring his illicit activity; US troops were not adequately prepared for nor overly interested in 'nation-building'; civilian agencies were not included in the planning process; the rationales for intervening were smoke-screens for a more personal dispute between Bush and Noriega; and the excuses themselves were not entirely legitimate according to international law. Thomas Carothers argued that, in Central America, this was a typical pattern because the US government often found itself pursuing democratic reforms after years of empty rhetoric.[62]

As discussed earlier in this chapter, the US military and civilian policy makers learned valuable lessons from this intervention, lessons that would impact on US involvement in future peace support operations. For instance, many US democratisation agencies, including USAID, were involved in pre-intervention planning for Haiti. Reconstruction

---

[60] Data supplied by the World Bank on the Web (www.worldbank.org).
[61] See, for example, *The Economist*, 29 June 1996, p. 47.
[62] Thomas Carothers, 'Comparing Perspectives on Promoting Democracy in Panama', in Loser, ed., *Conflict Resolution and Democratization in Panama*, p. 83. See also Carothers, *In the Name of Democracy*, for more information.

necessarily requires co-operation by civilian and military agencies, and the strong relationship between the two was also in evidence throughout the peacekeeping phase (see chapter 4 for more details). Significantly, the US administration and military have both agreed since Panama that political reconstruction should not be controlled by the military, although one of the six missions of US Army South (based in Panama) today remains 'Support for democracy in Panama and throughout the region'.[63]

In Panama, the hand-over from the military to the civilian agencies was not achieved in the desired time frame because the US military far outnumbered the civilian agencies, they had a longer history of involvement in Panamanian affairs, and civilian agencies were not included in strategic planning. This transition issue was resolved by Haiti, where the development role was integrated from the start. Other concerns, such as the use of ICITAP and the reluctance of this organisation to work with the military, will recur in interventions as turf wars are inevitable, and civil–military distrust will likely be a factor for some time to come.

Why such extensive involvement in Panama by the US government? Despite active US participation in most Central American countries throughout the twentieth century, especially during the Cold War, Panama has often been referred to, somewhat sarcastically, as the fifty-first American state because of its strategic value. For decades, the military presence has been enormous: there were so many troops stationed in Panama at the time of the invasion that only about half the total needed to be transported there – most of the soldiers simply relocated from within the country. The logistical problems that would accompany later US interventions therefore did not exist in Panama. This long-standing, intrusive presence may also account for the belated semi-success in implanting democracy, as opposed to what transpired in Somalia, for example, because US troops remained in Panama, unlike in Somalia when all US soldiers were withdrawn.

Having democracy 'restored' by the US government after a military intervention, and the Panamanian leader transported to a foreign country where he was tried and imprisoned, despite his unpopularity, were humiliating episodes in a country that has long tried to exclude US influence in domestic affairs. Moreover, a vocal minority of Panamanians continue to be upset that the US has refused to compensate

---

[63] From the US Army home page on the Web (www.army.mil/USARSO/mission.htm).

families of several hundred civilians killed during the invasion.[64] Panamanians vacillate in opinion between wanting the US presence to remain after the complete hand-over of the canal scheduled for 31 December 1999 and provide financial assistance, and opting instead to control their own affairs.

The US administration, however, is not particularly interested in maintaining a large presence in Panama now that its strategic importance has declined, and military budget cuts are forcing reductions sooner rather than later. A base is planned in Panama for a multilateral counter-narcotics centre (funded mainly by the United States), primarily because of its proximity to Colombia, which would give both Panama and the United States an excuse to keep US troops on the isthmus.

The role of the media in US policy making was also becoming a factor at the time of the invasion, and would be a determinant for later interventions. Americans watched Noriega's thugs physically abusing other Panamanians – visual aids that prompted them to push for change. And as in the subsequent cases discussed in this book, US policy waffling, public humiliations by 'tin pot dictators', drug trafficking, or refugee flows that directly affect the United States (or Europe in the case of Bosnia), and international media coverage, all ensured that the military option was ultimately chosen.

Were the four goals articulated by Bush achieved?

1.   *Save American lives.* More American lives were lost during the invasion than in the run-up to *Just Cause* (twenty-three US troops as against one), and interestingly, these deaths did not factor into American public opinion as it later would in Somalia. This change can possibly be accounted for by the lack of media coverage of the deaths of the US soldiers in Panama in real time, in direct contrast to what occurred in Somalia. In addition, hundreds of Panamanian civilians were killed during the invasion.

2.   *Restore democracy.* There was no democracy to restore, yet an inchoate democratic government has been in place since troops landed, which might not have occurred as quickly without the invasion. Senior members of the US military also established healthy working relationships with the GOP, and assisted in relaunching the GOP immediately after the invasion.

3.   *Preserve the canal treaties.* Even though there was no apparent threat

---

[64] *The Economist*, 29 March 1997, p. 28.

to the canal, the US government had already agreed to transfer control to Panama by the end of the century.

4. *Apprehend Noriega.* Fully accomplished. Initially, the US government announced a $1 million reward for his capture, as he had been on the run since troops arrived. This cash reward tactic later proved to have a detrimental effect in Somalia, and was also initiated by the same person (Jonathan Howe).

Panama may now be a better place to live than it was prior to the invasion, but it also does not entirely resemble the one described by President George Bush in his 1990 State of the Union Address:

Think back just twelve short months ago to the world we knew as 1989 began. One year, one year ago the people of Panama lived in fear under the thumb of a dictator [sic]. Today democracy is restored. Panama is free. 'Operation Just Cause' has achieved its objective.

The same would erroneously be said by other US government representatives about Somalia, the next US-led military intervention – undertaken this time solely for humanitarian purposes – with no underlying pretext.

3   Disappointed and defeated in Somalia[1]

UNOSOM I, *Operation Restore Hope* and UNOSOM II – which together endured from April 1992 to March 1995 – plunged the international community headlong into its first post-Cold War encounter with a collapsed state. For US President George Bush, still heady from his victories in the Cold and Gulf Wars (and to a lesser extent, in Panama), and UN Secretary-General Boutros Boutros-Ghali, eager to test the potential of an organisation that had been in a Superpower stranglehold since its inception, Somalia provided the perfect opportunity.[2] Vietnam was by then a mere after-thought. The intervention in Somalia, however, did not live up to expectations. Much of Somalia today has slipped back into the situation of sporadic lawlessness that prevailed before foreign troops arrived – albeit not the famine – despite the enormous infusion of funds ($2.3 billion spent by the US government, and $1.64 billion by the UN), and invasion of untold numbers of aid workers and foreign soldiers (close to 50,000 troops at its peak).[3]

The Somalia intervention set in motion the recent evolution of the non-interventionary norm and established a pattern in the 'new world order', because the decision to use military force was justified purely on humanitarian grounds. There were no strategic, economic or narco-

[1] Some sections of this chapter draw on an earlier article by K. von Hippel and A. Yannis, 'The European Response to State Collapse in Somalia', in Knud Erik Jøergensen, ed., *European Approaches to Crisis Management*, The Hague, Kluwer International Press, 1997. The author would like to thank Dr Yannis for his assistance.

[2] It is also true that President Bush had already been defeated in the US presidential election when he decided to intervene, and thus he did not have to worry about an electoral backlash linked to his decision. Bush probably believed that this operation would give him good marks in the history books as it would be his last official foreign policy move.

[3] The total spent by the UN comes from the UN Department of Public Information, while for the US military, that figure comes from John G. Sommer, 'Hope Restored? Humanitarian Aid in Somalia, 1990–1994', Refugee Policy Group, November 1994, p. C-5.

interests that propelled the UN and the United States into action, nor foreign territory that had been invaded or seized by an errant state. Vice-Chair of the US Joint Chiefs of Staff, Admiral David Jeremiah, confirmed this when he said that there 'was nothing of geopolitical value in Somalia that should engage US interest . . . the intervention therefore had only one motivation – humanitarian'.[4]

Significantly, the intervention took place without the official consent of the government concerned, but with the approval of the UN. Supporters argued that the intervention did abide by the traditional norm: there was no sovereign state and consequently no authority to grant consent. The overwhelming endorsement at the UN for the intervention was indeed garnered because the state imploded and the formal institutions of government disappeared, leaving the population unprotected from the ravages of a civil war that began in 1988, the resultant manmade (or war-lord-inspired) famine, and the local war-lords themselves, who were committing human rights violations on a massive scale. Members of the UN Security Council did, however, emphasise the 'unique', 'extraordinary', and 'exceptional' circumstances surrounding the situation in Somalia, in an attempt to safeguard the non-interventionary norm.[5]

Once the intervention was underway, the Security Council passed Resolution 814 on 26 March 1993, which set a further precedent by mandating the UN to assist in all aspects of 'nation-building'. This chapter analyses the changes in operations that led to Resolution 814, then examines the problems encountered while promoting a political agenda, and concludes with a synopsis of lessons learned and ongoing efforts to rebuild the state. Before proceeding, a brief account of Somalia's recent history follows.

Somalia, the United Nations, and the United States

Creating the crisis

The antecedents of the conflict can be traced back to 1960, when Britain and Italy departed from their colonial outposts – Britain from the

---

[4] This quote is paraphrased from Andrew S. Natsios, 'Humanitarian Relief Intervention in Somalia', in Walter Clarke and Jeffrey Herbst, eds., *Learning From Somalia*, Boulder, CO, Westview Press, February 1997, p. 78. Natsios attended the NSC meeting when Jeremiah made this remark, in his capacity as assistant administrator of USAID during the Somalia relief operations.

[5] Mats Berdal, 'The United Nations in International Relations', *Review of International Studies*, 22, 1996, p. 105.

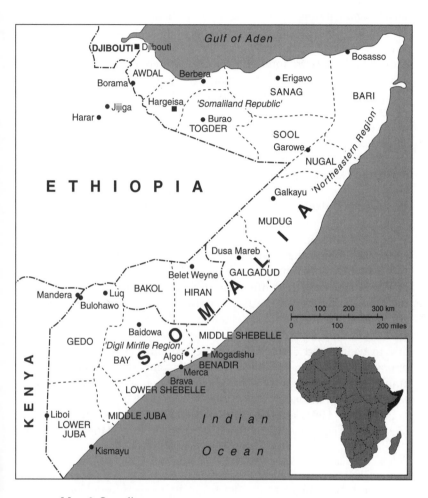

Map 2 Somalia

north-west (the British Somaliland Protectorate) and Italy from the southern trusteeship territory – and the two parts joined to form the Somali Republic. Although the new country established a multiparty democracy, it disintegrated fairly soon due to immense political and social fragmentation, administrative and financial mismanagement, and as John Drysdale explained, 'the unimaginative application of alien systems of government'.[6] Just nine years after independence, General Mohamed Siad Barre took over the Somali Republic in a military coup.

Siad Barre was to rule this country – populated predominantly by pastoral nomads – for over twenty years through shrewd manipulation of clan politics and rivalries, military coercion, and the exploitation of state resources and foreign assistance. Formally he proclaimed that the all-pervasive yet very 'uncentralised' clan-structure that permeated Somalia would no longer dominate. In reality, however, Siad Barre favoured the Darod clan-family (of six major clan-families), especially his own Marehan clan, his mother's clan (Ogaden), and the clan of his son-in-law (Dulbahante) for all important public posts.[7]

During the Cold War, the Soviet Union supported Somalia and, from 1974, Ethiopia as well. The war between Somalia and Ethiopia (1977–78) forced the Soviet Union to choose between its two allies, and Ethiopia came out on top. This exchange, coupled with Somalia's defeat in the war, thereafter placed Somalia under the patronage of the United States, and the country then became dependent on western foreign aid to sustain its economy.[8] Peace with Ethiopia was not formalised until 1988, but by then, the economy had all but collapsed due to widespread corruption, erratic economic policies, a financially draining civil war in north-west Somalia, and the massive influx of ethnic Somali refugees from the Ogaden region of Ethiopia. A nationwide civil war ensued.

In January 1991, after the various rebel movements had taken over most of Somalia, President Siad Barre finally fled Mogadishu. Four

---

[6] John Drysdale, *The Somali Dispute*, London, Pall Mall, 1964, p. 21, cited in Matt Bryden, 'Strategy and Programme of Actions in Support of Local and Regional Administrations in Somalia in the Field of Institution-Building', A Draft Proposal to the EC Somalia Unit (unpublished), October 1996, para. 2.

[7] For more details, see I.M. Lewis, *A Modern History of Somalia: Nation and State in the Horn of Africa*, Boulder, CO, Westview Press, 1988.

[8] Throughout this period (and including the subsequent civil war), the country was flooded with arms. Today most male Somalis possess automatic rifles, while many have access to heavier weapons.

months later, the north-west region of Somalia declared its independence from the rump state as the 'Somaliland Republic' (it has yet to be recognised by a single member of the UN). Also in 1991, most foreigners were evacuated from Mogadishu.

During its tenure, the civil war caused immense devastation, with enormous numbers of refugees (at least 500,000 going to neighbouring Kenya, Ethiopia, and Djibouti), internally displaced persons (another 500,000 IDPs), and civilian deaths, most of which were famine-related (estimated at 350,000). The grain-growing region between the Shebelle and Juba rivers in the south was particularly ravaged, and famine thus spread rapidly throughout the country.

By the early 1990s, foreign food aid could no longer get through to affected Somalis. Instead, war-lords plundered relief supplies to feed their militias and exchange the aid for more weapons. The humanitarian relief agencies remaining in Somalia were forced to hire thug Somalis to protect them and their work (usually from the self-proclaimed protectors). Relief workers watched helplessly while most of their food aid filtered through this corrupt system, in the vain hope that some of it would trickle down. The aid only enhanced the role and strength of the militias, while the population at large continued to starve.

The UN Security Council, indecisive and hesitant in its response to the looming disaster, on 23 January 1992 passed Resolution 733, which called for a total arms embargo and the establishment of an immediate cease-fire. By February, the parties to the conflict agreed to the cease-fire, mediated through the co-ordinated efforts of the UN, the League of Arab States, the Organization of African Unity (OAU), and the Organisation of the Islamic Conference (OIC). Yet the situation on the ground remained conflictual.

International intervention soon crystallised as the number of refugees, IDPs, and deaths from hunger ballooned: approximately 23 per cent of the population were directly affected, while up to 70 per cent were reportedly in the queue. Moreover, extensive media coverage of emaciated Somalis ensured a suitable international outcry (the 'Do Something' response), although some have since argued that the state of emergency was vastly exaggerated by the media.[9] The media were greatly assisted in this effort by the relief agencies who, together with interested members of the US Congress, launched one of the more successful public relations campaigns in history with the hope of raising

---

[9] See Michael Maren, 'Feeding a Famine', Forbes MediaCritic, Fall 1994.

funds for their work and putting a stop to the famine.[10] Such an alliance left the international community with relatively few options.

UNOSOM was therefore conceived through Security Council Resolution 751 (24 April 1992) to facilitate the delivery of humanitarian assistance. That same month, Mohamed Sahnoun was confirmed as the Special Representative of the Secretary-General (SRSG). July witnessed the arrival of the first 50 military observers who comprised the initial security force for UNOSOM I, which grew to 500 by mid-September.

It quickly became apparent, however, that the provision of widespread relief needed a much larger organisation than UNOSOM to secure food delivery.[11] Hence in December 1992, the United States initiated *Operation Restore Hope* (also known as the Unified Task Force, or UNITAF), transporting 37,000 troops to the African continent to do just that. Because of fears of 'mission creep', UNITAF was to last only five months, with its primary aim the protection of food relief. A hand-over to a multi-national, peace-enforcement operation – UNOSOM II – was therefore arranged for May 1993, with the United States providing some troops and the new SRSG (retired Admiral Jonathan Howe, who arrived two months earlier in March, when UNOSOM II was established by Security Council Resolution 814).

On 5 June 1993, General Mohamed Farah Aideed's men ambushed a contingent of Pakistani soldiers, killing twenty-four and wounding many more (Aideed was one of the men responsible for the overthrow of Barre). From that day forward, the operation veered off course and soon came to a crashing halt. The next day, the Security Council passed Resolution 837, which explicitly called for the detention and trial of those responsible. What started out as an impartial peacekeeping operation to feed starving women and children soon turned into an unsuccessful all-out man-hunt in pursuit of Aideed, culminating on the night of 3 October when 18 US Army Rangers were killed and 77 wounded after an attack on an Aideed meeting place in Mogadishu. The Somali casualty list was even higher: an estimated 300 were killed, another 700 wounded, with up to 30 per cent of the victims women and children. This was the bloodiest confrontation of any UN operation.

---

[10] For more information, see Warren P. Strobel, 'The Media and US Policies Toward Intervention: A Closer Look at the "CNN Effect"', in Chester Crocker, Fen Osler Hampson with Pamela Aall, eds., *Managing Global Chaos: Sources of and Responses to International Conflict*, Washington, DC, US Institute of Peace, 1996, pp. 360–6.

[11] In August, the US Air Force had launched a food airlift from Mombasa in Kenya, but it too was insufficient.

Americans once again reacted strongly to media coverage on CNN; this time it was not starving children but rather a dead US soldier being dragged through the streets of Mogadishu by Aideed's men.[12] The 'Do Something' cries were rapidly replaced by a rousing chorus of 'Get Out', as the US public could not understand why Somalis were killing their troops – troops who were sent to Somalia purely on a humanitarian mission. By now President, Clinton then promised to have all US soldiers out by March 1994 (US troops briefly returned in March 1995 to provide protection off the coast during the final force withdrawal, *Operation United Shield*).[13]

In early January 1994, Boutros-Ghali recommended scaling back the mission, and the following November (just as the United States was going into Haiti), the UN Security Council set March 1995 as the final date of operation for UNOSOM II. The operation stumbled on until its termination, on schedule, without accomplishing political reconstruction, disarming of the factions, or a resolution of the conflict – all of which were stated aims of the intervention. It did put a stop to the famine – an estimated 100,000 lives were saved by the intervention (President Clinton claimed one million) – yet the human cost was 156 peacekeepers and several thousand Somali civilians.

Traditional or trailblazing?

If international support for the Somali intervention was amassed because the state collapsed, an equally valid point is that many of the problems encountered by the international community were due to the inability of a traditional peacekeeping operation to function in a society with no government. As Mayall and Lewis explained,

---

[12] This incident would not be easily forgotten. During the 1996 Olympics in Atlanta, the Somali soccer team could not find a hotel in Atlanta and had to go to a nearby town where residents took them in.

[13] Although US public opinion has been cited as the reason for withdrawing from Somalia, some researchers believe that the US government misread public opinion, which was in fact supportive of escalation, despite (or because of) their outrage. For more information, see Steven Kull, I. M. Destler, and Clay Ramsay, *The Foreign Policy Gap: How Policymakers Misread the Public*, College Park, MD, Center for International and Security Studies at Maryland, 1997. Roy Licklider explained that an event such as the Ranger deaths, 'mobilizes new participants in the debate – both at the elite and mass level – who speak out loudly for the first time, while those who had supported the intervention keep quiet, and policymakers get the impression that everyone wants out'. From personal correspondence with Dr Licklider.

the situation lay so far beyond the experience of UN peacekeeping that had developed over the previous forty years – there were simply no precedents for deploying UN forces on a humanitarian rather than a peacekeeping mission when there was no government with which to negotiate and where the practical decision, therefore, was always going to be whether to appease those with the power on the ground or oppose them by force.[14]

In Somalia, both options were chosen, with disastrous consequences.

Technically, UNOSOM I was a small, traditional peacekeeping operation that was intended to separate the warring parties (who had already agreed to a cease-fire). UNITAF then took over as a US-led, UN-endorsed peace-enforcement operation to secure urgent humanitarian assistance. It was a non-blue helmet operation precisely because of the flexibility it allowed a member state – in this case, the United States – to take certain actions to maintain or promote peace and security. The bulk of the financial costs of UNITAF were thus borne by the United States (approximately 75 per cent instead of the normal 30 per cent of peacekeeping), in exchange for a non-UN command and control operation. Yet this supposed flexibility was not realised as intended in Somalia.

Similar to subsequent operations in Haiti, Bosnia, and Albania, the three objectives of UNITAF were: to secure the seaports, airstrips, and food distribution points; to protect relief convoys and ensure the smooth operation of relief agencies; and to assist UN agencies and non-governmental organisations (NGOs) in providing relief to the famine-stricken population.[15] The provision of security also entailed voluntary disarmament and storing weapons in secure areas in exchange for money or food, and retraining Somalis for civilian employment. UN military escorts were used so that Somali security guards, riding in 'technicals', could no longer profit.[16] Finally, a UN Civilian Police training unit (CIVPOL) assisted in the re-establishment of local police forces

---

[14] James Mayall and Ioan Lewis, 'Somalia', in James Mayall, ed., *The New Interventionism, 1991–1994: United Nations Experience in Cambodia, former Yugoslavia and Somalia*, Cambridge, Cambridge University Press, 1996, p. 109.

[15] According to Lt. Gen. McCaffrey, cited in Clement Adibe, *Managing Arms in Peace Processes: Somalia*, Geneva, United Nations Institute for Disarmament Research, 1995, pp. 58–9.

[16] A technical is a basic pick-up truck, mounted with a machine gun. They have been utilised by all faction leaders in Somalia, as well as the international aid community. The term was coined by the NGOs and IGOs during the civil war because they hired Somali escorts to protect them, and then justified their payments to these Somalis under the heading, 'technical assistance'.

and the restoration of the rule of law. This last task was not as much of an obstacle as it would be in Haiti and Bosnia, since Somali police were well known for their professionalism. If the UN had succeeded in re-establishing a Somali state, the CIVPOL programme would have been accorded plaudits.

When plans for UNOSOM II were drawn up, the United States signalled a willingness to let US troops serve as members of a UN force once the transition had taken place.[17] The reality, however, did not measure up to the plans, especially after the hand-over was completed. At the peak of involvement in UNOSOM II, 17,700 US troops served under separate US command, while 3,000 US personnel worked in non-combat, UN logistical units.[18]

The method of transition from the US-military led operation, UNITAF, to the one run by the UN, UNOSOM II, has emerged as a pattern for US military planners, derived from the lessons learned in the Vietnam War and the subsequent desire to avoid 'mission creep'. Based on the 'Powell Doctrine', the emphasis is on initial, overwhelming force, with the baton passed to a multi-national operation within a short time period. This format has been typical of US involvement in peace support operations, and integral to the planning and execution of all the post-Cold War operations.

What complicated the Somalia operation was the overt emphasis on 'nation-building' in a situation of prolonged state collapse, officially tacked on after the operation began. UNITAF had managed to sidestep this issue, although the US government was fully aware that political reconstruction needed to be addressed in order to prevent the situation on the ground returning to the *status quo ante*, i.e., internecine warfare and possibly another famine.[19] President Clinton remarked, 'We didn't

---

[17] In the past, US troops have participated as observers in US-led, non-UN multi-lateral forces (e.g., in Sinai), and have provided logistical support for peacekeeping operations. Indeed, US military personnel have taken part in UN peace support operations since 1948.

[18] A US president has never *relinquished command over US forces*, yet, as mentioned, US troops have served under the *operational control* of foreign commanders (as occurred in World War I, World War II, and Operation Desert Storm). For further information, see Clinton Administration Policy on Reforming Multilateral Peace Operations (PDD 25), released on the Web by the Bureau of International Organizational Affairs, US Department of State, 22 February, 1996 (www.state.gov).

[19] See, for example, Remarks by President Bill Clinton to the Congress from the White House Office of the Press Secretary, 13 October, 1993.

want to go there, pull out and have chaos, anarchy, starvation return [*sic*].'[20]

Because of the extent and duration of state collapse in Somalia, plans to rebuild the state were even more comprehensive than in Panama, and like Panama, they resembled in many ways those of the Allied occupation of Germany and Japan. Embodied in Security Council Resolution 814 (26 March 1993), the relevant points of what would later be referred to as 'the Mother of all Resolutions'[21] are listed below:

Noting the need for continued humanitarian relief assistance and for the rehabilitation of Somalia's political institutions and economy . . . Requests the Secretary-General

- To assist in the provision of relief and in the economic rehabilitation of Somalia;
- To assist the people of Somalia to promote and advance political reconciliation, through broad participation by all sectors of Somali society, and the re-establishment of national and regional institutions and civil administration in the entire country;
- To assist in the re-establishment of Somali police, as appropriate at the local, regional or national level, to assist in the restoration and maintenance of peace, stability and law and order;
- To create conditions under which Somali civil society may have a role, at every level, in the process of political reconciliation and in the formulation and realization of rehabilitation and reconstruction programmes.[22]

US Ambassador Madeleine Albright remarked that the passage of this resolution signified 'an unprecedented enterprise aimed at nothing less than the restoration of an entire country'.[23] For the first time, the international community recklessly jumped into uncharted territory in attempting to rebuild a collapsed state, without having a very clear idea as to how this would be done. Initially, political reconstruction did not appear so daunting a task, as the very same war-lords who instigated the civil war had, since the start of the UN operation, signed various

[20] Remarks By The President To The Pool, The White House, Office of the Press Secretary (New Haven, Connecticut), 9 October, 1993.
[21] From Walter Clarke, 'Failed Visions and Uncertain Mandates in Somalia', in Clarke and Herbst, eds., *Learning From Somalia*, p. 18.
[22] Security Council (SC) Resolution 814, 26 March 1993.
[23] US–UN Press Release 37-(93), 26 March 1993.

agreements that were to lead to the formation of new political structures. It is to this subject that we now turn.

Nation-building

We can rebuild it: we have the technology

Before the UN operation was underway, attempts at reconciliation had been made by various groups of Somali intellectuals, e.g., the Manifesto signed by 144 Somalis in May 1990; by Somali war-lords or 'politicians', e.g., Ali Mahdi's planned, and later abandoned, national reconciliation conference in early 1991;[24] by foreign governments, e.g., Italian and Egyptian initiatives in November and December 1990; and by regional states (Ethiopia, Kenya, and Djibouti), e.g., Djibouti-sponsored meetings in mid-July 1991.[25] Yet none of these was successful because they could not generate enough support amongst Somalis, and critically, the war-lords, who never agreed to the terms for long enough for them to be implemented. This did not change once the UN became embroiled.

Between 1991 and early 1995, seventeen national-level and twenty local-level 'reconciliation initiatives' were attempted, not all under the auspices of the UN.[26] Many were held in Somalia, but some were also convened in neighbouring states – one was even held in the Seychelles! A dozen peace agreements emerged from these (and from post-UNOSOM efforts). Most of the agreements called for the reformulation of local administrative councils, national and local police, employment and vocational training, primary education, livestock and agriculture services, the return of refugees and IDPs, the development of a food security system, increased access to basic health care, potable water and sanitation services, with emphasis placed on including women in the political process. They also called for a cease-fire and disarmament.

One particular national reconciliation conference that attracted

---

[24] Ali Mahdi (Hawiye/Abgal) had been declared interim President, which was contested by General Mohamed Farah Aideed (Hawiye/Habr Gedr).

[25] For more details of these and other attempts, see Mohamed Sahnoun, *Somalia: The Missed Opportunities*, Washington, DC, US Institute of Peace, 1994; and John L. Hirsch and Robert B. Oakley, *Somalia and Operation Restore Hope: Reflections on Peacemaking and Peacekeeping*, Washington, DC, US Institute of Peace, 1995.

[26] Ken Menkhaus, 'International Peacebuilding and the Dynamics of Local and National Reconciliation in Somalia', *International Peacekeeping*, 3, 1, Spring 1996, p. 43.

considerable attention occurred in March 1993 in Addis Ababa, Ethiopia, when a 74-member Transitional National Council (TNC) was devised to provide an immediate structure and pave the way for a more permanent solution. The TNC proposed to include representatives from the eighteen regions, with local and central divisions of power, and seats reserved for women.[27] Prior to this meeting, Boutros-Ghali had warned Somalis that a transitional government would be imposed if they could not agree to future structures at this March meeting.[28]

Optimism followed the Addis Ababa agreement and the assumption that something tangible would emerge from the resultant peace accords. Indeed, this enthusiasm led the European Commission (EC) to appoint a Special Envoy to assist with the reconstruction of Somalia.[29] Article 45 of the Draft Transitional Charter of Somalia (1 November 1993), also conferred a quixotic picture of the TNC: 'With the first meeting of the TNC, a new era of security, nationalism, brotherhood and work shall begin, and shall end the era of tribalism, hostility, looting, division and all forms of brutality'.

As with the other agreements, satisfying the stipulations *and* the parties involved eventually proved impossible. The precise demarcation of the regions was another insuperable obstacle, while the issue of self-determination for Somaliland was not broached. Finally, little progress was made because of the erratic implementation of this agreement by UNOSOM II.

Primarily the TNC failed because the focus remained too heavily tilted towards the war-lords, which would have only given them more power in a future government and made compromise between them virtually impossible as they would have all wanted to control the new government. One UN document noted in planning for the TNC that a consultative body should be formed with members nominated by fifteen factions as well as by the regional councils.[30] The inclusion of non-

---

[27] For further information, see the Addis Ababa Agreement of the First Session of the Conference on National Reconciliation in Somalia, 27 March 1993, and the *Draft Transitional Charter of Somalia*, 1 November 1993, Mogadishu.

[28] John Drysdale, *Whatever Happened to Somalia? A Tale of Tragic Blunders*, London, Haan Associates, 1994, p. 115.

[29] In June 1993, Mr Sigurd Illing arrived in Nairobi as the EC Special Envoy to Somalia, armed with a mandate to prepare for the re-establishment of the European Delegation in Mogadishu. The delegation office in Mogadishu has not yet been re-established due to security concerns, although an EC liaison office was opened in 1995 in Mogadishu, and other liaison offices subsequently opened in Bosasso and Berbera.

[30] UN Document, 'Next Steps in Somalia – Political', 750–13/4, date unknown.

faction members was a late decision – the Transitional Charter Drafting Committee was originally composed of only faction representatives. Ironically, the UN established a Committee on Peaceful Settlement of Disputes, first formed with *only* faction representatives (this was also expanded to include members of civil society).[31]

Despite the plethora of agreements reached on peace, national unity, and the formation of a central government, they were organised in a fairly haphazard manner, without any overall coherency or strategy to implement them, and consequently, not one of the national-level meetings experienced any success. Moreover, apart from the Addis Ababa accords, these initiatives also failed because they focused almost exclusively on a rapid revival of a central state – without the prior elaboration of constitutional arrangements that could have accommodated the centrifugal realities of Somali society and built confidence among the various actors in the peace process.[32] Finally, the national-level agreements foundered because they included more war-lords than traditional leaders from civil society, and these war-lords could not fully control their claimed constituencies. As Mayall and Lewis explained, 'These [warlords] have been consistently endowed with a degree of power and authority which they would very much like to have, but do not actually possess – as has been demonstrated time and again by their failure to deliver on their various promises.'[33]

Local-level agreements attained more results, especially in Somaliland (and more recently, in the north-east with the drafting of the Puntland regional charter in mid-1998), through the organisation of many small, local meetings. These gradually transformed, over the course of a year, into regional conferences. The Boroma 'national' conference, held between February and May 1993, capped this process. Here, elders agreed on a National Peace Charter for the 'Somaliland Republic', which assisted in resolving clan conflicts. Later in 1993, a similar initiative, the Sanaag conference, also concluded with positive results, and as in the former, it evolved out of many grassroots meetings. Significantly, neither initiative received much external, financial assistance.[34]

---

[31] UNOSOM II Political Strategy Timelines, March 1993–March 1995.

[32] Alexandros Yannis, 'Perspectives for Democratic Governance in Somalia', paper presented at the 6th International Congress of Somali Studies, Berlin, Germany, 6–9 December 1996. This belief would later inspire the European Union to launch its project on decentralised structures, discussed at the end of this chapter.

[33] Mayall and Lewis, 'Somalia', in Mayall, ed., *The New Interventionism*, p. 123.

[34] Not all local meetings achieved success; for example, the Jubaland Accord, reached in August 1993 after two months of negotiating in Kismayu, pro-

Over-exertion and under-achievement (814 or bust)

Somalis bear the ultimate responsibility for the crisis that has undermined their society, albeit endeavours of the international community, well-intentioned though they may have been, exacerbated the situation. From the onset of the civil war through the interventions, and relevant to the above-mentioned problems that beset the peace conferences, the difficulties encountered while promoting political reconstruction can be attributed to certain Somalis, the United Nations, the US government and military, and the relationship between the United States and the UN.

Somali solecisms

Somali war-lords induced the wide-scale famine via the plundering and pillaging that normally accompanies civil war. Years of dependence on foreign aid also provided these Somalis with ample experience of manipulating that assistance, especially after the state imploded. It operated in the following manner (see Figure 3.1): A village is besieged, food supplies are stolen and disrupted, the foreign media hover and home in on the most severe cases of starvation, an international outcry ensues, more aid is sent in, that aid is subsequently stolen by the war-lords, who also offer their protection to aid workers at a price, and the spiral continues. Politics caused the famine that was to become an international issue in 1992; thereafter food plundering sustained the war economy. And significantly, as Clarke and Herbst explained, 'Where famine is man-made, stopping the famine means rebuilding political institutions to create order.'[35]

During the intervention, the meagre attempts to reconstruct political coalitions by Somalis never generated enough trust or sufficient guarantees to ensure adherence. The Prisoner's Dilemma was played out in full with respect to voluntary disarmament, implementation of peace agreements, and access to foreign aid. Although it was implicitly understood that full compliance would benefit the majority, the factions preferred to take the known risks associated with continued fighting and

duced constructive objectives and was sponsored at minimal cost to UNOSOM, but it was eventually invalidated by the militias. See Menkhaus, 'International Peacebuilding and the Dynamics of Local and National Reconciliation in Somalia', for more information on this and other initiatives.

[35] Walter Clarke and Jeffrey Herbst, 'Somalia and the Future of Humanitarian Intervention', Center of International Studies, Monograph Series, No. 9, Princeton University, 1995, p. 10.

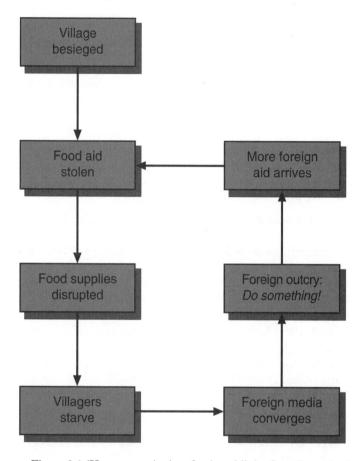

Figure 3.1 'How to manipulate foreign aid', by Somali war-lords.

plundering over the serious risk of disarmament, re-channelling efforts into peace, and allowing aid to arrive unhindered: the fear that others would not follow suit and thereby profit at their expense.

A great majority of Somalis worried that these agreements would not be observed once the UN left; thus they maintained large stockpiles of weapons. Many others preferred to wait out the intervention to see what it would leave behind. Finally, those Somalis who profited because the government imploded (as is typical in any war or terrorist campaign) also obstructed – and continue to obstruct – efforts at peace.

In such an insecure environment, rumours spread quickly, especially by faction leaders adept at manipulation. For example, Aideed was claiming that the UN supported his then rival, Ali Mahdi, which served to undermine any wholesale Somali embrace of the UN. Some of these stories were seemingly confirmed as the numbers of Somali civilians killed during UNOSOM II mounted, deaths often caused by UN soldiers, but also because the war-lords used civilians, especially women and children, as human shields, fully cognisant of the propaganda coup to be won both at home and abroad.

UNcertainties

The UN also played a principal role in the unfolding Somali tragedy for many reasons, particularly the following:

1   poor co-ordination (and turf wars) between New York and Mogadishu staff;
2   over-concentration on Mogadishu at the expense of the rest of the country;
3   Jonathan Howe's culturally insensitive gaffe,[36] while serving as SRSG of UNOSOM II, of offering a $25,000 reward for Aideed's capture, dead or alive (the Secretary-General also reportedly declared that Aideed's 'physical elimination' would help the situation[37]);
4   the ramifications of the (alleged) mutual antipathy between Boutros Boutros-Ghali and General Aideed, based on Boutros-Ghali's supposed support for Siad Barre when he was Egyptian foreign minister;
5   Mohamed Sahnoun's resignation on 29 October 1992, after he initiated an effective, albeit slow, process of brokering peace between clans;[38]
6   the frequent change of the person acting as Special Representative of the Secretary-General (SRSG), and of the humanitarian co-ordinators – a total of five of each rotated through Somalia within a three-year time period; and

---

[36] This move only made Somalis rally around Aideed, even if they did not like him.
[37] From *La Repubblica*, 15 July, 1993, cited in Gérard Prunier, 'The Experience of European Armies in *Operation Restore Hope*', in Clarke and Herbst, eds., *Learning From Somalia*, p. 147.
[38] In fact, Sahnoun is still regarded by many as one of the most effective international actors involved in the Somali crisis, even though he only served for six months.

7   unclear rules of engagement and on the use of force, and for civil–
     military relations.

An overview of these factors could subsume them under the umbrella
of management problems, which can threaten and impede any peace
support operation. It is also nearly impossible to by-pass the personality
variable in situations heavily reliant on human relations and cultural
sensitivities. The differences between the management styles of
Mohamed Sahnoun and Jonathan Howe, the SRSGs of UNOSOM and
UNOSOM II respectively, could not help but confuse Somalis who
were still attempting to understand what the UN was doing there in the
first place.[39] Such disparities in leadership can account for the derail-
ment or the smooth running of an operation (in Haiti, by contrast, good
management permeated the entire operation).

The building blocks necessary to reconstruct the state, especially in
terms of regaining control over security in this heavily-armed, faction-
ridden society, were also not in place. Boutros-Ghali sought to disarm
the Somalis from the beginning of the operation, using whatever force
necessary, yet he was unable to incorporate this aim until Security
Council Resolution 814 was passed in March 1993. His aspiration was
never realised due to the US military, which did not want to participate
in a door-to-door disarmament campaign as it was guaranteed to be
bloody, while the removal of such vast quantities of weapons was
realistically beyond the capacity of US troops.

Although a thorough disarmament programme could feasibly have
helped lay the foundation for implementing political reforms – and
Somalis today say that the failure to do so initially was a missed
opportunity as most Somalis were willing to disarm at the start of
the operation – US planners believed it would transform the mission

---

[39] Sahnoun resigned in October 1992 due to several conflicts between himself
and the UN, including differences over time scales necessary to accomplish
certain tasks. Sahnoun was a slow and patient negotiator, well-respected by
Somalis because he was knowledgeable of traditional Somali consensual
decision making and utilised it to his benefit during UNOSOM. Boutros
Boutros-Ghali wanted to see results very quickly and thus was frustrated by
Sahnoun. Moreover, Sahnoun had publicly criticised the work of UN agencies in Somalia. For Sahnoun's account, see Sahnoun, *Somalia*. Howe's work,
on the other hand, was hampered by the command structure in Somalia –
the military component of the operation was under separate control. Finally,
the overall intent of the intervention never was very clear to Somalis. Many
Somalis today still erroneously insist that the US decided to intervene in the
first place because of the possibilities of oil off the Somali coast.

of their troops, from providing an impartial food security service to directly participating in the conflict.[40] Ironically, this occurred anyhow. The little disarming that did take place was sporadic and voluntary, while eventually most of the weapons were stolen from the cantonment sites.

The mad Aideed man-hunt invalidated any residual pretensions of impartiality, and instead boosted Aideed's image amongst Somalis.[41] In addition, General Aideed's radio broadcasts in early June 1993 were also interpreted by the UN as direct counter-attacks on UN efforts to promote political reconciliation and reactivate the Somali judicial system. Finally, as mentioned, any UN contact with the war-lords inevitably conferred more legitimacy on them, which only served to wrest control from many of the elders who traditionally held more influence, and potentially had the prestige to assist in reconstruction.

UNOSOM II gave Boutros-Ghali his first opportunity to execute his *Agenda for Peace*, with the 'largest multinational force ever assembled under [his] direct control'.[42] Yet experimentation, by definition, is a trial-and-error process. Political rehabilitation was ill-co-ordinated and applied patchily in Somalia, without any overall sharing of information between UN agencies, the military, and NGOs. Fortunately, as became evident in Haiti, many of these mistakes were rectified.[43] What was expected of the UN, in any case, was without doubt beyond its reach due to the lack of resources and experience in this area.

American obfuscation

Not only did the UN commit itself to rebuild the state, but so did the US government, despite some assertions to the contrary by US officials. As Clarke and Herbst explained, 'When US troops intervened in December 1992 to stop the theft of food, they immediately disrupted the entire political economy of Somalia. The US, therefore, immediately

---

[40] See, for example, Roy Licklider, 'State Building After Invasion: Somalia and Panama', presented at the International Studies Association annual convention, San Diego, CA, April 1996, p. 21. The information on disarmament provided by Somalis was obtained by author interviews in Somalia.

[41] It is unclear what other options were available to the UN. Obviously the UN could not let troops be killed without reprisals. Many suggestions have since been made, albeit none very satisfactory. See Ameen Jan, 'Peacebuilding in Somalia', IPA Policy Briefing Series, International Peace Academy, New York, July 1996, for one alternative.

[42] Adibe, *Managing Arms in Peace Processes*, p. 64.

[43] See chapter 4 for more information.

stepped deeply into the muck of Somali politics because the most funda-mental institution in any country is order.'[44]

The Americans boasted of excellent overall co-ordination, pointing to attendant results: at the close of UNITAF, some court and prison sys-tems were up and running in a few cities, with police training at more advanced stages (e.g., more than 3,000 men were back at work in Mogadishu). According to Hirsch and Oakley, these reforms were not given prolonged support after the transition, and consequently, they soon disintegrated.[45] This assertion stretched the truth somewhat; for example, by the time the US Marines left on 4 May 1993, only two Somalis were in prison in Mogadishu.[46] Other components of UNITAF also disappeared along with the US troops, such as the Civil–Military Operations Center (CMOC), which held daily briefings with representa-tives from all the relief organisations, UN personnel and military staff, and most of the Civil Affairs (CA) and Psychological Operations (PSYOPS) units. Again, opinion was mixed as to the effectiveness of the CMOC in Mogadishu.[47]

Although UNOSOM II could have benefited by continuing these activities if they had the resources and the political will (neither of which existed), it is also true that US policy decisions were not as harmonious as alleged, both in the field and at home. For example, there was little interaction between the American SRSG of UNOSOM II, Jonathan Howe, and the US Marine field commander of UNITAF, Lt.-Gen. Robert B. Johnston, during the transition. In addition, Howe also was not in charge of the military component of UNOSOM II, which ensured that the operation would be divided and therefore less effective, a mis-take also made in Panama.

Back in the United States, on 10 August 1993, US Ambassador to the UN Madeleine Albright claimed that troops would 'stay as long as needed to lift the country and its people from the category of a failed state into that of an emerging democracy'.[48] Along with her earlier

---

[44] Clarke and Herbst, 'Somalia and the Future of Humanitarian Intervention', p. 5.
[45] Hirsch and Oakley, *Somalia and Operation Restore Hope*, p. 92. Oakley served as US Special Envoy to Bush during UNITAF and then was appointed again by Clinton after the Rangers were killed.
[46] From personal correspondence with Walter Clarke, who was deputy chief of mission at the US Embassy in Mogadishu in 1993.
[47] From personal correspondence with Col. Gary Herring, director of the Civil Military Operations Center (CMOC) in Haiti from 20 September 1994 to 1 February 1995.
[48] Hirsch and Oakley, *Somalia and Operation Restore Hope*, p. 124.

comments after the passage of Resolution 814, she left a firm impression that the US administration would hold its course while Somalia underwent the transition to a reconstructed state. Two weeks later, on 27 August, US Defense Secretary Les Aspin argued in a policy speech for paring down the nation-building mission.[49]

Two months later, President Clinton did more than pare it down: he decapitated it. On 7 October, he said, 'It is not our job to rebuild Somalia's society or even to create a new political process that can allow Somalia's clans to live and work in peace'[50]. One week later, he claimed, 'The US military mission is not now nor was it ever one of "nation building".'[51] In fact, Clinton had been pressured by Congress to jettison the nation-building component after the October deaths.[52] Ironically, it was also pressure applied early on by influential members of Congress that led to Bush's decision to intervene in the first place.[53]

UN–US unstable alliance

The UN and the US government share responsibility for many of the mistakes made during the interventions in Somalia – and each accordingly has blamed the other – which can partially be attributed to the clashing and often antagonistic struggle for control of the mission based on an unclear chain of command. If Somalis can be characterised as having constantly changing political loyalties, and living according to the Bedouin Arab maxim 'myself against my brother; my brother and I against my cousins; my cousins and I against the world',[54] those who

---

[49] Cited in Hirsch and Oakley, *Somalia and Operation Restore Hope*, p. 125. This could also be attributed to different policies promoted by the various departments in the US government, which in this case were the State Department and the Department of Defense.

[50] Cited in Richard N. Haass, *Intervention: the Use of American Military Force in the Post-Cold War World*, Washington, DC, Carnegie Endowment for International Peace, 1994, p. 46.

[51] Remarks by President Bill Clinton to the Congress from the White House Office of the Press Secretary, 13 October, 1993.

[52] From Harry Johnston and Ted Dagne, 'Congress and the Somalia Crisis', in Clarke and Herbst, eds., *Learning From Somalia*, p. 201. Johnston was a senior member of the House International Relations Committee and the former chair of the Subcommittee on Africa (1993–4).

[53] The Congressional Black Caucus played a strong role in encouraging the USA to intervene, as they also did in Haiti. See Congressional Record, 103rd Congress, H2745, 25 May, 1993 (and H2748) and Senate and House Resolution 45 from February 1993.

[54] For more details, see I.M. Lewis's, *Blood and Bone*, New Jersey, The Red Sea Press, 1993; *A Modern History of Somalia: Nation and State in the Horn of*

work with Somalis tend to ape that behaviour within a short time period. Such poor co-ordination has rarely been witnessed in a peacekeeping operation, and was aptly illustrated during the transition from the American-run UNITAF operation to UNOSOM II, when not one UN planner was sent to Somalia before the Commander and Deputy Commander arrived to ensure a 'seamless transition' and provide the overlap necessary to become fully apprised of the distinct operational requirements.

Additionally, UNOSOM I had not been fully phased out when UNITAF became operational, and instead remained active until UNOSOM II began, which confused the mission and served to increase friction between the UN and the US government. Senior UN staffers in Mogadishu also insisted on taking orders from headquarters in New York instead of from field commanders and directors, while member states participating in the operations, such as Italy and the United States, often acted on orders from their respective capitals without informing the UN, which inevitably meant a delayed reaction to events on the ground (as occurred in UNOSOM II when the Pakistani soldiers were ambushed).[55] Mayall and Lewis added, 'With the prominence of US logistical support and special forces, this inevitably gave UNOSOM II a strongly American orientation which, when UN forces became embroiled in actual fighting, made it difficult to decide whether the Pentagon or Dr Boutros-Ghali was calling the shots.'[56]

Resource allocation also proved inadequate to accomplish mission mandates, as transpired in Bosnia during UNPROFOR: the mandates did not match the means.[57] UNITAF's mandate was limited, while its budget constraints were few. UNOSOM II, on the other hand, was supposed to operate throughout the entire country, on restricted funding.[58] And the financing that was available arrived sporadically, thus impeding the operation throughout.

Africa, Boulder, CO, Westview Press, 1988; or *A Pastoral Democracy*, New York, Africana Press, 1982.

[55] In mid-1993, the UN Under-Secretary-General for Peacekeeping Operations, Mr Kofi Annan, requested that General Bruno Loi, the Italian Commander of UNOSOM II, be dismissed. General Loi had been instructed by headquarters in Rome to obey its orders rather than those emanating from UN command in Mogadishu.

[56] Mayall and Lewis, 'Somalia', in Mayall, ed., *The New Interventionism*, p. 116.

[57] See chapter 5 for more information on UNPROFOR.

[58] *Comprehensive Report on Lessons-Learned from United Nations Operation in Somalia*, April 1992–March 1995, Friedrich Ebert Stiftung, Germany; Life and Peace Institute, Sweden; Norwegian Institute of International Affairs; in Co-operation with the Lessons-Learned Unit of the Department of Peacekeeping Operations, UN, New York, December 1995, p. 5, para. 14.

In addition to poor co-ordination and inadequate funding, which have plagued other peace support operations, the UN and the US government had been considering political reconstruction of the Somali state since UNOSOM I, and unrealistically assumed that impartiality could be maintained. The US government knew that it could not pull off another Panama-style operation in a collapsed state without expecting the conditions to revert back to the *status quo ante* once troops left (as indeed eventually happened, except without the famine); the earlier Clinton quote demonstrated this understanding ('We didn't want to go there, pull out and have chaos, anarchy, starvation return [*sic*])'.[59] Yet the Americans were (understandably) unclear on the means to accomplish this task, and therefore tried to foist political reconstruction onto the UN, while publicly committing only to undertaking the temporary, stop-gap assignment of securing food delivery. Unfortunately, the UN also had no overall conception of how to accomplish political reform, apart from their involvement in rebuilding local councils.

Not only did the Americans strive to avoid the responsibility for political reconstruction, but senior administration officials, including both Bush and Clinton, denied that they ever even considered it a feasible option. On 4 December 1992, Bush declared, 'Our mission [in Somalia] is humanitarian. . . We do not plan to dictate political outcomes.'[60] (See also quotes from Clinton at the end of the previous section.) Moreover, many Americans supported the myth that the UN altered the scope of the operation with the passage of Resolution 814. Failure, therefore, could not be attributed to the US government, as clearly explained by a US military analyst: 'While the long-term objectives of the UN Secretary General were not met, the United States had never intended to meet them.'[61]

Besides public speeches of both Bush and Clinton in which they admitted that they did consider political reconstruction a necessity, it is also true that the military decisions that went wrong during UNOSOM

[59] Remarks By The President To The Pool, The White House, Office of the Press Secretary (New Haven, Connecticut), 9 October, 1993. Clarke and Herbst also wryly noted, 'simply stopping the warlords from stealing food for a few weeks was hardly an adequate solution'. Clarke and Herbst, eds., *Learning From Somalia*, p. 243.

[60] Cited in 'White Paper: An Analysis of the Application of the Principles of Military Operations Other Than War (MOOTW) in Somalia', Mr Hunter et al., The Army–Air Force Center for Low Intensity Conflict, February 1994.

[61] 'White Paper: An Analysis of the Application of the Principles of Military Operations Other Than War (MOOTW) in Somalia', Mr Hunter et al., The Army–Air Force Center for Low Intensity Conflict, February 1994.

II, such as the pursuit of Aideed, were all approved by the command authorities in the United States, as were those related to nation-building. As Clarke and Herbst explained, 'At the doctrinal level, it is simply not true that the UN greatly broadened the mission that the US had decided to limit. In fact, all of the major Security Council resolutions on Somalia, including the March 1993 "nation-building" resolution, were written by the United States, mainly in the Pentagon.'[62]

An examination of the resolutions emanating from the Security Council also confirms this point: of the seventeen resolutions on Somalia passed by the Security Council and the five presidential statements during the interventions, all the resolutions and four of the statements mentioned support for political reconciliation and rehabilitation. It is also true that Resolution 814 went into greater detail as to how political reconstruction was to occur and the extent of UN involvement, but from very early on it was evident that the UN and the US government were aware they would be involved in nation-building, as can be seen in the six resolutions that preceded 814.[63] And UNITAF became partial and involved in politics anyway by virtue of securing food deliveries and choosing representatives in villages to assist with the distribution.

External involvement in political reconstruction is by definition controversial and complex. Arguably, the USA and the UN erred in pressing solutions on Somalis without properly involving them at different stages of the process or assisting them to develop their own revenue-raising capacity to sustain these institutions. Even the programmes that were considered more successful, such as the establishment of local and regional councils, did not prove viable, primarily because there was no over-arching authority in place.[64] Additionally, the UN, which managed

[62] Clarke and Herbst, 'Somalia and the Future of Humanitarian Intervention', p. 4.
[63] See Security Council resolutions and presidential statements on Somalia, found in 'Reference Paper: The United Nations and the Situation in Somalia, United Nations Department of Public Information', April 1995, United Nations Web page (www.un.org).
[64] By the end of 1994, fifty-four of eighty-two district councils had been formed, and regional councils were established in eight of thirteen regions (both excluding Somaliland). Most of these councils disappeared as quickly as they were set up once UNOSOM decamped, although in areas of Somalia today where local councils have emerged, such as in the Bari region, training from UNOSOM has probably factored into the relative success of these administrations. From personal correspondence with Dr Bernhard Helander, an anthropologist who specialises in Somalia, and UNOSOM II documents on the district and regional councils (e.g., 'Governance: District and Regional Councils, their Legitimacy, Effectiveness and Role in Reconciliation and

the project, was more concerned about hastily setting up councils rather than ensuring that the councils functioned as intended. Most were established within one or two weeks after the first consultations with UNOSOM.[65]

Conclusions

Lessons learned – lessons to learn

The international community, particularly the UN and the US government, received a rude awakening in Somalia, which inevitably caused a great deal of soul-searching. Mistakes made during the intervention have been publicly disclosed, and policy altered accordingly, most notably in Haiti and Bosnia, as will be discussed in subsequent chapters. At UN headquarters, a Lessons-Learned Unit was created in 1995 in the Office of Planning and Support to analyse peacekeeping operations at different stages and make recommendations. Significantly, the report on Somalia concluded the following:

> Evaluation of UNOSOM at all levels has concluded that the Operation's mandate was vague, changed frequently during the process and was open to myriad interpretations. The mandate changed from protecting the delivery of humanitarian assistance, to encouraging and assisting in political reconciliation, to establishing and maintaining a 'secure environment', to capturing a leader of one of the factions at one stage and, later, to encouraging negotiations with that same leader. These mandates were, in many respects, contradictory, and most often the changes were decided upon with little explanation to Member States, troop-contributing countries, the humanitarian community operating in Somalia or the Somali people. As a consequence, UNOSOM was bedeviled with disagreements among the various players ... which, in the end, even led to clashes between UNOSOM and some elements of the Somali community.[66]

It has also been recognised that in order to avoid repeating the mistakes made in Somalia, a primary objective of peace support operations should be to *integrate diplomatic, military, and humanitarian relief operations*. As Kenneth Allard explained, 'With the benefit of hindsight, it is possible to see that operations in Somalia were successful when they

Development', 22–24 June 1994, UN orientation seminar for newly arrived UNV specialists; 'Meeting on Workshop for District Councillors in Somalia', and 'UNOSOM II: District Councillors' Workshops', 10–11 August 1993).
[65] Establishment of District Councils, 23 August 1993, UN Document, date unknown.
[66] *Comprehensive Report on Lessons-Learned from United Nations Operation in Somalia*, p. 4, para. 10.

recognized this trinity of diplomatic, military, and humanitarian actions – and remarkably less so when they did not.'[67] In planning the intervention, there was 'no contact at the operational level' between US military planners and representatives of relief organisations (as indeed also occurred in Panama due to the secrecy of the operation). Kevin Kennedy remarked, 'What parties the MEF [the Marine Expeditionary Force] would be working with, their expectations, and the scope of their requirements were largely unknown to the military forces charged with carrying out the humanitarian intervention.'[68] And once the operation was underway, the military command remained separate from the civilian, leading to a range of associated problems.

In Haiti this mistake would not be repeated: the SRSG insisted that the development role be incorporated in the overall peacekeeping mission from the start, military and civilians were trained together before deployment, both were under the command of a civilian, the CMOC was rigorously maintained throughout, and the mandate was explicit from the beginning.[69] That these lessons have been applied in Haiti can be partly attributed to the synergism of several recent *changes at the UN*: the above-mentioned Lessons-Learned Unit and a Training Unit, the consolidation of the Department of Peacekeeping Operations (DPKO, established in 1992), and the empowerment of a 'Framework for Co-ordination' between the DPKO, Political Affairs, and Humanitarian Affairs. The latter supervises all aspects of peacekeeping activities, 'from the early warning signals to close-down of a peacekeeping operation'.[70]

The experience in Somalia also taught planners that *Chapter VII peace enforcement operations need to be phased out before a Chapter VI peacekeeping operation takes over*, which also occurred in Haiti.[71] In Somalia, UNOSOM I (Chapter VI) and UNITAF (Chapter VII) co-existed, with UNOSOM I not officially phased out until UNOSOM II (Chapter VII) took over, further confusing the command and control of the mission.

---

[67] Kenneth Allard, *Somalia Operations: Lessons Learned*, Institute for National Strategic Studies, National Defense University Press, 1995, p. 9.

[68] Kevin M. Kennedy, 'The Military and Humanitarian Organizations', in Clarke and Herbst, *Learning From Somalia*, p. 100. Kennedy was formerly the commander of the CMOC in Somalia.

[69] In Bosnia, however, as will become evident in chapter 5, the military and civilian elements of the NATO operation were separated on purpose, and therefore it is uncertain whether this lesson has been fully learned.

[70] *Comprehensive Report on Lessons-Learned from United Nations Operation in Somalia*, pp. 28–9, para. 94.

[71] The same troops could work in both types of operations; the point is that they should not be operating simultaneously.

Furthermore, even though the Security Council resolutions that created UNITAF and UNOSOM II gave both broad Chapter VII mandates, in practice, the two functioned in many respects as if they were Chapter VI operations, or as some argued at the time, Chapter $6\frac{1}{2}$.[72]

Other difficulties arose over the *nation-building* aspect, although it was inevitable that this focus would be adopted. For the US government and military, this was nothing new, as mentioned in chapter 1. In Germany and Japan after World War II, nation-building worked: the highly educated   populations   supported   democracy   because   fascism, imperialism, and militarism had let them down, thus enabling democratic reforms to take root. In Panama, at least there was a democratically elected government that could be restored and supported by the US government, even if that was the extent of it.

Yet the US government did not direct the political reconstruction in Somalia, even though it was heavily involved behind-the-scenes. Arguably, the US government should have maintained the focus on nation-building instead of forcing the UN to manage it, since the United States has more experience in this sphere than the UN.[73] Moreover, Somalia, like Panama, had no direct practice in democracy (apart from a few years of unsuccessful experimentation after the Europeans left in 1960), and no strong foundation on which it could be built.

According to World Bank estimates, adult literacy rates in Somalia hover at approximately 25 per cent, while UNDP figures give the average Somali a life expectancy of 41–43 years. Somalia today would rank at the bottom of the index of the UNDP Human Development Report, if enough data were available even to include it in the reports for 1997 and 1998. In 1996, it was ranked at 172 of 174 countries[74]. In addition, unlike Panama, where US troops had been stationed for years and therefore could provide competent intelligence on the political situation, the pastoral tradition and culture in Somalia was little understood. Attempts at nation-building were furthermore undertaken in a situation of prolonged state collapse, a first for the international community. In many

---

[72] Walter Clarke, 'Failed Visions and Uncertain Mandates in Somalia: Abandoning Hope in a Troubled State', in Clarke and Herbst, *Learning From Somalia*, p. 8. The interpretation of the mandates in this way launched a debate on whether there should be Chapter $6\frac{1}{2}$ interventions.

[73] This point will be addressed more fully in chapter 6. Most of the UN's democratisation experience took place during the decolonisation of Africa and Asia from 1960 through to the mid-1970s.

[74] Human Development Report, Somalia 1998, New York, UNDP, p. 12. See also   general   UNDP   Human   Development   Reports   on   the   Website www.undp.org for the years 1996–8.

ways, therefore, this nation-building failure resembles that which occurred in Vietnam in terms of a poor understanding of the culture and the ways of adapting democracy to it.

This latter point – how to *tailor the operation to the specific needs of the particular culture* – will continue to plague future peace support and nation-building operations. As John Drysdale remarked, '*Operation Restore Hope* demonstrated that when humanitarian peacemaking becomes a compelling necessity . . . diplomacy must be carried out with full knowledge of local political, social, and cultural norms.'[75] Clarke added, 'Inability or unwillingness to discern the essential political dynamics of the country and to effect remedial measures to foster civil society – out of expedience, disinterest, or naïve "neutrality" – lie at the root of the world's failure in Somalia.'[76] These points do not necessarily signify that a deep understanding of Somali culture would have ensured success, as many international organisations employ fully qualified staff in this regard and they still encounter difficulties in Somalia, but rather that some mistakes were certainly avoidable, such as the original failure to disarm, the bond on Aideed's head, the man-hunt, and the treatment of Somali radio stations in a predominantly oral culture. It is difficult to say whether political reconstruction might have been more effective if the peace support operations had been better managed, but the odds are high.

For the United States, Somalia taught the military establishment that there are certain limits – or 'bright lines' – that should not be exceeded, most notably the *involvement of the military in nation-building*, 'a mission for which [US] forces should not be primarily responsible'.[77] In Somalia, military involvement at senior levels consisted of preparing UN resolutions on nation-building, while at the junior levels, soldiers became involved in politics by their control of food delivery, and later in their pursuit of General Aideed. Military involvement did not reach the levels experienced in Panama, however, and by Bosnia, it would be reduced even further.

Although the military has extensive experience in this field, both military and political analysts agree that there are certain tasks that the military should continue to do. For example, they could prepare the groundwork for political reconstruction by securing conflict regions and

[75] John Drysdale, 'Foreign Military Intervention in Somalia', in Clarke and Herbst, *Learning From Somalia*, p. 134.
[76] Walter Clarke, 'Failed Visions and Uncertain Mandates in Somalia', in Clarke and Herbst, *Learning From Somalia*, p. 4.
[77] Allard, *Somalia Operations: Lessons Learned*, p. 89.

involving Civil Affairs (CA) and PSYOPS units (most of which are staffed by reservists) during the peace support operation. Meanwhile the responsibility for political rehabilitation should be borne by civilian agencies and local organisations. In Somalia, the CA and PSYOPS units that were in evidence during UNITAF were not maintained after the transition to UNOSOM II, which was surprising after the success experienced by CA troops in Kuwait after the Gulf War in helping to re-establish the police and judiciary – not to mention their widespread use in Germany and Japan after World War II, and in Panama.[78] In Haiti, these units comprised a healthier percentage throughout the operation.[79]

Since Somalia, the UN has tried to adhere to the maxim that *peace-keeping forces should not enter a conflict area if there is no political will among the parties towards reconciliation*.[80] Unfortunately, applying this tenet to international crises could confine the international community to the sidelines. In Rwanda in 1994, where undoubtedly there was little political will among the parties for peace, the state imploded during a period when international despair was at its peak because of the Somalia débâcle, and thus nearly a million were killed while the world silently watched. An early, substantial intervention might have prevented the Tutsi genocide, yet except for France, which conducted its own controversial intervention, there was little international interest. Of course, political will notwithstanding, it is unclear whether the well-oiled and

---

[78] Martin R. Ganzglass, 'The Restoration of the Somali Justice System', in Clarke and Herbst, *Learning From Somalia*, p. 20. Ganzglass also mentioned that the original plan for *Operation Restore Hope* included the use of more Civil Affairs units, which would have been especially helpful to the police and judiciary, but the Joint Chiefs of Staff decided against it (p. 23). Ganzglass was a former legal adviser to the Somali National Police Force and a special adviser to the State Department during *Operation Restore Hope*.

[79] In Haiti during the initial Multi-National Force intervention there were 80 CA and 70 PSYOPS out of a total of 20,000 troops, while during the peace-keeping part of the operation, or UNMIH, there were 60 CA, 70 PSYOPS, and 400 Special Forces, out of a total of 2,000 US troops (6,000 UN troops). In Panama, over a thousand CA troops participated in the invasion and the aftermath, while after the Gulf War 300 CA were sent to northern Iraq. In sharp contrast, there were only 7–30 CA troops participating in UNITAF at any one time, and these were all sent home by UNOSOM II. Information compiled from various US Army sources on the World Wide Web, from 'Civil Affairs in *Operation Just Cause*', *Special Warfare*, 4, Winter 1991, and from correspondence with Col. Doug Daniels, who was in charge of Civil Affairs in Haiti in 1995.

[80] *Comprehensive Report on Lessons-Learned from United Nations Operation in Somalia*, p. 27.

organised genocide could have been halted.[81] The UN's lesson pertaining to political will needs greater redress, as the proposed solution is obviously unsatisfactory.

Disarmament will continue to be thorny and intractable for peace support operations, where mostly second-hand light weapons circulate with ease and little documentation exists as to where they are or came from. Disarmament and demobilisation of soldiers and militia members may be best achieved through intensive capacity building exercises, but they can only be realised if there is some semblance of government. After all, what did the UN imagine would happen once all the weapons were destroyed? Without adequate political and civic institutions to provide basic daily needs and ensure security, voluntary disarmament is unrealisable. New arms can always be found, and they do not have to be sophisticated to obstruct political reconciliation and rehabilitation efforts.

In addition, *the fear of body bags* in the United States, which ultimately undermined this operation, will have to be overcome. Interestingly, as noted in the previous chapter, the deaths of twenty-three US soldiers in Panama did not cause a comparable uproar. This distinction can largely be attributed to the significant increase in media attention paid to the Ranger deaths. US soldiers are professionals, and are fully aware when they enlist that their lives may be at risk, as are police officers in inner cities, or aid workers and journalists in many foreign states embroiled in civil wars. Jonathan Howe raised this point in terms of the US–UN relationship that will need to be reconciled for future humanitarian operations. He asked 'why the United States would no longer put its soldiers at risk when the Pakistanis had suffered similar losses and persevered'?[82] Why indeed.

Finally, *the interventions bestowed too much legitimacy on the faction leaders, at the expense of traditional leaders,* by including more of the former in the internationally sponsored attempts at national reconciliation. As Lee Cassanelli remarked,

Peacekeeping operations . . . must invariably put their resources into dealing with those who are most capable of and prone to disturbing the peace – that is, those with weapons. In the Somali case, it was unfortunate but perhaps inevitable that in attempting to bring the war-lords together for national-level

[81] For more information, see Gérard Prunier, *The Rwanda Crisis: History of a Genocide, 1959–1994*, Kampala, Fountain Publishers, 1995.

[82] Jonathan T. Howe, 'Relations Between the United States and United Nations in Dealing with Somalia', in Clarke and Herbst, *Learning From Somalia*, p. 183. Interestingly, Howe also noted that the United States should be blamed for providing an American SRSG (himself) for UNOSOM II! (p. 189).

negotiations, the United States and the UN also effectively legitimated their authority and gave them added leverage in their local wars for land.[83]

Gérard Prunier added, 'dealing with the war-lords from the start as Special Envoy Robert Oakley chose to do, especially without bothering to seriously reduce the amount of weaponry under their control, was a fatal mistake'.[84] The jury is still out on the extent to which conflict instigators should participate in mediation. Excluding the war-lords is arguably ineffective (although to some extent it worked in Bosnia) since they control the situation on the ground and will need to relinquish their hold if peace is to be given a chance, as occurred in Haiti.[85]

The Aideed man-hunt also conferred more authority on him. Somalis not only rallied behind one of their own in opposition to the UN, and especially the United States, but they witnessed the international community elevating him to a loftier position than he in fact merited. Some of these war-lords even benefited in financial terms from manipulating (and outright pilfering) a large percentage of the foreign funds used to pay for the intervention.

Overall the war-lords have thrived on the absence of a government. For example, before his death in August 1996, General Aideed was reportedly earning $100,000 a month on the banana trade (most of the bananas going to Europe, since the annual export quota of 60,000 metric tonnes is still applicable for Somalia – even though there has been no internationally recognised government since 1991 to certify the origin of these bananas). His interests – both financial and 'political' – were therefore threatened by attempts to reformulate central authority that were out of his control, and he took every opportunity to sabotage such attempts at reconciliation.[86]

Vicious circles vs. on-going efforts to rebuild the state

Although the seemingly endless supply of foreign aid has been reduced dramatically since the state collapsed and the UN departed, and diplo-

---

[83] Lee V. Cassanelli, 'Somali Land Resource Issues in Historical Perspective', in Clarke and Herbst, *Learning From Somalia*, p. 75.

[84] Gérard Prunier, 'The Experience of European Armies in *Operation Restore Hope*', in Clarke and Herbst, *Learning From Somalia*, p. 141.

[85] In Bosnia, Karadjic and Mladic were both excluded from Dayton, although if Milosevic was indeed in overall control, as some have argued, then this point is irrelevant. This will be discussed in greater detail in chapters 4, 5 and 6.

[86] The EC Somalia Unit held two seminars on decentralised political structures in June and November 1996 in Kenya for Somali intellectuals and traditional

matic representation has either moved to Nairobi or been withdrawn, the international community has not fully abandoned Somalia. Some donors and experts are convinced that no more foreign assistance should go into Somalia until a national government has been restored, as aid has historically only served to compound the problem as well as create a situation of dependency.[87] Before the state collapsed, foreign aid comprised 70 per cent of the national budget, and itself became the source of conflict.

Many Somalis erroneously believe that a restored central government, based in Mogadishu, will once again cause the foreign aid floodgates to open at similar levels to those prior to state collapse. Mogadishu therefore remains the most hotly contested piece of real estate in the country, and the most destroyed, while the north-east, or Puntland, and the north-west, or Somaliland, have been re-establishing order and rudimentary administrations. In these areas, trade was flourishing with export revenues exceeding pre-collapse rates – without large infusions of foreign aid – until the ban on livestock from Gulf states was imposed early in 1998 (it was lifted in June 1999). Significantly, these are also regions where UNOSOM did not interfere. Organic change normally inspires greater loyalty than externally imposed efforts due to feelings of ownership.

Even if a democratic central government were reconstructed in Somalia, the country – and indeed most African states – would still be on the bottom of the donor list as it is no longer a priority for western governments, despite recent US policy statements to the contrary.[88] Somalis, moreover, argue that they cannot put their government back together without foreign aid. Although some major donors have been asserting that money will not arrive until a government is in place, since the World Bank and the IMF are restricted by their articles of agreement to working *only* with established governments, other donors have recently modified their rules to continue projects – albeit at greatly reduced levels – in this collapsed state.

Following the departure of UNOSOM, the European Union (EU) – now the leading donor in Somalia – adopted three guiding principles for involvement in the country:

and religious leaders (discussed in the final section). Aideed denounced the first seminar, while his son denounced the second, declaring that the EC was attempting to reimpose colonial rule and 'dismantle' the Somali state.

[87] For an extremely negative version of the ill-effects of foreign aid, see Michael Maren, *The Road to Hell: The Ravaging Effects of Foreign Aid and International Charity*, Amazon Press, 1997.

[88] *The Economist*, 26 April 1997, pp. 20, 61.

1. strict neutrality with respect to the fighting factions;
2. non-recognition of any government that is not broadly representative; and
3. no direct mediation role but rather encouragement and support for initiatives by the UN and the OAU.[89]

These principles allow the EU, and the NGOs funded by the EU, to work where local authorities are in place and where security (mostly) prevails. They were established due to the lessons learned from the UNOSOM experience.[90]

In 1994 at the Fourth Co-ordination Meeting on Humanitarian Assistance for Somalia, the Somalia Aid Co-ordination Body (SACB) was established to serve as the permanent co-ordination body for donors, UN agencies, NGOs, and other international organisations. Since 1994, the SACB has provided the international community with an alternative framework for involvement in a state that has no effective government, and therefore no official counterparts on the ground. After UNOSOM II departed, it became the only international forum where political, security, and humanitarian questions were debated and policy adopted in a series of committees. The SACB has actually filled the role often provided by a UN agency, e.g., in Bosnia, UNHCR was lead co-ordinator until Dayton.

At the national level, the EU initiated a governance project, based on the aforementioned conviction that the initiatives sponsored by the UN and Somali leaders between 1991 and 1995 failed to reach a settlement of the Somali conflict because they hastily tried to reconstruct a central state without elaborating constitutional arrangements compatible with traditional 'uncentralised' Somali culture.[91] Additionally, they concentrated primarily on the war-lords at the expense of members of civil

---

[89] For example, see speech by Roberto di Leo, Ambassador, Embassy of Italy, Representing the EU Presidency, delivered to the participants at the 'First Seminar on Decentralised Political Structures for Somalia', sponsored and organised by the European Commission–European Union, Lake Naivasha, Kenya, June 1996. For more information on the EU's involvement in the Somali crisis, see von Hippel and Yannis, 'The European Response to State Collapse in Somalia' in Jøergensen, *European Approaches to Crisis Management.*

[90] Between 1994 and mid-1996, the EU rehabilitation programme sponsored 125 micro-rehabilitation projects across Somalia in regions with relative peace and stability.

[91] Alexandros Yannis, 'Perspectives for Democratic Governance in Somalia', paper presented at the 6th International Congress of Somali Studies, Berlin, Germany, 6–9 December 1996.

society.[92] Ken Menkhaus commented, 'The ability to destroy had been confused with the ability to govern. The power to govern, it turned out, had devolved to a much more localized level.'[93] The EC Special Envoy to Somalia, Mr Sigurd Illing, thus launched the Somalia Project, commissioning a group of academic consultants at the London School of Economics and Political Science (LSE) to prepare *A Study of Decentralised Political Structures for Somalia: A Menu of Options* (August 1995).[94]

This project was inspired by discussions between the EC Special Envoy and Somalis from all political and social affiliations, who agreed that the only way to ensure that another dictator would not usurp power at the centre was to decentralise all aspects of government. At the March 1993 conference in Addis Ababa, Somalis maintained that the centralised political governments in Somalia from 1960 to 1991 were no longer 'acceptable' since 'the trust reposed in over-centralised governments has been abused, especially since 1969'.[95] As in many resource-starved, under-developed states, if there are no power-sharing arrangements worked out in advance, those excluded tend to destroy whatever has been made.

A Somali proverb explains this in blunt fashion: *Cadyohow (Somaaliyeey) ama ku cunay, ama ku ciideeyey*, which means 'O, thou beautiful cut of meat [the state], either I will eat you all by myself or I will ensure to soil you in the dirt so that no other can have you.'[96] Although many Somalis concurred that a decentralised state was desirable and compatible with their 'uncentralised' political organisation, they did not fully understand the complexities of the different models and their successes and failures in other parts of the world. Nor did they have the resources to commit to such an undertaking.

The LSE report therefore outlined four models of decentralised government, including three territorially-based models (the

---

[92] Security Council Resolution 814 made specific reference to support for civil society, but in practice this was not undertaken to a significant degree.

[93] Ken Menkhaus, 'Stateless Somalia', draft article later published in *Current History*, May 1998.

[94] See J. Barker, E.A. Brett, P. Dawson, I.M. Lewis, P. McAuslan, J. Mayall, B. O'Leary, and K. von Hippel, *A Study of Decentralised Political Structures for Somalia: A Menu of Options*, London School of Economics and the European Union, commissioned by the European Union, EC Somalia Unit, with the Assistance of the United Nations Development Office for Somalia, August 1995, 130 pp.

[95] Drysdale, *Whatever Happened to Somalia?*, p. 117.

[96] Proverb noted by S. Samatar, in *Somali: Africa's Problem Child*, found on NomadNet on the Web (http://www.users.interport.net/mmaren/somarchive. html).

confederation, federation, and decentralised unitary state), and a community-based type of power-sharing known as consocation. Following its publication, in 1996, the EU organised two seminars in Kenya, and in 1997, several more inside Somalia, for Somali traditional and religious leaders, intellectuals, professionals, former politicians, women, and other representatives of Somali civil society to provide the forum for these Somalis to deliberate the study in greater detail as well as contribute their expertise to the overall debate.[97] The *Menu of Options* and the subsequent seminars have provoked considerable public debate in Somalia and in the diaspora as to how decentralisation could be accommodated within a future Somali constitution. Additionally, these discussions contributed to a Somali-led effort in mid-1998 to prepare a regional charter for north-east Somalia based on democratic, power-sharing principles. Unfortunately, the departure of the EC Special Envoy subsequently led to the termination of this project at the EC by his successor.

Somalis, particularly leaders from traditional and civil society, as well as many political figures, have thus far supported the concept of establishing 'a decentralised state with constitutional guarantees for the full autonomy of the constituent units'.[98] There remains a strong perception, however, amongst other parts of the Somali political leadership based in Mogadishu that international recognition of a government in Mogadishu would sooner or later be followed by international financial and military support to enable the central authority to impose its rule over the entire Somali territory, irrespective of its political legitimacy. This perception, shared by many Somalis and even by some members

---

[97] The present author was the project manager for the LSE report, and was responsible for organising the seminars in Kenya and Somalia. See reports prepared by Karin von Hippel, entitled *First Seminar on Decentralised Political Structures for Somalia*, Lake Naivasha, Kenya, June 1996; and *Second Seminar on Decentralised Political Structures for Somalia*, Lake Nakuru, Kenya, November 1996. Both reports were sponsored and organised by the European Commission Somalia Unit of the European Union. The Naivasha and Nakuru seminars were recognised in the recent Report of the UN Secretary-General on the Situation in Somalia, S/1997/135 of 17 February 1997. Other relevant activities included the production of the Somali-language version of the *Menu of Options* on cassette, which has been distributed to radio stations within Somalia as well as to the BBC Somali Service. Future activities will concentrate on further information dissemination inside the country.

[98] Statement by Participants, 'Second Seminar on Decentralised Political Structures for Somalia', sponsored and organised by the European Commission–European Union, Lake Nakuru, Kenya, 16–18 November 1996.

of the international community, is currently one of the main obstacles to the establishment of a democratic and secure Somali state.

Since 1997, a regional Cold War has interfered with efforts to establish an effective government. The competition first was between Kenya and Ethiopia for control of the peace process, then between Ethiopia and Egypt due to their long-standing dispute over the Nile, with each country supporting different, opposed war-lords and political leaders in both northern and southern Somalia. Complicating the equation was the Eritrean–Ethiopian war, which fully erupted in early 1999 and was responsible for an upsurge in arms flows inside Somalia. Eritrea has reportedly supplied Hussein Aideed with weapons, so that he would in turn provide some to the Oromo Liberation Front on the border with Ethiopia to help in their cross-border incursions; on its part, Ethiopia has allegedly been supplying arms to the Rahanwein Resistance Army, who have been fighting Aideed for several years now in an attempt to regain control of Bay and Bakool regions. Yemen and Libya have entered the picture and have also been accused of supplying arms to different actors as well. All these states have additionally continued the earlier damaging policy of negotiating possible settlements only with the war-lords (giving them large sums of money to attend the so-called peace talks and sign agreements that cannot be implemented). As mentioned, these war-lords are incapable of delivering on their promises, or their claimed constituencies.

In November 1998, Ethiopia, acting as the lead country within IGAD (Inter-Governmental Authority on Development), along with other interested members of the international community, set up the Standing Committee on Somalia, which is a group comprising IGAD member states (e.g., Ethiopia, Kenya, Sudan, Eritrea), members of the IGAD Partners' Forum Liaison Group (e.g., the European Commission, Egypt, Italy, the United Nations, the United States), and interested countries and organisations (e.g., Yemen, the League of Arab States). The purpose of this committee is to attempt to speak and act with one voice internationally with regard to Somalia, which would in turn allow the 'peace process' to move forward. The Standing Committee is also preparing a step-by-step plan to assist Somalis to rebuild their state, although the jury is still out on whether this committee will provide the necessary leadership and authority.

Currently it is difficult to predict whether Somalia will be reincarnated as one state or several states, or if it will continue to comprise several fluid mini-fiefdoms, some more economically and politically viable than others, with no central authority. This type of organisation, where it works, is called functional co-operation.[99] Somalis might even argue that the state was an artificial western imposition, and not compatible with their traditional 'uncentralised' political culture. While some analysts argue that 'restoration of stateness is dependent on reaffirmation of the precollapsed state',[100] others recommend that alternatives to the existing nation-states be formulated for Africa.[101]

In Somalia, the dynamic emergence of strong patterns of local sovereignty now competes with the assumption that state sovereignty will sooner or later be restored at the centre. The appearance of functioning and legitimate patterns of local administration not only constitutes a political and social adaptation of Somali society to the prolonged collapse of the Somali state,[102] but it also emphasises the tendency to consider sub-state political formations as entities qualified to achieve political legitimacy and, possibly, some form of international recognition and support. Moreover, these local authorities are unlikely to yield their recently acquired power to a central authority and should help to ensure that a future Somali state (or states) is very decentralised. At the same time, in the areas of Somalia that remain relatively chaotic, particularly most of southern Somalia, the duration of state collapse and the negative ramifications from almost complete infrastructural damage will also complicate reconstruction. The longer this situation of lawlessness endures in these parts, the harder it will be to convince those in control of strategic resources to relinquish them and, subsequently, to help rebuild the state.

State collapse, however, has not yet been incorporated into the normative structure of the international system.[103] Experience in Somalia during the intervention demonstrated that the international community

[99] See David Mitrany, *A Working Peace System*, Chicago, Quadrangle Books, 1966, p. 27, for more information.

[100] I. William Zartman, 'Putting Things Back Together', in I. William Zartman, ed., *Collapsed States: The Disintegration and Restoration of Legitimate Authority*, Boulder and London, Lynne Rienner Publishers, 1995, p. 268.

[101] See Jeffrey Herbst, 'Alternatives to the Current Nation-States in Africa', *International Security*, 21, 3, Winter 1996/7.

[102] Ken Menkhaus and John Prendergast, 'The Political Economy of Post-Intervention Somalia', *Somalia Task Force Issue Paper 3* (published on the Internet), April 1995, p. 1.

[103] 'The situation in Somalia will continue to deteriorate until the political will exists among the parties to reach a peaceful solution to their dispute, or until the international community gives itself new instruments to address the phenomenon of a failed state': *The United Nations and Somalia (1992–1996)*, The United Nations, Blue Books Series, Volume VIII, Department of Public Information of the United Nations, New York, 1996, p. 89.

addressed the phenomenon of state collapse mainly through subsidiary
policies of humanitarian, peacekeeping, and peace enforcement operations, and not through the establishment of constitutional structures
and devolution of power. The international community certainly contributed to the collapse of Somalia, though the blame also rests with
Somalis themselves.

The unfortunate combination of centuries of competition over scarce
resources, years of dependence on foreign aid, and an imploded government has magnified the natural corrupt tendencies manifest in all
human beings. During his tenure, Siad Barre and his cronies monopol-
ised the limited resources in the country, while also abusing military
power, and thus the state itself became the focus of the conflict. The
original famine that led to the intervention may be over, though humanitarian disasters have continued to plague the region (e.g. floods in 1997,
draught in the northeast in 1999). Nascent political administrations do
exist in several parts of the country, yet Somalia did not (and does not
today) resemble the rosy picture painted in 1995 by Chester Crocker,
former Assistant Secretary of State for African Affairs, when he claimed
the following:

Operation Restore Hope . . . dramatically strengthened Somalia's vestigial civil
society and challenged the war-lords' political monopoly. By stopping the fac-
tional strife, it also froze in place the military situation, denying the initiative to
the stronger factions and protecting, for a time, the weaker. In this way, a new
state of affairs developed to replace the hideous one that prompted the intervention.[104]

In the subsequent US-led military intervention in Haiti, the operation
encountered fewer problems because the government did not implode,
and because the US government and the UN redressed many of the
mistakes made in Somalia, although other concerns have impaired political reconstruction in Haiti.

---

[104] Foreword by Chester Crocker in Hirsch and Oakley, *Somalia and Operation
Restore Hope*, p. xvi.

4   Heartened in Haiti

Operation Uphold Democracy, the misnomer for the US-led military intervention in Haiti, has entered the post-Cold War political lexicon, reflecting the recent prominence enjoyed by advocates of democratisation. Of greater significance is the precedent set when the UN Security Council formally sanctioned the use of force to implant – or 'uphold' – democracy by invoking Chapter VII of the UN Charter. While the Somalia intervention challenged the non-interventionary norm because of the humanitarian pretext, international approval of the denial-of-democracy excuse in Haiti advanced this process even further. As Thomas Buergenthal explained, 'Once the rule of law, human rights and democratic pluralism are made the subject of international commitments, there is little left in terms of governmental institutions that is domestic.'[1] As in Somalia, however, the Security Council recognised the 'unique character of the present situation in Haiti and its deteriorating, complex and extraordinary nature, requiring an exceptional response', to protect whatever remained of this norm.[2]

This chapter examines the third post-Cold War military intervention that would become a nation-building operation – and the first in which the motive behind the intervention naturally led to the nation-building component. It explains the manner by which the fundamental elements necessary to establish a democratic state have, in fact, been implanted in Haiti through a bizarre combination of erratic US behaviour prior to the intervention, with considerate and efficient US and UN activity during the operation. The chapter concludes with an analysis of lessons learned and the prospects for upholding democracy in Haiti.

[1] Thomas Buergenthal, *CSCE Human Dimension: The Birth of a System*, 1 Collected Courses of the Academy of European Law, No. 2, at 3, 42–43 (forthcoming) as cited in Thomas Franck, 'The Emerging Right to Democratic Governance', *The American Journal of International Law*, 86, 46, 1992, p. 68.
[2] Security Council Resolution 940, 31 July 1994.

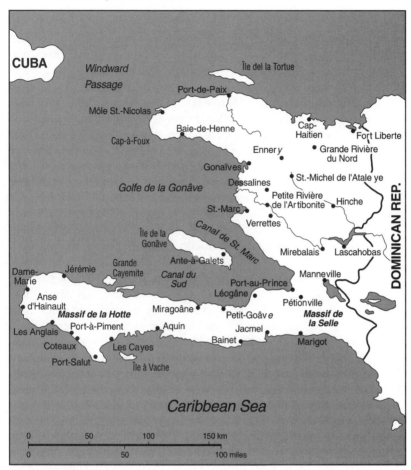

Map 3 Haiti

The run-up to intervention

Democratisation and international security

Before concentrating on Haiti, however, a brief analysis of how democratisation matured into such a position of primacy in the United States
is necessary, as this development foreshadowed official UN sanction of
the Haiti intervention.[3] As noted in chapter 1, the concept of *democratis-*

---

[3] This brief analysis should complement the historical overview of nation-
building presented in chapter 1.

ation evolved from the Reagan and Bush years, when it was equated with the policy of containment of international communism. The translation of this policy in Central America during that period essentially meant arming the Nicaraguan Contras (in Panama, it provided a pretence for the removal of Noriega and the embarrassing drug link).[4] Under Clinton, democratisation has been modified, with the basic motive now the promotion of democracy for international peace and security reasons. The campaign has taken on added weight due to the demise of communism and the western fear of Islamic fundamentalism.

The underlying supposition, usually attributed to Immanuel Kant, is that liberal democracies *rarely* go to war with one other; instead they channel discontent through existing multilateral or bilateral institutions, such as the UN or the World Trade Organization (WTO).[5] Moreover, as Bruce Russett explained, 'In the absence of direct attack, institutionalised checks and balances make democracies' decisions to go to war slow and very public.'[6] Samuel Huntington thus remarked, 'the spread of democracy in the world means the expansion of a zone of peace in the world'.[7] In addition, democracy proponents believe that democratisation can help to undermine oppressive and authoritarian regimes. Notwithstanding the controversy surrounding these arguments, such assumptions now inform US policy.[8]

The United States has put democratisation (or the promotion and support of democracy) on the policy-making agenda as a means of safeguarding international society, while multilateral organisations increasingly require it for full membership. The promotion of democracy has

---

[4] See chapter 2 for more information about the use of the democracy excuse in Panama.

[5] More recently, Thomas Friedman of the *New York Times* has formulated the 'Golden Arches Theory of Prevention', which asserts that 'No two countries that both have a McDonald's have ever fought a war against each other.' As cited in *Yale Alumni Magazine*, March, 1998, p. 8.

[6] Letter to the editor, *The Economist*, 29 April 1995.

[7] Samuel P. Huntington, *The Third Wave: Democratization in the Late Twentieth Century*, Norman, Oklahoma, University of Oklahoma Press, 1991, p. 29.

[8] See, for example, Thomas Carothers, 'The Democracy Nostrum', *World Policy Journal*, 11, 3, Fall 1994, pp. 47–53, who argued that this rationale is out-dated. Supporters of the theory include Bruce Russett, who explained, 'Over the past 50 years, pairs of democratic states have been only one-eighth as likely as other kinds of states to threaten to use force against one another, and only one-tenth as likely to carry out these threats. Democracies have also been less likely to escalate disputes with one another, and more likely to avail themselves of third-party mediation,' Letter to the editor, *The Economist*, 29 April 1995.

been one of the three main objectives of President Clinton's foreign policy, and one of the four redefined aims of the United States Agency for International Development (USAID). In May 1994 President Clinton declared, 'Now the greatest opportunity for our security is to help enlarge the world's communities of market democracies; and to move toward a world in which all the great powers govern by a democratic plan.'[9] Funding has kept pace with this commitment: the United States now invests vast amounts of time and resources in democratisation (approximately 13 per cent of the budget allocated to the State Department in 1995, for example), significantly more than other countries and multilateral institutions.[10] Today the State Department now also has a Bureau of Democracy, Human Rights and Labor Affairs, with the responsibility of 'promoting democracy world-wide, formulating US human rights policies, and co-ordinating policy in human rights-related labor issues.'[11] Democracy promotion continues to be a fundamental national security concern.[12]

Besides promoting democracy through the many different democratisation organisations, the US government also applies economic pressures, suspends aid, and often vetoes or abstains in votes for World Bank and IMF loans. In most of the western hemisphere, which historically has been the priority region in the drive to democratise, the campaign has been generally successful, with the impetus for change emanating primarily from the countries themselves, although often with covert and overt pressure from outside, and in some instances, following military intervention. Currently all thirty-four active OAS member states have democratically elected governments. Cuba is the only country in the region that has not held elections, but it is not a participating OAS member,[13] while Haiti's membership was suspended until

[9] Remarks by the President in CNN Telecast of 'A Global Forum with President Clinton', The Carter Center, Atlanta, Georgia, 3 May 1994.

[10] Relatively speaking, these figures are much less than that which was spent in Germany and Japan after World War II.

[11] See http://www.state.gov/www/global.human—rights/index.html for more information.

[12] See, for example, the 1997 National Security Strategy, in which support for democratisation remained a strategic goal of the US government, or USAID's Web page on democracy (http://www.info.usaid.gov/democracy/).

[13] At the closing session of the 8th Meeting of the Consultation of Ministers of Foreign Affairs, which took place on 31 January 1962, the OAS approved several resolutions (Communist Offensive in America, and Special Consultative Committee on Security Against the Subversive Action of International Communism), which prevented Cuba from participating in the organisation. Information supplied by the Columbus Memorial Library, Organisation of American States.

after the US-led military intervention. Indeed, the path to democracy in Haiti has proved to be full of potholes, with the possibility of reform only coming about because of yet another US intervention.

Haiti's tragic history

Father Jean-Bertrand Aristide's triumphant return to Haiti on 15 October 1994, after three years of forced exile, may have been somewhat diminished because he arrived aboard a US military aircraft. Yet for the majority of Haiti's 7.3 million inhabitants, his return was all that mattered, and if it could only come about in the presence of 20,000 US military escorts, so be it. This non-forced, US-led military intervention ('peaceful deployment' in UN-speak) has set the poorest country in the western hemisphere on a democratic course.

Like other countries in the region, such as Panama and Nicaragua, Haiti's history has been marred by political violence and US intervention. As summarised in the *Haiti Handbook for US Personnel* (given to troops who participated in the September 1994 operation), 'For a variety of internal and external reasons far too complex to address here, Haiti did not fare well over the last 200 years.' In 1915 the United States ordered the Marines to occupy Haiti out of concern for widespread civil unrest and US business interests. US troops left nineteen years later without establishing any sort of democratic foundation, and the country reverted to chaos with the army emerging as the dominant faction. Elections were finally held in 1956, and François 'Papa Doc' Duvalier won. He stayed in office until his death in 1971 because he had learned early in life how tenuous Haiti's leadership could be, and significantly, what actions were necessary to maintain control. Mark Danner explained:

In 1907, in a modest house not far from the National Palace, François Duvalier was born... This was during the military dictatorship of Nord Alexis, though when François was one year old General Antoine Simon overthrew Alexis. He was four when a revolution ousted Simon and five when an explosion reduced the old wooden Palais National and President Cincinnatus Leconte along with it to splinters. Duvalier was six when President Tancrède Auguste was poisoned; his funeral was interrupted when two generals began fighting over his succession... One Michel Oreste got the job, but he was overthrown the following year by a man named Zamor, who in turn fell a year later to Davilmar Théodore. President Théodore lasted barely three months before Vilbrun Guillaume Sam marched a detachment of irregulars down from the north and overthrew him; President Sam had reigned five months when, with another revolution spreading from the north, he ordered a hundred and sixty-seven political prisoners, most of them members of elite families, massacred, and took refuge in the French Embassy – whence, on the following day, a mob dragged him out, impaled him on the Embassy's spiked fence, and tore his body to pieces. . . When the marines marched ashore, François Duvalier was a child of eight; by the time they left, he was a nationalist intellectual of twenty-seven.[14]

A typical Papa Doc reprisal after an attempted coup, of which there were many during his reign, occurred in the summer of 1964, when a group of exiled mulatto aristocrats invaded from the north. Papa Doc's *tonton macoutes*[15] murdered most of them, but two received special treatment: they were executed at the National Cemetery, in front of live television and crowds of children. Papa Doc then had his *macoutes* parade the wealthy, European-educated families of the plotters naked through the streets of Jérémie to the airport, where they were publicly killed with daggers, by order of age: the infants and children first (to enrage the parents), the women next (to enrage the husbands), and finally the men.[16] After his death, Papa Doc's enormous and famously stupid son, Jean-Claude, or 'Baby Doc', assumed control at the age of nineteen, reinforcing and consolidating his father's repressive style of rule.

Although the United States eventually facilitated the departure of Jean-Claude Duvalier in 1986, their continued support of the violent regimes that followed Duvalier once again eroded the faith that the Haitian public had placed in the USA. The United States backed the interim governments partly out of a belief that they were pursuing democratic policies and genuinely wanted to hand over power to an elected civilian government. In addition, support given to the Haitian leaders was also based on the US fear of the spread of communism in the region, particularly emanating from neighbouring Cuba. US democ-

[14] Mark Danner, 'A Reporter at Large: Beyond the Mountains I', *The New Yorker*, Part II, 4 December 1989, p. 111. Part of this quote was cited by Danner as coming from a book by Bernard Diederich and Al Burt, called *Papa Doc*.

[15] 'Tonton macoute' in Creole stands for Uncle Knapsack, the opposite of Tonton Noël – or Uncle Christmas. Tonton macoute is the one who grabs bad children, throws them in his deep and very dark sack and takes them off into the night. In Haiti, the *macoutes* were the 'unofficial, voodoo-linked authorities' who were 'evil and all-powerful'. Mark Danner explained, 'As every Haitian knew, Papa Doc was the incarnation of Baron Samedi, the voodoo *loa* who trafficked with the dead. And the Macoutes were his creatures . . . [they] were Papa Doc's instruments; by virtue of him they were above the law.' The *macoutes* worked on a voluntary basis, but survived by blackmail. See Danner, 'A Reporter at Large', pp. 127–8 for more information.

[16] This story was taken from Danner's article, though Papa Doc was famous for such executions.

racy assistance to Haiti during this period was mainly directed at the holding of elections, and not at the many other societal changes that were necessary for sustained democratic reform, albeit there were some projects that focused on civic and political education, for example.

The continuous barrage of verbal and economic pressure from the US government finally wore down the Haitian rulers, and elections took place in December 1990. Provisional President Ertha Pascal Trouillot, the Provisional Electoral Council, and leaders of the major political parties invited international observers, and their presence reassured voters that a slaughter, like that which occurred in the cancelled 1987 election, would not be repeated at the polls.[17] Indeed, the elections were run in a relatively peaceful manner, with Aristide, a radical populist priest, winning 70 per cent of the national vote.

International response to Aristide's overthrow: the last straw

One month after the election, there was a coup attempt by Roger Lafontant, the former Interior Minister under Duvalier and head of the dreaded *tonton macoutes*. Lafontant failed because Aristide supporters rioted, and he was arrested. Nine months later – in September 1991 – after Aristide attempted to raise the minimum wage from $3 to $5 a day, he was overthrown in yet another coup and went into exile.[18] General Raoul Cedras, Philippe Biamby, and Colonel Michel François assumed *de facto* control of Haiti, and held it until the United States forced them out three years later.[19]

During its tenure, the Cedras regime was responsible for various acts of barbarity, including the arrest, torture, rape, murder, and destruction of property of thousands of ordinary Haitians and many prominent Aristide supporters. Five thousand Haitians were killed, tens of thousands fled the country, while an estimated 300,000 were unable to live at home for fear of persecution, and therefore internally displaced. The international community, prodded by the United States, the UN and the OAS, responded to these events by increasing pressure on the junta

[17] Because Haiti's population is largely illiterate, the election ballots had pictures of party members as well as representative symbols from their parties.
[18] The attempt to change the minimum wage did not directly cause the coup, but it was Aristide's last official act in office.
[19] Cedras had originally been appointed by Aristide as Commander in Chief of the Armed Forces, while the latter two were graduates from the US Army Infantry officer basic course at Ft. Benning in Georgia, USA. Later, in March 1997, François was indicted in Miami on charges that he helped smuggle 66,000 pounds of Colombian cocaine and heroin into the United States.

to allow Aristide to return and resume the presidency through the imposition of ever-tightening sanctions and diplomatic pressure.[20]

In addition to these typical diplomatic measures, the US government
also acted in a somewhat unpredictable and bizarre fashion. Historically,
the US administration maintained strong ties to the leadership in Haiti –
including both Papa Doc and Baby Doc Duvalier – much as it did with
Manuel Noriega in Panama. Also reminiscent of Panama, press reports
revealed that the CIA had trained many Haitian military officers and
kept them on the CIA payroll – even after the 1991 coup – despite
documentation that they had been engaged in drug trafficking since the
mid-1980s. In fact, the major incentive for the junta to cling to power
for so long was the huge return on their illegal activities: they were
reportedly earning more than $500 million a year.

At the same time that these reports were surfacing, there was a growing anti-Aristide movement among senior conservatives in the United
States. Henry Kissinger, Jesse Helms, Elliott Abrams, Bob Dole, and
Dick Cheney all publicly denounced Aristide. The CIA's senior Latin
America analyst, Brian Latell, testified to Congress that Aristide was
mentally unstable and that he had spent time in a psychiatric hospital
in Montreal. The *Miami Herald* received permission from Aristide to
check his medical records, and no such stay was in evidence. Other
reports revealed that even after the 1991 coup, the CIA had been paying
Aristide's enemies in the military for information on him.

In 1992 Latell, who worked directly for former CIA Director R. James
Woolsey, met with and praised Marc Bazin, prime minister just after
the coup, and Bazin's team (which included General Cedras), calling
them 'the most promising group of Haitian leaders to emerge since the
Duvalier family dictatorship was overthrown in 1986'.[21] He also added
that, contrary to popular belief, there was no widespread violence and
repression and that 'Gen. Cedras impressed me as a conscientious military leader who genuinely wishes to minimize his role in politics. . . I
believe he is relatively moderate and uncorrupt [*sic*].'[22] Democracy promotion was thus hampered by the peculiar goings-on in the United

---

[20] See OAS Document CP/RES.567 (870/91), 30 September 1991; OAS Document MRE/RES.1/91, 3 October 1991; OAS Document MRE/RES. 2/91, 8
October 1991; OAS Document MRE/RES. 3/92, 17 May 1992; and UN
Security Council Resolutions 841 (1993), 873 (1993), 875 (1993) and 917
(1994).

[21] 'Haiti Leaders on CIA Payroll', *The International Herald Tribune*, 2 November
1993.

[22] 'CIA Memo Discounts "Oppressive Rule" in Haiti', *The Washington Post*, 18
December 1993.

States, the reluctance of the junta to leave, and Haiti's unfortunate familiarity with discord – as encapsulated in the Haitian proverb: *Deye mon, gen mon* (Beyond the mountains, more mountains).

Non-compliance meets a military response

On 3 July 1993 Aristide and Cedras signed the Governors Island Accord, in which both agreed that Aristide would return in October and the junta would leave, in exchange for amnesty. On 12 October 1993, US Secretary of Defense Les Aspin ordered the USS *Harlan County*, a naval vessel, to depart from the Port-au-Prince harbour without disembarking due to the violent protests that greeted its arrival. On board was a small team of UN peacekeepers who were to assist with the implementation of the Governors Island Accord and set up the UN Mission in Haiti (UNMIH). This incident took place just nine days after the eighteen US Army Rangers were killed in Somalia. The US administration was extremely anxious about a similar débâcle occurring in a situation that was also not 'secure'.

By May 1994, comprehensive sanctions were in place because the junta had not complied with the agreement, and violence and political repression continued. At this time, only humanitarian aid was allowed through. On 21 July 1994, US Ambassador to the UN, Madeline Albright, requested permission from the Security Council to remove the junta with whatever means were necessary, after Aristide sent a letter to the Security Council in endorsement. She received permission ten days later, embodied in Resolution 940. Approval by the Security Council occurred primarily because Aristide, who represented the 'legitimate' government of Haiti, supported the intervention. The relevant sections of the resolution read as follows:

Acting under Chapter VII of the Charter of the United Nations, authorizes Member States to form a multinational force under unified command and control and, in this framework, *to use all necessary means* to facilitate the departure from Haiti of the military leadership, consistent with the Governors Island Agreement, the prompt return of the legitimately elected President and the restoration of the legitimate authorities of the Government of Haiti, and to establish and maintain a secure and stable environment that will permit implementation of the Governors Island Agreement.[23]

The resolution also clarified the tasks of UNMIH, which would take over after the multi-national force (MNF) achieved its objective.

---

[23] Security Council Resolution 940, 31 July 1994. The vote had twelve votes in favour with two abstentions, Brazil and China. Emphasis added.

Why military force?

Clinton was the first US president to appeal for permission to intervene from the UN but not from the US Congress, many members of which were opposed to the plan. The United States requested authorisation from the former because this administration did not want other regional powers to think they could have free rein in their supposed spheres of influence *without* UN sanction. Additionally, because Aristide had requested the military option (as well as many of the earlier sanctions imposed by the OAS and the UN), Clinton could claim that the operation was not a request for war, and therefore, could legally avoid Congressional involvement in his decision.

The following justifications (some more credible than the others) were cited by officials, since Clinton had to explain (or overstate) why force was necessary in a small country that in no way threatened international peace and security:[24]

1. *Haiti is in the US sphere of influence.* The United States has assumed paternal responsibility for the region ever since the Monroe Doctrine. Hence the invasions of Grenada and Panama, and the covert operations in El Salvador and Nicaragua. Clinton supported this argument by pointing to other major power involvement in their respective regions, e.g., European activity in Bosnia, and Russian military intervention in Georgia, 'at the request of the government of Georgia, [and] willing to abide by United Nations standards'.[25] He made this remark just one year before the United States became militarily involved in Bosnia.

2. *Democracy was denied to a country in the western hemisphere.* Bush had claimed this as one of the rationales for his Panamanian venture, as Reagan had in Grenada, but without securing UN approval. This pretext was also put forward by Clinton to avoid having to threaten Cuba with intervention (where no comparable elections have been held). Clinton argued that such intervention 'helps to end human rights violations that we find intolerable everywhere but are unconscionable on our doorstep'.[26] Further, the OAS, with backing by the United States, had

---

[24] In fact, Cuba, Mexico, Uruguay, and Venezuela opposed the intervention on the grounds that the situation in Haiti did not threaten international peace and security, and that other means beyond the use of force were more suitable for this case.

[25] Interview of the President by Wire Reporters, 14 September 1994. This point ignores the reality that the Russians were responsible for much of the instability in Georgia in the first place, created in order to coerce Georgia into joining the Commonwealth of Independent States.

[26] *International Herald Tribune*, 26 September 1994.

recently agreed to uphold democracy in the region, and to take steps to counter any action that threatened it.[27]

3. *The refugee problem was threatening to overwhelm the United States.* Haiti maintained its high position on the political agenda since the 1991 coup primarily because of the refugee crisis, although Cuban refugees were arriving in large numbers in late August and early September, and no similar threat was made to Cuba. Approximately 20,000 refugees left Haiti during June and July 1994, which was the busiest period in Coast Guard history for Haitian refugees, and it was rumoured that 300,000 more lay in wait. Further, by the time the intervention occurred, the Haitian refugees held at the US military base in Guantanamo, Cuba had already cost the US government $200 million; their maintenance was estimated at $14 million a month.[28]

More important, the state government in Florida had already initiated a lawsuit for $1 billion against the federal government for education, health care and social welfare spending on illegal immigrants over the years; the Haitian refugee dilemma reinforced Florida's claim and apprehension. Clinton did not want to alienate Florida's voters, and thus reneged on his campaign promise that he would not repatriate Haitian refugees without proper hearings as Bush had done. That promise had given hope to other Haitians, and was partially responsible for the increase in numbers.

4. *The US administration had suffered continual humiliations by the ruling junta since the 1991 coup*, culminating in the USS *Harlan County* incident, just as Bush had done from Noriega and Saddam Hussein. The *de facto* rulers of Haiti needed to be taught the lesson that the United States meant what it said, and respected international agreements (Governors Island) and commitments (UN and OAS resolutions). There was additional pressure at that time in Clinton's presidency to demonstrate that he was capable of carrying out a coherent foreign policy, especially in America's own backyard. This message would serve as a warning to other errant leaders world-wide. As Clinton later remarked, 'We sent a powerful message

---

[27] In fact, the OAS passed Resolution AG/Res. 1080 in 1991, which set out the procedure to be used when a democratic government in the western hemisphere was overthrown by non-democratic elements. This resolution was first used to impose sanctions on Haiti after the coup. This and subsequent resolutions on promoting democracy at the OAS stopped short of advocating force by noting that efforts to promote democracy should observe 'due respect for the principle of nonintervention' (see any of the resolutions on democracy for the years 1994–8, e.g. AG/Res. 1551 (XXVIII-0/98) on the OAS Web page, www.oas.org).

[28] Most of the 14,000 Haitian refugees who were waiting in Guantanamo have returned since Aristide's restoration.

to the would-be despots in the region: democracy in the Americas cannot be overthrown with impunity.'[29]

5. *Human rights abuses were severe.* Clinton spoke of murderers, rapists, and torturers among the ruling junta. Drug dealing among Haitian leaders also became a factor, as it eventually did in Panama.

6. *Concern for US citizens living in Haiti, albeit a small number.* This was also put forward as a major reason for the Panama and Grenada invasions.

7. Finally, in the most implausible rationale of all, Clinton claimed that the situation in Haiti caused '*the total fracturing of the ability of the world community to conduct business in the post-Cold War era*'.[30]

Other reasons not cited by the administration – but equally important – included Randall Robinson's hunger strike, which embarrassed Clinton, and demands by the Congressional Black Caucus, as well as pressure exerted by representatives of the 1.5 million Haitian-Americans. Extensive media coverage ensured that the majority of Americans were fully cognisant of the scope of the problem in Haiti – as well as of the refugee crisis that was plaguing Florida. In fact, during the year prior to the intervention, most of the stories on Haiti could be found in the 'domestic' sections of the US press, signifying how Haiti's predicament was viewed as more of a domestic US issue than a foreign one, and the important place in the debate that it then occupied. As in earlier cases, factors such as increased refugee flows, the media, defiance by Cedras and company, and sanctions – albeit couched among other more noble rationales – eventually forced the administration to 'Do Something'.

President Clinton summarised the situation four days prior to the intervention: 'In Haiti, we have a case in which the right is clear, in which the country in question is nearby, in which our own interests are plain, in which the mission is achievable and limited, and in which the nations of the world stand with us.'[31] The only really clear points were that Haiti was indeed nearby and that the military mission was certainly achievable.

Closer collaboration: US and UN co-ordination

Intervention, not invasion

The eventual intervention, officially underway at 12.01 a.m. on 19 September 1994, with the support of twenty-seven countries that comprised

[29] Remarks by the President at the Opening of the Commemoration of '50 Years After Nuremberg: Human Rights and the Rule of Law', Storrs, Connecticut, 15 October 1995.

[30] White House Press Conference, Interview with the President, 14 September 1994.

[31] Remarks by the President in Television Address to the Nation, 15 September 1994.

the multi-national force, such as Nepal and Bangladesh (there were approximately 2,000 non-US personnel), was 'non-forced' due to last-minute diplomacy conducted by former President Jimmy Carter, General Colin Powell, and Sam Nunn.[32] Cedras had been in touch with Carter prior to the intervention, and Carter requested permission from the Clinton administration to mediate. The agreement with Cedras was reached because of Carter's negotiations, backed by the imminent threat of arriving troops, or to paraphrase Clinton, through 'the successful combination of the credible threat of force with diplomacy'.[33] This formula would again work in Bosnia.[34]

The US administration was pleased with the results of Carter's mediation, which surely spared many US and Haitian lives, but there was some resentment that Carter chose to act as a free agent. At one point he admitted to being ashamed of US policy in order to reassert his authority after rumours were circulating that the intervention had already begun before the negotiations terminated. There was also controversy over Carter and Powell labelling Cedras 'a man of honour', just after Clinton had publicly described him as a murderer. Aristide was not pleased either because the deal signed did not stipulate that the junta had to leave the country, as Clinton had earlier promised, and because it allowed Cedras to stay in office for another month.[35] Aristide was eventually arm-twisted into a public display of gratitude to the United States a few days later. Meanwhile, the UN Special Envoy to Haiti, Dante Caputo, resigned over the lack of consultation with him and the UN during the Carter negotiations.

MNF to UNMIH to UNSMIH to UNTMIH to MIPONUH: *transition to peacekeeping and operation shrinkage*

After approximately six months of the multi-national force (MNF), which operated under a Chapter VII mandate, in March 1995 the baton

[32] Colin Powell was the former Chair of the Joint Chiefs of Staff, and Sam Nunn the former Head of the Senate Armed Services Committee.

[33] See any of the press briefings by President Clinton just after the intervention, e.g., 'Remarks by the President in Bipartisan Leadership Meeting', The White House, Office of the Press Secretary, 20 September 1994.

[34] A US official attempted to explain the last-minute change that occurred once the operation was underway, and how an invasion becomes an intervention: 'There was a question on rules of engagement because we had built them for an invasion. And in fact, we intervened without an invasion. So there was a tweaking of the rules of engagement to ensure that they matched the situation that we had on the ground.' Background briefing by Senior US Officials, 27 March 1995, The White House.

[35] All three military rulers eventually left the country: Cedras and Biamby both went to Panama, while François went to the Dominican Republic.

passed to the UN Mission in Haiti (UNMIH), which was a Chapter VI peacekeeping operation, staffed by 6,000 personnel, with less than half being US employees. UNMIH was to remain until 29 February 1996, just three weeks after the first democratic transition in Haiti ushered in the new president and friend of Aristide, Réné Préval. Instead, UNMIH was prolonged until the end of June 1996, at Préval's request.

US troops withdrew entirely along with UNMIH, due to Clinton's long-overdue promise to have all US troops out of Haiti one year after their original arrival in September 1994, even though the US administration did agree to pay the bulk of running costs for the remaining Pakistani battalion. Separately, however, 450 American military personnel, most of them belonging to engineering and medical units, remained in Haiti – not as part of the UN contingent, but rather for 'training' purposes (called US Support Group Haiti, which has no official link with the UN mission).[36] In 1996, they staged two separate military exercises in Haiti, and such manoeuvres, along with the presence of other international troops, will continue to serve as a physical reminder of the US and UN commitment to uphold the fragile democracy in Haiti – and also as a warning to future coup plotters.

From July 1996, the mission continued under the auspices of the United Nations Support Mission in Haiti (UNSMIH), approved by Security Council Resolution 1063.[37] UNSMIH comprised approximately 1,300 UN personnel (Canadian and Pakistani) – 700 of whom were not officially part of the UN team but under separate control of the Canadian government, while 300 of the total were police trainers (Canada spent an estimated US $8 million per month on the operation). The troop composition, command structure and financing of UNSMIH resulted from a last-minute compromise reached in the Security Council due to China's objections to the maintenance of a larger force.[38] After the transfer to UNSMIH, the operation became a *de facto* US and Canadian endeavour – despite the non-participation by US troops in the UN operation, and with the involvement of Pakistani troops.[39] Officially, however, the operation remained under the mantle of the UN.

[36] Reuters, 13 May 1997.
[37] Security Council Resolution 1063, 28 June 1996.
[38] Before the earlier extension of UNMIH to 28 June 1996 was granted, China attempted to delay this extension but eventually conceded just minutes before the mandate for UNMIH was due to expire at midnight on 29 February. The Chinese were upset because Aristide had invited the Taiwanese to President Preval's inauguration.
[39] Canadian leadership has been welcome in Haiti and supported by most of the members of the UN due to Canada's extensive experience in peacekeeping and the ability of many of their troops to speak French.

Additional requests by Préval extended UNSMIH, first until the end of November 1996, and then to July 1997 (this was the fifth such extension). Préval claimed that the fifth request would be his last appeal for a mandate extension, while the Security Council also issued a statement that it would not renew the mandate of its peace force after the July expiry date; continued unrest and slow progress on police training have, however, caused the decision to be reversed, and the mandate extended, under yet another name.

From August to November 1997, 300 members of the UN Transition Mission in Haiti (UNTMIH) continued police training, as well as providing security for UN employees. The Special Representative of the Secretary-General remained lead co-ordinator for institution-building activities, national reconciliation efforts and economic rehabilitation work. This extension was authorised by Security Council Resolution 1123 (30 July 1997).

Reforms had still not been implemented to a satisfactory degree, and thus the Security Council passed resolution 1141 (28 November 1997), which established the UN Civilian Police Mission in Haiti (MIPONUH). MIPONUH's strength resembled UNTMIH, with an estimated budget of $44 million from its inception to 30 June 1999. The original mandate ran to November 1998, and on 25 November 1998, the Security Council extended MIPONUH's mandate until 30 November 1999.[40] Significantly, and unlike the previous three missions, it has no military component. Its mandate is to continue to reform and professionalise the Haitian police force.

The police training is likely to continue for some time after this latest mission expires because the costs are low and the risks of complete withdrawal are high. Indeed, all the extensions have been granted by the Security Council to uphold the 'secure and stable environment' that has been evident since the operation began, because for the near future at least, this stability can only be sustained while foreign troops and police are visible and foreign funds are buoying the economy. Even though costs have been reduced drastically, $316 million was spent on the multi-national force and UNMIH, a further $56 million on UNSMIH, $20.6 million on UNTMIH, and finally an estimated $44 million for MIPONUH; these funds have made a significant contribution to this poor economy.[41] What has the international community intended to

---

[40] See Security Council Resolution 1212, 25 November 1998.
[41] According to several UNMIH, UNSMIH, UNTMIH, and MIPONUH documents, obtained on the Web (www.un.org).

achieve in Haiti during all these missions, and has there been sufficient progress towards these goals?

Limited mandates

Haiti has a long way to go before it resembles its Caribbean cousins. Because of mistakes made in Somalia and in Bosnia during UNPRO-FOR, the objectives for the Haiti intervention, spelled out in Security Council Resolution 940 and UNMIH documents, were realistic, limited, and fundamental for activating much-needed reforms in this extremely impoverished nation. They were to be achieved in three phases. During the first, the MNF met its two targets in a brief time period: it deployed troops within several days, and secured key posts in the capital and other major cities; and it administered vital humanitarian assistance, such as the provision of food and medicine, within a six-month period while upholding security. The MNF avoided any involvement in nation-building tasks.

Responsibility was then transferred to UNMIH (and subsequently to UNSMIH, UNTMIH and MIPONUH), in the second phase, with four additional aims, the first a carry-over from the military operation: to maintain a secure environment with multinational troops, and protect international personnel and key installations; to professionalise the Haitian armed forces, create a new police force, and improve the functioning of the justice system (including penal institutions); to prepare the country for free and fair elections, and assist in their execution; and to promote economic development. The fourth aim of the UN peace support operation and the third phase of the operation will be fully passed on to UN development agencies and international and local NGOs when the UN operation finally terminates. Significantly, this is the first peace support operation where the development role has been fully integrated since the start in recognition of the need to link security and democratic reforms with development. The UNDP Resident Representative simultaneously served as the Deputy Special Representative of the Secretary-General (SRSG) in order to smooth this transition.

There have thus been three shifts, each of which has overlapped with the subsequent one: from the military to the peace support operations to the development agencies, who have the most challenging job, although all are important and necessary if Haiti is to become a stable democracy. Significantly, no *comprehensive* 'nation-building' component was included, as in Somalia; rather the focus has been on assistance in preparing for and promoting democratic reforms, which were envisaged to continue for many years.

All the aims were approved and have been supported by the government of Haiti, which was the intention from the start – that the operation be a collaborative effort. Reforms have been instigated to achieve the latter three, with difficulties, especially in reforming the police and judiciary, though this is to be expected due to Haiti's extreme poverty and dearth of democratic experience.

Nation-building part I: police, military and judicial reforms

Prior to implementing democratic reforms and necessary to upholding them, the state needs to re-establish a sufficient degree of security. In Haiti, the fledgling democracy was unable to do this on its own. The re-establishment and maintenance of governmental control over security is contingent upon police, military and judicial reforms. The UN Secretary-General noted that a major aim of the intervention was to establish a new police force that would be separate from the armed forces, and that this objective would be ratified by the Haitian Parliament 'at the earliest opportunity'.[42]

A competent police force was considered vital for the rehabilitation of Haiti, which is why the majority of foreign personnel who have remained in Haiti after the many reductions in the UN force have been tasked primarily to continue the police training programme, as well as provide a rapid reaction force to deal with emergencies. As in Panama, the Haitian police had only ever served to instil terror in the population, and certainly not trust. At the same time, no corps of competent and available Haitians who could be trained to replace the dysfunctional police (or paramilitary) was on hand. To avoid repeating the mistakes made in Panama when the US military trained the new police force – which in fact was not 'new' as it was composed primarily of old PDF members – and similar to what occurred in Somalia, in Haiti, police trained other police. (In Bosnia too, the same would occur.)

The approach adopted by the UN civilian police trainers (CIVPOL) gradually weeded out former security personnel as new recruits became more fully trained, up to the hoped-for total force deployment of 6,726. The initial force was called the Interim Public Security Force (IPSF), created from former armed forces personnel who were not tainted by association with the previous regime as well as Haitians from abroad

---

[42] Report of the Secretary-General on the United Nations Mission in Haiti, UN, S/1994/828, 15 July 1994, para. 9(d).

(including refugees from Guantanamo). These recruits received six days of training in the United States, and by the end of 1994, the IPSF comprised nearly 3,000 members.[43]

The permanent force, the Haitian National Police (HNP), eventually absorbed the competent members of the IPSF. Those members of the IPSF who were phased out were retrained for civilian employment, when possible. This phasing-out of former members of the paramilitary force was important for instilling public support and trust in the new force throughout the country, so that the new force could replace the traditional Haitian method of self-policing, which often was embodied in violent forms of retribution, such as 'necklacing'.[44]

Yet difficulties were encountered – and expected. By mid-1997, the new police force was not entirely confident, nor were the desired total number fully trained, while many members of the CIVPOL were 'significantly ignorant' about their role in the peacekeeping operation.[45] In addition, several violent incidents occurred due to the police failing to do their job, while some members of the new force were accused of committing human rights abuses (by February 1997 approximately fifty civilians had been killed by the police). One year later, the UN Secretary-General reported that 'there has been little change in the level of criminal activity, including organised crime related to drug trafficking, which has been a constant worry to the Haitian authorities'.[46]

The increase in violence in various parts of the country has also been attributed to Haitian anxiety about the impending departure of UN troops, although the police training unit will continue under the direction of the US or Canadian government if the UN pulls out entirely: donors agreed in late July 1996 to maintain the programme in some capacity for another five years.[47] The US government remains commit-

---

[43] *Managing Arms in Peace Processes: Haiti*, United Nations Institute for Disarmament Research, Disarmament and Conflict Resolution Project, UN, Geneva, 1996, p. 22. See also MICIVIH Report on Haitian National Police (as listed on the OAS Web page, www.oas.org).

[44] The term has come to represent a form of community revenge in which a suspect is killed usually by placing some object of harm around the neck, such as a burning tyre.

[45] United Nations Mission in Haiti (UNMIH), Mid-Mission Assessment Report, April 1995–February 1996, The Lessons-Learned Unit, DPKO, New York, March 1996, p. 18, para. 51. Approximately half of the 5,000 Haitian police officers have been based in the capital, while the rest are dispersed throughout the country.

[46] Report of the Secretary-General on the United Nations Civilian Police Mission in Haiti, 20 February 1998, section II, para. 12.

[47] *The Economist*, 27 July 1996, p. 39.

ted to maintaining a secure environment, as demonstrated on 28 February 1997, when the US National Security Advisor Sandy Berger and Deputy Secretary of State Strobe Talbott went to Haiti to assess the overall progress of the mission, with a special focus on the efforts to establish an independent judicial system and the new police force.

Because of such problems, UN police and troops have interfered on several occasions to restore order, which partially undermined the hoped-for domestic confidence in the new force. The Haitian government has also taken control and punished misbehaviour accordingly: by the end of January 1998, the Inspector-General's office had dealt with over 2,000 complaints of crimes, such as murder, robbery, brutality and drug dealing, and dismissed over 200 members of the force, while it also suspended 500 others.[48] Moreover, by the end of 1997, the Haitian police had dismantled 40 criminal gangs, seized 2,180 kilograms of drugs, and confiscated 276 illegal weapons.[49]

Other concerns included the lack of functioning equipment for the new force (everything from radios to cars to suitable jails), which will remain a problem for some time due to inadequate funds and great demand. International donors have been asked to provide funds for this purpose, but in many cases when equipment has been provided, the Haitian police have not maintained it.[50] Additionally, the US government, which by early 1997 had already spent $65 million on training, sent forty Haitian-American, Creole-speaking police officers to Haiti to assist CIVPOL, and they have been deployed to trouble spots, such as Croix De Bouquet, where violence has escalated.[51]

These new trainers have been serving as mentors for the burgeoning force. They accompany Haitian recruits into the different communities throughout the country to explain to the local population what to expect from their police. By late spring 1997, there were 300 civilian police trainers from French-speaking countries, together with the 40 Creole-speaking Haitian-Americans, working in police stations throughout the country. And although problems remain, progress is in evidence. In early

---

[48] *Voice of America*, 14 February 1997, and Report of the Secretary-General on the United Nations Civilian Police Mission in Haiti, 20 February 1998, section IV, para. 20.

[49] Report of the Secretary-General on the United Nations Civilian Police Mission in Haiti, 20 February 1998, section IV, para. 18.

[50] Author interviews with CIVPOL trainers and the director of CIVPOL, Haiti, October 1995.

[51] See, for example, Sandra Marquez Garcia, 'Cops Cope with Scandal, Disarray', *The Miami Herald*, 22 February 1997, for more information.

1998, the UN Secretary-General commented that the Haitian National Police,

has become less dependent on the United Nations civilian police, has improved its management and has strengthened reporting relationships both by building an effective cadre of commissaires and inspecteurs and by redeploying rank-and-file agents throughout the country to improve the balance in police coverage between the capital and the provinces.[52]

Linked with police reform was reform of the armed forces. In early 1995, Aristide officially dismissed the members of the armed forces, including most of the officer corps. By mid-1996, the remaining 1,500 members of the officer corps were also disbanded, along with the Ministry of Defence.[53] Many of those dismissed joined the police force, while others were reintegrated into civilian life under a scheme operated by the International Organization for Migration, in co-operation with the Haitian government.

The US government preferred a reduced army over no army at all to protect the border with the Dominican Republic and the coastline. Additionally, the Americans believed an entirely disbanded army would lead to more insecurity, but Aristide did not give in to US pressure.[54] Some disgruntled and unemployed former officers do remain at large – giving the Haitian government cause for concern, especially since many of those who were given vocational training have not been able to find jobs. A rally was held in June 1996 by former officers who were demanding pay, but they were also reminding the government that they were still a force to be reckoned with.

Judicial and penal reforms have also been hampered by the dire state of the judiciary, based as it is on inadequate laws. Several foreign democratisation organisations, such as the USAID-sponsored International Criminal Investigative Training Assistance Program (ICITAP), have been working in this sector to help construct a reliable and impartial justice system. In co-operation with the government of Haiti, ICITAP has been training new applicants for the police force as well as judges and lawyers throughout the country.[55]

Prisons remain overcrowded, and many accused of crimes are forced to wait months in prison before their trials, despite the law that states

[52] Report of the Secretary-General on the United Nations Civilian Police Mission in Haiti, 20 February 1998, section IV, para. 18.
[53] *The Economist*, 27 July 1996, p. 38.
[54] *Managing Arms in Peace Processes: Haiti*, p. 27.
[55] *Managing Arms in Peace Processes: Haiti*, p. 22.

that they can only be held for a maximum of forty-eight hours before their hearing. The prison reform project initiated under the auspices of the UN, however, has significantly improved procedures in prison administration.[56] A functioning judicial and penal system is a prerequisite to bolster police reforms.

Nation-building part II: strengthening democratic institutions

The UN mandate merely stipulated that the international community assist in the realisation of elections, which has been accomplished, albeit with some difficulties. Other democracy promotion activities, however, have been integral to the operation since its inception. International democratisation groups, notably the International Civilian Mission in Haiti (MICIVIH), have been working with Haitians in many spheres of electoral support, including voter education and political party training. Enthusiasm for democracy initially generated a turn-out of over 80 per cent of eligible Haitians who voted in the 1990 elections, yet five years later (and one year after international involvement), only 29 per cent participated.

Legislative elections were re-run several times because of intimidation and poor co-ordination in some areas, and several major parties boycotted them altogether. Turn-out continued to decline: by April 1997, a mere 5 per cent voted in the first round of Senate elections. The UN can at least point to partial success in executing three rounds of elections, even if participation was reduced to minimal numbers, most likely due to impatience over the slow pace of reforms.

Elections are indeed crucial to establishing democracy, but even more important are functioning political parties and a legislative system to sustain democratic reforms. Improvements are underway, but the challenge is enormous in a country that has never had even a rudimentary democratic base. For example, in 1995 elections, many lame duck mayors abandoned office the day the results came in, leaving empty posts for several months until the new term started.[57] A prevailing fear of the international community and some Haitians is that Haiti will once again surrender to over-centralised state control, even though the largely rural population (70 per cent) and the natural tendency to run things locally would make Haiti an ideal testing ground for decentralisation options. The 1987 constitution even points to the need to decentralise public administration.

---

[56] Report of the Secretary-General on the United Nations Civilian Police Mission in Haiti, 20 February 1998, sectionVI, para. 32.

[57] Author interviews with UNMIH electoral officers, Haiti, October 1995.

Long-term political prospects seem particularly daunting. Concern that the former *de facto* rulers are biding time until foreign troops leave haunts US intelligence experts, causing pressure to mount on democracy promotion groups to accomplish the near impossible in a country with no real familiarity with democracy and much experience with corrupt and repressive rule.[58] Similar to the beginning of the twentieth century, presidential rule continues to be an ephemeral occupation: during the ten years from 1987 to 1997, Haiti witnessed ten changes in the presidency.

Finally, political parties lack strong platforms and pedigrees, and are hard to distinguish from one another, especially since early 1997 when Aristide split with Préval and formed another branch of the Lavalas party, the Lavalas Family. Prime Minister Rosny Smarth resigned over what he considered were flawed elections in April 1997, and the country had been without a functioning government for almost two years, which also held up $100 million of foreign aid. At the end of March 1999, Préval appointed a new government by decree. Whether this government will be able to begin the long process of reconstructing the government is unclear. The political situation has been held up by Aristide, who is planning to run again for the presidency in 2000, and who opposes the privatisation of poorly run state assets. He was banned from running against Préval in 1996 because the constitution forbids successive presidencies, but it does allow a candidate to run again after a period out of office.

Nation-building part III: economic development

The third and final phase of the planned reconstruction effort, which in fact has been underway since the beginning, is the promotion of economic development. Aristide's sound-bite, that he wants to help Haitians move from 'misery to poverty with dignity', is a realistic aspiration. For years the economy has been in decline, compounded by nearly two centuries of corrupt and brutal rule.

Haiti's high growth rate (one of the fastest in the western hemisphere) caused the population to jump from 4.5 million in 1970 to 7.3 million by 1997. The lethal combination of deforestation, soil erosion and the subsequent decline in arable land, along with urbanisation, outward migration (normally of skilled labour) and the recent embargo, which caused unemployment to increase to 70 per cent by the time US troops arrived, left the rump economy in a drastic state. The 1996 UNDP Human Development Report ranked Haiti at 145 of 174 countries on

---

[58] Author interviews with intelligence officers, Haiti, October 1995.

its Human Development Index; one year later it dropped to 156, and by 1998, it was at 159.

Reducing unemployment, which today persists at 60 per cent, is a major challenge for the international community. For example, foreign agencies have been experiencing difficulties promoting job training schemes in Haiti because few companies retain employment records, while most public employees lack basic managerial and accounting skills. USAID compiled a skills data-bank of many Haitians living abroad by tapping into the records of various international agencies, yet no similar data can be found for Haitians at home.

Because of the intervention, however, Haiti will continue to receive critical assistance, funding and attention in the immediate term, which should give its economy a kick-start. Total financial commitments by multilateral and bilateral donors and creditors for October 1994 to 2000 were $1.7 billion, with the bulk of the funds to be dispersed by 1997. In 1997, international donors declared that the remaining $400 million, designed primarily for infrastructure improvements, would only be distributed if the Haitian government could demonstrate that the funds would be used judiciously, including the privatisation of nine state-owned enterprises, such as the telephone and electricity companies, and the Port-au-Prince port and airport.[59]

Since he left office, Aristide has been campaigning against the sale of these government assets, even though he agreed to it when he was president. His opposition has been mostly responsible for the delay in the privatisation plans due to consequent popular protest (and the governmental impasse, as mentioned). In addition, government application of the World Bank and IMF Structural Adjustment Policy has been unpopular with the majority of the population because of the concomitant negative economic effects. The European Union has also committed 148 million ECUs (US $175 million) for 1996–2000. The bulk of EU funds will be allocated to agriculture, economic, infrastructure, transport and judicial sector projects.[60]

These short-term commitments by donors do not necessarily imply that funding will stop after the year 2000: in April 1997, for example, after a meeting with President Préval, Canadian Foreign Minister Lloyd Axworthy promised that his country's development assistance to Haiti would persist over the next five years.[61] The benefits from all these funds should have a multiplier effect in a country where only 45 per cent of the urban population and 3 per cent of rural dwellers have electricity, where literacy hovers

---

[59] *Voice of America*, 27 February 1997, and Reuters, 8 February 1997.
[60] Agence Haïtienne de Presse (AHP), Port-au-Prince, 6 March 1997.
[61] Reuters, 2 April 1997.

at 35 per cent, where annual per capita GDP persists at $250, and every day one thousand tons of garbage is washed into the Port-au-Prince harbour.[62] Improvements are already visible. The refugee crisis has abated, even though the flow has not entirely stopped.[63] Inflation has declined since troops arrived, taxes are being collected, and GDP has grown and is expected to continue in this direction over the next few years.[64] The UN Secretary-General reported in early 1998 that, in the opinion of international development banks, 'the country is well-placed to move into a path of steady economic growth . . . which, combined with an improved regulatory environment and a continued emphasis on privatiz-ation, would be sufficient to create a climate of confidence for increased local as well as foreign direct investment'.[65]

Yet until that time, economic expansion will continue to be based on foreign assistance, all of it public. The government of Haiti's 1995 budget had external sources accounting for 66 per cent of the total, while the 1996 budget increased that figure to 70 percent.[66] The focus for all projects has been on involving the government as much as possible since foreign troops will only be around temporarily, and donors are questioning the need to direct so much of their foreign assistance to one tiny country.

Expansion of the Haitian economy will take many years, and this point has been recognised by the international community and, signifi-cantly, by Haitians. In January 1997, President Préval commented, 'Give us 18 months to two years and I would expect to begin to see the fruits of the actions we are taking today. What we want to do is lay good foundations for development.'[67]

---

[62] Associated Press (AP), 16 December 1995. These figures persist at similar levels today (see, for example, 'Haiti: Profile', *The Courier*, No. 161, January–February 1997, p. 43).

[63] Before he left office, Aristide was using the threat of refugees as a bargaining chip, warning of increased numbers if foreign aid did not arrive as pledged.

[64] The United States has also been assisting with infrastructure projects, such as paving roads and planting millions of trees. During 1996, Prime Minister Rosny Smarth noted that inflation reached 30 per cent – which was in fact a significant reduction from the figures cited during the embargo – while growth was only 2.8 per cent. Haiti's balance of trade was also uneven in 1996: exports reached US $100 million while imports totalled $450 million, and the country has been forced to import 34 per cent of its food (compared with thirty years ago when Haiti satisfied nearly all its food needs). 'Haiti: Profile', *The Courier*, No. 161, January–February 1997, p. 43.

[65] Report of the Secretary-General on the United Nations Civilian Police Mis-sion in Haiti, 20 February 1998, section VI, para. 28.

[66] 'Haiti: Profile', *The Courier*, No. 161, January–February 1997, p. 43.

[67] 'Interview with Réné Préval: The President of Last Resort', *The Courier*, No. 161, January–February 1997, p. 41.

Assistance by foreign troops

In the tasks outlined in the Security Council resolutions, foreign troops, in co-operation with civilian organisations and police trainers, participated in promoting the overall aims. For example, by 1 October 1995, US Civil Affairs (CA) troops completed 332 infrastructure rebuilding projects, and were continuing another 375. These troops worked with Haitians, who provided some funding, manpower, assisted in planning, and eventually took over their running once CA troops left. Most of the projects were proposed by Haitians, who prioritised their needs at local levels, and then worked with foreign troops stationed in their region to accomplish the tasks. The emphasis was on decentralisation as much as possible, for the flexibility of the foreign troops and their varying expertise, to accommodate the particular needs of different communities, and because international funding was not available to pay for all the projects.[68]

Initially, in October 1994, the US Ambassador requested and received deployment of 37 Civil Affairs soldiers to work in different cabinet offices in Haiti, assisting the new government to establish their offices and accomplish administrative tasks.[69] A total of 80 CA and 70 Psychological Operations (PSYOPS) troops participated during the MNF, while 60 CA, 70 PSYOPS, and 400 Special Forces took part in UNMIH. These troops comprised a healthier percentage of the peacekeeping operation (e.g., less than 1 per cent of the MNF as against 9 per cent of UNMIH). The utility of these special forces had been recognised in Panama (over a thousand CA troops participated), and after the Gulf War (300 CA troops were sent to northern Iraq). In sharp contrast, there were only 7–30 CA troops participating in UNITAF in Somalia at any one time, and all were sent home at the start of UNOSOM II.[70]

Conclusions

The Haiti endeavour culminates the self-taught course, Nation-Building 101, in the western hemisphere for the US government (democratisation in Cuba has never been on the syllabus). After years of promoting democratic reforms through the provision of low levels of public assist-

---

[68] Author interviews with CA and PSYOPS troops in Haiti, October 1995.
[69] *Managing Arms in Peace Processes: Haiti*, p. 18.
[70] Information compiled from various US Army sources on the World Wide Web and from correspondence with Colonel Doug Daniels, who was in charge of Civil Affairs in Haiti in 1995. These figures were also mentioned in the previous chapter.

ance in the entire region (e.g., election monitoring), sporadic high levels of covert aid, and occasional intervention, the US engagement in Haiti has not ostensibly drifted out of orbit. And even though US proponents of democratisation, especially those in the administration, have severed their link with the crusade against communism, the government's approach to the intervention in Haiti was littered with inconsistent policies, covert support of military leaders and specious arguments that so marked many earlier US interventions.

Indeed, the operation can be seen as a typical case of 'regional power projection' by the US government in its area of influence: some of the reasons the intervention transpired were self-serving and it was not undertaken merely out of concern for Haiti. Yet the intervention deviates from the norm in several critical ways. *Operation Uphold Democracy* was not unilateral, the prelude to it was very public, and UN involvement after it has been significant.

Moreover, the Clinton administration does not deserve the entire blame for the bungling in Haiti prior to the intervention because it inherited many unresolved international problems from Bush – Somalia and Haiti among the most prominent. It is extremely unlikely that Clinton endorsed the anachronistic CIA activity, and he responded to the accusations in appropriate fashion, with promises to expedite reforms for all US intelligence agencies. And despite the muddled process, the end result could be that ordinary Haitians may finally have a chance to live without fear and rebuild their economy, neither of which would have come to pass in the near future without US interference.

Notwithstanding the erratic period prior to the intervention, the multinational force and the peace support operations have been efficiently managed and considered successful in terms of co-ordination and implementation of the international mandate. This achievement can also be attributed to the existence of several important factors in Haiti: there was a strong will amongst the local population in support of the intervention, an elected government to replace the illegitimate rulers, a powerful and wealthy neighbour with a stake in the outcome, and on the ground, modified UN behaviour due to 'lessons learned' from past operations in both the military and civilian spheres.

Lessons learned and applied: militarily

First and foremost, *the military concentrated primarily on security*, to prepare the way for the humanitarian operation. They did not become involved in nation-building activities to the same extent as they did in Panama. During the MNF operation, US troops avoided repeating the mistakes made in Somalia by not crossing what Sir Michael Rose termed the 'Mogadishu Line' and getting entangled in internal warfare.

Other lessons were learned from Panama, when US troops were unprepared for the looting that took place, and *Operation Desert Storm*, when they were surprised by the massive Kurdish flight to the hills. *Planning for Haiti included thorough post-intervention strategies.* To avoid the Panamanian-style chaos, Cedras was permitted to remain in office for an additional month after troops landed (he left on 15 October), which would provide some continuity of authority before Aristide returned to replace him. Further, the Chapter VII operation (the MNF) was fully phased out before Chapter VI (UNMIH) took over.

The MNF and troops in UNMIH also attempted some *disarmament*, though not a comprehensive programme, even though Canada applied pressure on the US government to do so. As a senior US official stated, 'There was a decision from the very beginning that we were not going to go house to house looking for weapons in Haiti.'[71] (Haiti's constitution permits private ownership of guns, as in the United States.) US troops did collect light weapons that were visible as well as establishing a voluntary buy-back programme.

Unlike in Somalia, when disarmament was sporadic and weapons were merely stored in secure areas, to be stolen at a later date, the weapons collected in Haiti were mostly destroyed, with a small percentage retained for the new police force. This programme, funded by the US Department of Defense, was responsible for 13,281 weapons collected between September 1994 and March 1995 at a cost of almost $2 million, while another 17,000 were seized.[72] The disarmament project was officially terminated in February 1996, although by early 1997, there were still complaints that Haiti was an 'arms bazaar'.[73]

The costs borne by the military operation were also low, due to international pressure, much of it coming from the US Congress, since the US government was footing a hefty percentage of the bill. For example, many projects initiated by Civil Affairs troops in the MNF and UNMIH, such as rebuilding roads and other community projects, were undertaken at minimal cost. As mentioned, Civil Affairs soldiers enlisted members of the local community to provide the labour, often only in exchange for food, and CA troops provided the technical know-how.

---

[71] Background briefing by Senior US Officials, The White House, 27 March 1995.

[72] *Managing Arms in Peace Processes: Haiti*, pp. 24, 35.

[73] See, for example, *The Economist*, 27 July 1996, p. 39.

This helped to ensure that the Haitians felt ownership of the projects, and therefore would expend greater effort in their upkeep.[74]

Domestic support in the United States for attainment of the mission mandate (instead of a hasty withdrawal as in Somalia) was partially upheld through the fortunate coincidence of *low US casualties*. There were more suicides than soldiers killed (4:1) by the time US troops left. The US administration knew it had to tread cautiously with the memory of the harsh treatment of the US Rangers in Somalia still fresh in the minds of most Americans.

Finally, *co-operation between the civilian and military sides of the operation was excellent*. On-going meetings between senior staff of both took place at the Civil–Military Operations Center (CMOC) at UN mission headquarters, under the overall direction of a civilian. These meetings were responsible for keeping all parties informed, allowing opinions to be aired. The CMOC was maintained from the multi-national force through the peace support operations, unlike in Somalia, where it was shut down after the transition to UNOSOM II.

This enhanced co-operation may be the result of the *special training that civilians and military personnel who participated in the transition received prior to the handover*, another first for peacekeeping. The integrated sessions held at Fort Bragg, North Carolina gave participants the opportunity to understand their separate, albeit linked, roles in the operation, such as in projects concerned with engineering, communications, logistics, movement control, and receipt and inspection of goods.[75] Normally the military and civilian/humanitarian communities are wary of each other, even though they are at the same time becoming increasingly interdependent due to the upsurge in civil conflicts that result in peace support operations.

Lessons learned and applied: inter-agency co-operation and peace support operations

Since the operation began, *co-ordination has been extremely good* between the government of Haiti, and UN civilian and military personnel, as it has also been with the Friends of Haiti (Argentina, Canada, Chile, France, the United States, and Venezuela), international NGOs and

---

[74] Information provided through personal interviews with Civil Affairs soldiers in Port-au-Prince and Cap Hatien.
[75] Information on the training sessions was provided by Lt. Eisele and Col. Peter Leentjes, Chief Training Unit, DPKO, UN Headquarters in NY.

multilateral lending agencies.[76] Frequent meetings have been held throughout, with the military playing a supporting role, unlike in Panama where they directed the effort. During UNMIH, good co-ordination could be attributed to the excellent managerial skills displayed by the SRSG, Lakhdar Brahimi, who brought with him experience from successful peacekeeping and other international democratisation missions (e.g., he directed the UN election effort in South Africa). He was well respected by UN personnel, and reminded his staff that, above all, they must 'respect the dignity of the Haitian people'.[77]

The keen interest in the success of the peacekeeping operation emanating from the UNMIH leadership was contagious and permeated all levels. In Panama, the opposite occurred due to the lack of interest in political reconstruction from military headquarters. This well-run management operation, which continued after Brahimi was replaced by Enrique Ter Horst at the start of UNSMIH, can be sharply contrasted to that which occurred in Somalia, but it is not possible to guarantee good leadership in all peace support operations because so much is contingent on the managerial skills of the particular director.

Good co-ordination would not have been possible without advance planning. Indeed, *civilian planning for the peace support operation was very thorough*, unlike in Panama where only the military were involved in planning due to the secrecy of the invasion. UNMIH was originally set up to implement the Governors Island Accord in autumn 1993. Another year and a half passed before UNMIH was finally established, giving planners additional time to fine-tune the design for the mission.[78] Ironically, the major positive side-effect of the US government dithering for so long before deciding to intervene was the luxury of time afforded the

[76] During UNMIH, President Aristide, Kinzer (UN military commander), Brahimi, and Poulliot (head of CIVPOL) met twice a week, and these meetings also included US Ambassador Swing, Ossa (the UNDP Resident Representative and Deputy SRSG), Lannegrace (adviser on political affairs), and Seraydarian (Chief Administrative Officer). Of this group, Brahimi, Lannegrace, Swing, and Seraydarian all knew each other and had worked together during the South African elections, and most had experience working in several other peacekeeping missions. Brahimi is currently the UN's chief trouble-shooter, having subsequently served in Afghanistan and Angola.

[77] As told to me by both civilians and military personnel participating on the mission.

[78] See, for example, Security Council Resolutions 862 (31 August 1993) and 867 (23 September 1993) for more details of the early plans for UNMIH.

various civilian departments of the US administration and the UN (as well as the military) to map out detailed courses of action.

Inter-agency political-military planning and information-sharing within the US government was also unprecedented, but only after the military had been convinced of the need to proceed. The US Department of Defense (DOD) was initially reluctant to use force in Haiti, and avoided concentrating on the conflict until the spring of 1994 when DOD was directed by the Secretary of Defense William Perry to begin drawing up possible intervention plans. Perry's instructions included inter-agency planning, which took place in the Executive Committee (Ex-Comm) from May under the National Security Council. Agencies that participated included the Departments of State, Defense, Justice, Treasury, the CIA, and USAID.[79]

By May 1994 USAID had begun police training plans, while the military had prepared a forced entry plan. These were finalised in September, just before the operation began, when meetings were held with senior civilian and military planners. Although they obviously could not iron out all anticipated problems, the planners outlined areas that needed further attention. This tight co-ordination can be sharply contrasted to Panama and Somalia, where in the former there was no civilian involvement and little senior military interest, while in the latter, DOD and the State Department did not co-operate in advance of the intervention, they diverged on matters pertaining to nation-building, turf wars erupted frequently, and information was often not shared between and even within agencies.

The US–UN relationship in Haiti also proceeded smoothly, and both deserve credit for the skilful running of the operation. Bureaucratic in-fighting was negligible, unlike in Somalia. Again, this can partially be attributed to the personalities of those in charge of the operation, but the overall chain of command was also clear. Initially it was a US-led intervention, which then passed on to the UN, with the US government serving in an advisory capacity, both in Washington, DC, and through the US Ambassador in Haiti, who was involved in most

---

[79] Richard E. Hayes, 'Interagency and Political-Military Dimensions of Peace Operations: Haiti – A Case Study', edited by Dr Margaret Daly Hays and RAdm. Gary F. Weatley, USN (Ret.), Directorate of Advanced Concepts, Technologies, and Information Strategies, Institute for National Strategic Studies, National Defense University, NDU Press Book, February 1996. Information also provided to the author during interviews at USAID in Washington, DC, Winter 1994. Several of those interviewed indicated that they were anticipating the intervention, and this was over nine months in advance of its occurrence.

major decisions, in co-operation with the UN and the government of Haiti. The US government preferred burden-sharing, which helped to ensure that the operation was not unilateral, and instead had international support.

In terms of peace support operations, other lessons have been applied at the macro-level, such as the *incorporation of the international development role within the overall strategy*, as mentioned earlier. The Special Representative of the Secretary-General insisted from the start that his deputy be the UNDP Resident Representative, which was important in such an impoverished state, and even in the significantly pared down operation, MIPONUH, this pairing continues, which has allowed the UN mission and development activities to maintain their high level of co-ordination. Further, *the transitions were conducted thoughtfully*, with a carry-over of personnel to provide continuity – a lesson learned from Somalia where new teams were not properly briefed and there was little overlap of personnel. For example, when the transference from the MNF to UNMIH occurred in March 1995, two-thirds of the military and one-third of the CIVPOL training unit stayed on, helping to ensure what the UN calls a 'seamless transition'.[80]

The nation-building aims were also limited and achievable, unlike in Somalia where the international community was asked to take on too large a task for its limited experience and abilities. The organisational constraints on the UN, with 185 member states, were too great to accomplish the rebuilding of the entire Somali state. In Haiti, on the other hand, the mandate included four components: maintain a secure environment, retrain the armed forces and police, prepare the country for elections and assist in their execution, and promote economic development. Resolution 940 stated quite clearly that 'the goal of the international community remains the restoration of democracy in Haiti and the prompt return of the legitimately elected President, Jean-Bertrand Aristide, within the framework of the Governors Island Agreement'.[81]

Most of these goals have been achieved by the international community – at least insofar as stipulated by the UN mandate – albeit with problems with police and judicial reforms, and with political party development. As National Security Adviser Anthony Lake concluded:

[80] In fact, the *modus operandi* for the transition was outlined in Security Council Resolution 964 (29 November 1994).
[81] Security Council Resolution 940, 31 July 1994.

Given the chance, the Haitian people quickly focused on the ballot, not the bullet; on trade, not terror; on hope, not despair. In just a year and a half, with our civilian help, they have completed presidential, parliamentary and local government elections; trained a police force, that is as yet imperfect, but showing great progress. They have dramatically, despite problems, improved the human rights situation and begun to reverse the economic decline of the coup years. Haiti remains the poorest nation in the Americas. There is no guarantee democracy will take hold or the economy will prosper. But its people now have a real chance to build a better future for themselves and their children – and for the US forces who have acted in Haiti with such strength and with such skill are leaving when we promised they would, we can say 'mission accomplished.'[82]

Finally, and significantly, the *political will was there*: the majority of Haitians sanctioned the intervention, as was amply demonstrated as troops arrived, and even though grumbling is getting louder because immediate economic recovery is not in evidence, the UN is still popular.

Reversing the downward development spiral

The fourth and most difficult task of the UN mandate, economic development, will be fully passed on to the development agencies when the UN finally departs, which can only be achieved in co-operation with the government of Haiti. The US government will remain involved, however, through funding the various democratisation agencies as well as maintaining a small military base. It is certain that at least for the remainder of the Clinton presidency, attention will be paid to Haiti, partially because Haiti is considered one of Clinton's foreign policy successes.

Yet without the successful realisation of the international community's first priority, that of security, the goal of democratic reform will not be reached, which is why there may be some extension of the UN mission for some time. International investors remain wary of investing in Haiti because of security concerns and continued instability, and their support is vital for rebuilding and strengthening the economy. Overall, the problems encountered and discussed earlier in the chapter were expected, as noted in Lake's statement above, and will continue to plague Haiti for years to come. A quick solution was just not possible given the scope of Haiti's economic and political problems prior to the intervention.

Other obstacles will need to be overcome in Haiti before the country

---

[82] Anthony Lake, Assistant to the President for National Security Affairs, Remarks at George Washington University, 'Defining Missions, Setting Deadlines: Meeting New Security Challenges in the Post-Cold War World', 6 March 1996.

can be referred to as a relatively stable democratic state. Today Haiti is a significant transshipment point for drugs from Latin America that eventually end up on the streets of America. President Préval in 1996 began his own anti-corruption campaign with an attack on drug corruption within the government. For example, on 1 October, he ordered the arrest of one judge for releasing an alleged Dominican drug dealer, and he also removed another judge who had been accused of improper handling of narcotics-related cases. Several police officers have also been dismissed for drug-related activities. The US government has been financing a large proportion of the anti-drug activities, including the equipment and training for the Counternarcotics Unit based in the capital.[83]

Implications for the future: is Haiti a model?

Although there are many more success stories in Latin American and Caribbean democratisation than failures, it is the responses to the failures that receive the most attention and, significantly, set precedents. The invasions of Panama and Grenada supplied the United States with the ultimate resolution to the Haitian dilemma, and the experiences in Kuwait and Somalia institutionalised the process by garnering UN approval. The US government has also not learned how to veer off the seemingly inevitable path leading to military intervention by exercising non-military options, especially when the threats get too loud and errant leaders continue to defy international pressure. Extensive international media coverage of the crisis, the threat posed to US 'stability' by refugee flows, the alleged drug and CIA links with the junta, and the embarrassing and hasty USS *Harlan County* retreat, ensured the military response by entrapping the US government. Most of these factors would also contribute to the decision to use force in Bosnia, as they had done in Panama and Somalia.

It is also becoming increasingly apparent that sanctions, though effective at times, do not always achieve their desired aim of removing nasty dictators, as was learned in Panama, Iraq, and many other parts of the world. Instead they often lead to the use of force. In addition, sanctions are often inherently myopic. For example, the Haitian embargo affected long-term recovery because family planning programmes and health care facilities were forced to shut down due to the lack of available supplies and financing, and job creation in the agro-industry was almost completely wiped out, causing more migration to the United States and

[83] State Department Narcotics Report on Haiti, 28 February 1997.

greater economic instability. Haitian GNP in fact dropped by 26 per cent during the embargo (between 1991 and 1994).[84]

It would be imprudent to suggest that intervention produces democracy in all cases: Somalia is a blatant example that external 'nation-building' does not always succeed. No matter how unpopular and ill-conceived, however, most of the interventions in the western hemisphere have allowed democratic reforms to take root. Grenada and Panama are the most conspicuous examples, although they have a long way to go before becoming stable democracies.

The security rationale for democratisation is indeed becoming entrenched in western political thought. As the US National Security Adviser, Anthony Lake, concluded: 'The United States is not starry-eyed about the prospects for spreading democracy, but it knows that to do so serves its interests. Democracies create free markets that offer economic opportunity, and they make for reliable trading partners. They tend not to abuse their citizens' rights or wage war on one another.'[85] (And those living in democracies are less likely to flee their country in search of safety.)

This argument may be applicable over the long term, yet in the short term it is also the case that externally driven democratic reforms have contributed to state collapse, or partial collapse, in several instances, as will be discussed in greater detail in chapter 6. Another lesson the US government and the UN still need to come to terms with is that support for transitional elections in any country, such as in Haiti during the 1990 election, should be coupled with meaningful, post-election programmes that can cope with 'inexperienced, weak, democratically elected governments coexisting with powerful anti-democratic structures of power'.[86] The common assumption among many policy makers in the United States is that foreign troops can leave once elections have been held.

The underlying motive for the intervention is important (e.g., refugees and saving face), but it is of greater significance how the public debate is framed, as the record sets precedents and relays messages to other way-ward rulers. After the Haiti intervention, Clinton reiterated his claim that maybe now other countries would hesitate before embarking on an authoritarian path by rejecting the results of fair elections. Clinton made this

---

[84] 'Haiti: Profile', *The Courier*, No. 161, January–February 1997, p. 43.
[85] From an editorial in *The International Herald Tribune*, 24–25 September 1994.
[86] Tom Carothers, 'Lessons for Policymakers', in Georges A. Fauriol, ed., *Haitian Frustrations: Dilemmas for US Policy*, A Report of the CSIS Americas Program, CSIS, Washington, DC, 1995, p. 118.

impulsive assertion: 'the world knows that the United States will stand up for human rights and against slaughter, stand up for democracy, honor our commitments and expect those who make commitments to us to honor them as well'.[87] Common sense suggests, however, that the grey area is still fairly large, particularly outside the western hemisphere.

Certainly the right to democracy is not the universal entitlement that many claim it to be. Thus there has been no mention of possible interventions in other cases where elections have been overturned: Myanmar (Burma), Algeria (where the prospect of refugee flows to Europe poses a serious threat), Nigeria, or even the Dominican Republic, where the 1994 elections were apparently not so honest but the United States could not denounce them because it needed help in sealing the border with Haiti during the blockade. In 1995, Freedom House listed fifty-five countries as 'not free'. Should such countries be parcelled out to the regional power to invade? Because of the expense of such operations, the fear of casualties, and residual respect for the non-interventionary norm, military intervention because of denial-of-democracy will remain a last resort, and will not become the *modus vivendi* of western foreign policy.

Reaction to events in Bosnia occurred more rapidly than in Haiti, though effective intervention took several years, as will become evident in the next chapter. In Bosnia, however, the drive to democratise did not provide the impetus for the military response. Instead, as in Somalia, humanitarian concerns linked to state collapse once again took the stage.

[87] Remarks by the President aboard the *USS Eisenhower*, Norfolk, Virginia, 6 October 1994.

5   UNPROFOR, IFOR and SFOR: can peace be FORced on Bosnia?

The war in Bosnia persisted for over three years (March 1992–August 1995) before the international community responded in a decisive manner with the right combination of force and diplomacy, even though attempts at the latter began in 1991 and NATO planes first started bombing in April 1994.[1] Once again, the international community, led by the United States and Europe, became entangled in nation-building, this time through an attempt to end the most distressing conflict in Europe since World War II. What happened during the three and a half years it took the international mediators to achieve the fragile peace contrived at Dayton in November 1995? Will Dayton endure?

This chapter addresses these questions in three parts: the first looks at the failure of the European Community (later Union)[2] and the UN to stop the fighting through the application of sanctions, mediation-by-recognition and the establishment of the UN Protection Force (UNPROFOR); the second part examines the many different peace plans that did not deliver the promised peace, the one that did, and the force that was necessary to secure that peace; and finally, the concluding section analyses Dayton in practice, lessons learned and implications for the future Bosnian state. Although the collapse of Yugoslavia engendered four Balkan wars, this chapter focuses only on that in Bosnia because it was the bloodiest, the longest, attracted the most international attention, and ultimately dragged in the international community, which in turn caused the focus to shift to rebuilding state structures.[3]

---

[1] NATO provided close air support to defend troops on the ground starting from April, while air strikes first took place in February 1994.

[2] Because the European Community later became the European Union after the 1992 Treaty on European Union (which was not implemented until November 1993), and because the European Commission still exists and is referred to as the EC, references to the former European Community will be abbreviated as the EU to avoid confusion.

[3] For more information, see Richard H. Ullman, 'Introduction: The World and Yugoslavia's Wars', and Ullman, 'The Wars in Yugoslavia and the Inter-

International impotence

Serbian irredentism[4]

Through the constitution, which ensured that no group dominated the state, President Josip Broz Tito contained ethnic strife between the eight main ethnic groups (Slovenes, Muslims, Serbs, Croats, Albanians, Macedonians, Montenegrins, and Hungarians) during his reign over communist Yugoslavia, from 1945 to 1980. Of the six Yugoslav republics, Serbia was the most heterogeneous, but in Bosnia as well, Serbs, Croats, and Muslims co-existed in a relatively integrated and tolerant society.[5] Although ethnic problems erupted on occasion, they did not eclipse the relative stability in Yugoslavia until after Tito's death in 1980 and the implosion of the former Soviet Union later that decade.

The uneven democratic forces that swept through the former Soviet Union, eastern and central Europe – compounded by the economic crises accompanying the collapse of communism – yielded severe side-effects in regions that were home to mixed minority groups, many of which harboured grievances for past offences committed. Some of the reformed states were able to accommodate this resurgence of nationalism, which normally generated demands for minority recognition and the right to self-determination, as in Romania.[6] Others that could not faced either dissolution, as in the former Czechoslovakia, or war, as in Chechnya, or both, as in the former Yugoslavia.

Once nationalist passions are unleashed, it is difficult to stop their spread – and spread they did through all the Yugoslav republics, in their most brutal manifestations: war, genocide and ethnic cleansing (i.e., forced population transfers). Serbia's President, Slobodan Milosevic, who came to power in September 1987, is primarily responsible for stirring up this ethnic hatred throughout the former Yugoslavia by exploiting historic Serb grievances that eventually led to the disintegration of the state itself. Later, he would also play a major role in the

national System after the Cold War', in Richard H. Ullman, ed., *The World and Yugoslavia's Wars*, New York, the Council on Foreign Relations, 1996, pp. 1–41.

[4] 'Irredentism' refers to a historical claim made by one sovereign state to land and/or people outside that state's internationally recognised boundaries, justified on the grounds that the earlier separation was illegal or forced.

[5] See, for example, Noel Malcolm, *Bosnia: A Short History*, London, Macmillan, 1994.

[6] Although it has only been since early 1997 that Romania has been able to achieve this type of power-sharing.

Map 4 The republics of former Yugoslavia

termination of the war in Bosnia.[7] Most irredentist campaigns are 'top-down' phenomena, initiated and maintained by governments, and Milosevic's claim to a Greater Serbia was the vehicle he used to promote his own personal power and agenda, with the aim of a Serb-dominated Federal Yugoslavia – at the expense of an entire nation-state and 6 per cent of the population of Bosnia alone.

The formal collapse of the Socialist Federal Republic of Yugoslavia, comprising the republics of Slovenia, Croatia, Serbia, Bosnia-

---

[7] See Laura Silber and Allan Little, *The Death of Yugoslavia*, London, Penguin Books/BBC Books, 1995, for more information.

Herzegovina, Montenegro, and Macedonia, began on 25 June 1991, when Slovenia and Croatia declared independence, partly due to their fear of being swallowed by the aggressive Serb nationalist movement. This declaration prompted a ten-day war, the first of the four Balkan wars, between the Yugoslav People's Army (JNA) and Slovenia. After their quick defeat, the JNA withdrew.

Slovenia was forfeited for the larger prize of Croatia, where Serbs comprised 12 per cent of the population – and Croatian Serbs were determined to maintain their link to Serbia. Croatia's Serbs were understandably anxious about their future in an independent Croatia, whose nationalist president, Franjo Tudjman, had already adopted measures perceived to be discriminatory by many Serbs. The second and third Balkan wars were in fact fought between Serbia and Croatia: the Serbo-Croatian war, which also began at the same time as that with Slovenia, and the struggle in the Krajina in Croatia, which was populated in the majority by Serbs, to join with Serbia.

Montenegro then federated with Serbia, and the union called itself the Federal Republic of Yugoslavia, while the Bosnia-Herzegovina Parliament waited until 15 October 1991 to declare sovereign status. Bosnia might not have proclaimed independence, but Croatia's and Slovenia's earlier declarations implanted the fear that Serbia would have too much control over the Muslim minority in what then remained of the Yugoslav state. The formal declaration of independence was delayed until a referendum took place on 1 March 1992.

The results of the referendum demonstrated that an overwhelming majority of those who voted supported independence (99 per cent), but the referendum was boycotted by the Bosnian Serbs, who comprised 32 per cent of the population of Bosnia, and who were apprehensive about being out-numbered and out-voted in an independent state (at the time, 44 per cent of the population were Muslims). The Assembly of the Serbian People in Bosnia-Herzegovina, backed by the Bosnian Serb population, had already made an unsuccessful bid two months earlier (9 January) for the independence of the 'Serbian Republic of Bosnia-Herzegovina'. On 3 March 1992 President Alija Izetbegovic proclaimed the independence of the Republic of Bosnia and Herzegovina.

The European Community recognises new states

International recognition of the new states occurred in a piecemeal fashion, with Germany taking the first step when it recognised Croatia and Slovenia on 23 December 1991. Slovenia and Croatia had requested European Community (later European Union) recognition on 19 December, which was granted on 15 January 1992. Bosnia-Herzegovina and Macedonia requested the same on 20 December, but the privilege was not extended to Bosnia-Herzegovina until 7 April 1992, after the Bosnian referendum, while formal recognition of Macedonia was frustrated by Greece until 8 April 1993, due to Greek fears of Macedonian irredentism. The United States recognised Bosnia-Herzegovina, Croatia, and Slovenia on 7 April 1992, and the UN General Assembly accepted the three as full members on 22 May 1992, while the Federal Republic of Yugoslavia (FRY) – is still waiting for recognition from the UN, contingent on fulfilment of certain stipulations.[8]

Germany is often blamed for exacerbating the wars in the former Yugoslavia due to its early recognition of Slovenia and Croatia, but those wars would have persisted even without that recognition. Because Serb nationalism had permeated more than half of the former Yugoslavia by the time recognition took place, and the wars with Slovenia and Croatia had already started, the Greater Serbia campaign would have continued anyway, and consequently, the former republics would have declared self-determination with or without international recognition. Germany made the erroneous assumption that recognition would serve as a preventive measure against further conflict, yet the country also had another excuse for supporting Slovene and Croat claims to self-determination.[9]

Germany today is one of the few European countries without aggressive, separatist movements. This non-belligerent nationalist status can be attributed to the democratic fervour spawned by German reunification, compounded by residual guilt from the Nazi era: the ideals of self-determination were given greater weight in the larger German nation. Thus German endorsement of self-determination in Slovenia and Croatia was consistent with its own recent experience.

Additionally, German sympathy was naturally aligned with fellow

---

[8] Since Dayton, the FRY has established diplomatic relations with most countries, including the UK. In addition, Croatia, Macedonia, and Bosnia have signed mutual recognition treaties with the FRY. Slovenia has not, although the FRY recognises Slovenia. In order to join the UN, and obtain loans from the multilateral lending agencies, the FRY needs to implement Dayton, pay heed to human rights issues, and resolve the problem in Kosovo, which may not occur for some time.

[9] See Ullman, 'The Wars in Yugoslavia', in Ullman, ed., *The World and Yugoslavia's Wars*, pp. 16–18, for a further discussion of German motives.

Catholic Croats, many of whom were immigrants in Germany, and Germany feared more refugees crossing the border. Homogenous Germany also did not have to fear that support given to secessionist movements within another country would encourage similar claims within its own borders. This was in direct contrast to Spain, for example, which was bullied into recognising Slovenia and Croatia, and was initially opposed to it due to fears of similar claims coming from the Basque and Catalan nationalists at home.

The official European Community guidelines on recognition were formulated at a meeting of the Council of Ministers of the European Community held in Brussels on 16 December 1991. Recognition would be extended to those republics that satisfied the stipulations laid out at the meeting ('Guidelines on the Recognition of New States in Eastern Europe and in the Soviet Union'), and subsequently, in the four opinions delivered on 14 January 1992 by the Badinter Arbitration Committee. These required that the republics satisfy certain human rights and minority rights provisions, such as guarantees or some form of autonomy for interested groups.

The European Community stipulations were included in a vain attempt to counter ethnic conflict, particularly in Croatia. As Richard Caplan noted, 'It was out of probable concern that Croatia would not satisfy this requirement that Germany broke ranks and extended unilateral recognition to Croatia and Slovenia . . . on 23 December, before the Badinter Committee had offered its opinions on their applications.'[10] Three weeks later, the Badinter Committee reported that the new Croatian constitution did not include adequate safeguards for minorities and asked that the constitution be revised. President Tudjman consented and eventually adopted the legislation, European Community recognition ensued, but he never implemented the measures due to the war.[11]

Although the Bosnia-Herzegovina government had accepted the European Community provisions, the same committee concluded that a referendum must be held in Bosnia, as had occurred in the other republics, to ascertain majority opinion. As mentioned, the Bosnian Serbs boycotted the referendum and European Community recognition was extended on 7 April. The war in Bosnia began less than one month before recognition.

[10] Richard Caplan, 'The EU's Recognition Policy Towards Republics of Former Yugoslavia', paper presented at the IPPR Seminars on the European Union and Former Yugoslavia, 24–28 November 1995, p. 9.

[11] Tudjman disregarded the stipulations altogether after cleansing most of the Serbs from the Krajina and recapturing the territory just before Dayton.

Conflicting approaches

Many international actors were involved in negotiating an end to the crisis in Bosnia: multilateral organisations, such as the European Community (later Union), the United Nations, and the Conference on Security and Co-operation in Europe (CSCE, later the Organization, or the OSCE); defence alliances such as the Western European Union (WEU) and the North Atlantic Treaty Organization (NATO); and individual states, such as the United States. As James Gow explained, all were attempting to 're-orient . . . and re-establish [their] identity' in the aftermath of the Cold War, and the crisis in the former Yugoslavia hastened this evolution.[12] Such an array of actors, undergoing various transformations, inevitably would contribute to divergent opinions on managing the conflict, which accounted for the inability of the international community to act as a community, and also for the delay in implementing a solution to the crisis.

Since the US government no longer worried about containing communism, it was willing to relegate the crisis in the former Yugoslavia to the Europeans, who the US government believed had more leverage.[13] European member states, especially France and Germany, also encouraged this distancing on the part of the United States as they were eager to test the resolve of the European Community in foreign policy, particularly in a European conflict.[14] Jacques Poos, Luxembourg's Foreign Minister and former head of the EU presidency, remarked in the early days of the war that this was 'the hour of Europe, not America'.[15]

The United States was also preoccupied with Iraq's invasion of Kuwait, and subsequently, with Somalia's humanitarian crisis; the latter ironically seemed more manageable than the ethnic cauldron that was boiling in the former Yugoslavia. Moreover, the US government was in no mood to commit ground troops to a UN operation until a peace agreement was reached, if then. Troops were already in too many places, as far as the Americans were concerned. As the conflict

---

[12] James Gow, *Triumph of the Lack of Will: International Diplomacy and the Yugoslav War*, London, Hurst and Company, 1997, p. 3.

[13] David C. Gompert, 'The United States and Yugoslavia's Wars', in Ullman, ed., *The World and Yugoslavia's Wars*, p. 127.

[14] Spyros Economides and Paul Taylor, 'Former Yugoslavia', in James Mayall, ed., *The New Interventionism, 1991–1994: United Nations Experience in Cambodia, Former Yugoslovia and Somalia*, Cambridge, Cambridge University Press, 1996, p. 65.

[15] As cited in *The Economist*, 22 March 1997, p. 50.

progressed, this opinion was reinforced due to the perception that the US government and military had played a big enough part in the Gulf War, and it was now the turn of other major powers.

Despite overwhelming agreement that the Europeans should take control of the conflict, they were unable to display coherent leadership during the crisis, although they made many attempts. As the crisis unfolded, and reports of genocide and ethnic cleansing grew, the Americans increasingly became more involved and eventually advocated the use of force, but the Europeans, who had troops on the ground and therefore feared for their safety if a bombing campaign were underway, prevented this from taking place until early 1994. The future of the NATO alliance was therefore threatened by the inability of the Europeans and the Americans to agree on a firm policy towards the former Yugoslavia. The eventual bombing campaign, led by the United States, was partly initiated because America had to demonstrate that it could still lead NATO, and significantly, that NATO was still a credible and necessary alliance now that its counterpart, the Warsaw Pact, no longer existed.

Within the UN, there was also a preference that the European Community should take the lead, much as the United States had in Kuwait and Somalia, and would again in Haiti. This option was backed by members of the Security Council and by the Secretary-General. Yet the UN was also gradually forced into playing a more direct role from November 1991, when the European Community was still making vain attempts to broker a cease-fire.[16] From November 1991, Cyrus Vance intervened on behalf of the Secretary-General and mediated the end of the Serbo-Croatian war, which the European Community could not do as the organisation was viewed as being too anti-Serb, and had neither the experience nor the manpower to implement a cease-fire.

By mid-July 1992, Lord Carrington (the European Community representative) and others had persuaded the UN to become more involved in the conflict, while the Secretary-General accepted this in his report of 6 June 1992. When David Owen replaced Carrington in August 1992 in London, he officially merged the efforts of the UN and the European Community, creating the Vance–Owen partnership. This marriage was also not efficacious, however, and the UN would soon demonstrate, yet again, its inability to cope with and understand the complexities of state collapse.

---

[16] The EC's mediating role had been delegated by the CSCE.

Sanctions

As in the other interventions discussed in this book, sanctions were one of the first diplomatic tools wielded in the Yugoslav crisis. Unlike the earlier interventions, however, in which they only exacerbated the crises, sanctions against Serbia ultimately succeeded in forcing Milosevic's hand at Dayton. In the short term, however, they contributed to a more robust Serb nationalism in Serbia and Montenegro, Bosnia and Croatia, led to the introduction of UN troops, and eventually, along with other factors, to the use of overwhelming force. In their application, the European Community was the first out of the paddock.

In July 1991 the European Community imposed an arms embargo and freeze on aid in what was then still called Yugoslavia. These moves were soon backed up by UN sanctions: Security Council Resolution 713 in September 1991, acting under Chapter VII of the UN Charter, established a complete arms embargo in co-operation with European Community member states. Specific sanctions against the FRY were imposed in May 1992 by Security Council Resolution 757.[17] Further sanctions were imposed after the Vance–Owen peace plan was rejected.

As is typical in most sanction situations, a black market quickly appeared, and supplied the black-listed community with essential needs. Additionally, certain states, such as Greece and Russia, were accused of interfering with attempts at strengthening sanctions, and even of non-compliance, out of sympathy for fellow Orthodox Slavs (Serbs). Overall, sanctions hurt the Serbian economy, and it may take many years to return to the pre-war level (without considering the ill-effects that war had on physical infrastructure, lives lost, etc.).

Just eight months after the first sanctions were imposed, the UN Security Council established the peacekeeping mission UNPROFOR on 21 February 1992, through Security Council Resolution 743, with the intention of 'creat[ing] the conditions of peace and security required for the negotiation of an overall settlement of the Yugoslav crisis'.[18] The

---

[17] Security Council (SC) Resolution 757 (30 May 1992) included an almost complete trade embargo (except for foodstuffs and humanitarian supplies), the prohibition on transfer of funds to Serbia and Montenegro for trade purposes, on aircraft travel to and from the said territory, a ban on participation in sporting events, scientific and technical cooperation, and cultural exchanges. SC Resolution 787 (November 1992) prohibited transhipment of certain strategic goods through the FRY, while SC Resolution 820 (April 1993) banned the transhipment of all goods through the FRY.

[18] SC Resolution 743, para. 5, 21 February 1992.

deployment of troops for UNPROFOR was approved in Security Council Resolution 749 on 7 April 1992, with troops initially sent to Croatia, but later UNPROFOR was extended to Bosnia. The initial force deployed 6,500 peacekeepers, which expanded to 38,000 by the end of 1994, and included troops from Britain, France, and seven other western countries.

Difficulties at the UN

As in Somalia, UNPROFOR was intended to be a traditional peace-keeping operation and therefore impartial, yet its aforementioned task precluded any hoped-for impartiality – especially in the face of mounting genocide and ethnic cleansing. Despite the references to Chapter VII in many of the resolutions that applied to UNPROFOR, it remained a peacekeeping operation, and used its enforcement powers only to protect international personnel, until August 1995 when it was mandated with greater enforcement powers. This unhealthy *de facto* mix of Chapter VI and VII was also a problem in Somalia, though not in Haiti. The UN Secretary-General later remarked that the UN 'has come to realize that a mix of peacekeeping and enforcement is not the answer to a lack of consent and co-operation by the parties to the conflict'.[19]

Predictably, the task of UNPROFOR soon expanded to secure strategic centres, delivery of humanitarian aid and foreign personnel (e.g., Security Council Resolutions 757, 761, 770, 771 and 776). Yet as in Somalia, those executing these tasks on the ground were not supplied with the adequate resources to accomplish their duties. As UN commander in Bosnia-Herzegovina, Lieutenant-General Francis Briquemont, remarked, 'There is a fantastic gap between the resolutions of the Security Council, the will to execute those resolutions, and the means available to commanders in the field.'[20]

Indeed, between September 1991 and November 1995, when the cease-fire that preceded Dayton came into effect, a total of eighty-three resolutions on the former Yugoslavia emanated from the Security Council (an average of twenty per year). Interestingly, the number of Security Council resolutions on peacekeeping around the world has also increased significantly since the end of the Cold War. In the forty-one years between 1947 and 1988 there were a total of 348 resolutions on

---

[19] Boutros Boutros-Ghali, *Report of the Secretary-General on the Work of the Organization*, August 1995, document A/50/1, para. 600.

[20] As cited in Weiss, 'Collective Spinelessness', in Ullman, ed., *The World and Yugoslavia's Wars*, p. 64.

peacekeeping – an average of 8.5 per year – while in the short six-year time span covering 1989 to 1994, there were 296 resolutions – or 49 per year. Security Council resolutions on the former Yugoslavia therefore comprised a healthy percentage of the annual peacekeeping resolutions at 41 per cent.[21]

Funding and manpower provided for the operation thus could not keep pace with the number of resolutions, nor fulfil their demands. Although UNPROFOR and humanitarian aid cost the EU $2.4 billion between 1991 and 1994, while the estimate for the international community up until the first half of 1995 was approximately $9 billion, the money normally arrived too late and most of the promised troops never arrived at all.[22] The barrage of resolutions only served to separate the operation at UN Headquarters, where the Security Council was calling for a direct response to any misdeed, from the operation on the ground, which was overwhelmed by these demands because of its small size, unclear rules of engagement, and lack of resources. Troops were sporadically and thinly dispersed, were lightly armed, had an unclear and evolving mandate, lacked unity of command, often arrived months after ordered by the Security Council, and were unwilling to become partial in the face of massive infringements of human rights. UNPROFOR personnel were therefore prone to being taken hostage, which further limited their ability to react due to fears for their own safety.

In addition, UNPROFOR was blamed for sustaining ethnically cleansed areas. For example, the presence of UN troops in the Krajina and other Serb-controlled parts of Croatia served only to consolidate gains. At the end of 1992, President Tudjman of Croatia, upset at UNPROFOR because of this *de facto* acceptance of Serb territorial gains, threatened not to renew its mandate.

In early February 1993, Tudjman finally agreed to a one-year renewal, but only after it was renamed the UN Confidence Restoration Operation (UNCRO), the mandate formally redefined and troop numbers reduced from 14,000 to 8,750, who were to police the border between Serbia and Croatia (and not just the cease-fire in the Krajina).[23] As Thomas Weiss noted, 'The objective was to show that the Serb-occupied Krajina was still part of Croatia; to impede arms shipments from Serbia to Serb rebels; and to permit the UN soldiers to continue

---

[21] Author calculations.

[22] These costs did not include those borne by NATO. Vesna Bojicic, Mary Kaldor, and Ivan Vejvoda, 'Post-War Reconstruction in the Balkans', Sussex European Institute Working Paper No 14, November 1995, p. 18.

[23] UNCRO was established by UN Security Council Resolution 981 (31 March 1995).

holding the lid on the Bosnian cauldron.'[24] The UN was also blamed for facilitating ethnic cleansing because UN troops transported minority groups out of besieged areas, such as the Muslims from Bijelina in January 1994 and Srebrenica in April 1993, in an effort to save lives.

Finally, the UN and other international actors were even faulted for negotiating cease-fires, over thirty of which had reportedly come and gone by the end of UNPROFOR[25], such as the first UN negotiated cease-fire implemented on 23 November 1991. The cease-fires only gave the aggressors the breathing space necessary to rearm and ready themselves for the next attack. The UN Secretary-General summarised these limitations, with the difficulties ascribed to 'UNPROFOR's nature as a highly dispersed and lightly armed peace-keeping force that was not mandated, equipped, trained or deployed to be a combatant'.[26] It was not until August 1995 that troops were 'regrouped and consolidated' in central Bosnia, in order to reduce this insecurity.[27]

The media and refugees

As in the other interventions discussed in this book, sanctions and a muddled peacekeeping operation only served to ensnare the international community, and increased the likelihood that force would eventually be used. Two additional factors contributed as well to this outcome: the media and refugees. The media relayed the mounting atrocities, genocide, and ethnic cleansing in horrible detail, which, together with the aforementioned factors, induced the 'Do Something' response also evident in Haiti and Somalia, and to a lesser extent in Panama. For example, the murder and abuse of Bosnian Muslims in the concentration camps run by Serbs, first published in August 1992 in New York's *Newsday* and aired on Britain's television news channel, ITN, caused a predictable outcry. The ensuing publicity forced the US administration to demand international access to the camps, while the Security Council passed Resolution 770, concurring with this demand.

[24] Weiss, 'Collective Spinelessness', in Ullman, ed., *The World and Yugoslavia's Wars*, pp. 67–8.
[25] Weiss, 'Collective Spinelessness', in Ullman, ed., *The World and Yugoslavia's Wars*, p. 67.
[26] 'UNITED NATIONS PROTECTION FORCE', Prepared by the Department of Public Information, United Nations – as of September 1996, from the UN Web site.
[27] Weiss, 'Collective Spinelessness', in Ullman, ed., *The World and Yugoslavia's Wars*, p. 72.

The 5 February 1994 mortar attack on a Sarajevo marketplace, in which 69 civilians were killed and 200 wounded, led NATO to issue an ultimatum to the Serbs to remove their heavy weapons from around Sarajevo (which was accomplished after Russian mediation).[28] Coverage of the 28 August 1995 shell that landed in the same market, killing 36 and wounding dozens more, which a UN investigation attributed to Bosnian Serbs, resulted in NATO air strikes against Bosnian Serb targets. Finally, the continued attacks on all the UN-declared 'safe areas'[29] also pushed the international community into using force, especially after Srebrenica in July 1995, when Bosnian Serbs over-ran seventy Dutch UN peacekeepers and killed up to 20 per cent of the population.

Forty-two thousand Bosnian Muslims lived in Srebrenica at the time, and the majority were internally displaced people.[30] This was the worst massacre of civilians in Europe since World War II, and caused the International War Crimes Tribunal in The Hague to announce indictments against Radovan Karadzic, the political leader of the Bosnian Serbs, and General Ratko Mladic, the commanding officer of the Bosnian Serb army, for genocide and the deaths of up to 8,000 people. In fact, it was the earlier press and UN reports of brutality inflicted on civilians that originally contributed to the establishment of the War Crimes Tribunal.[31]

The increased refugee flows into neighbouring European states, especially Germany, was another important factor, as in Haiti and in Albania. And action was only taken after refugees started leaving their homes in large numbers: one of the motives behind establishing UNPROFOR was to provide protection in order to stop flows of refugees and IDPs travelling to neighbouring countries in search of

---

[28] There was an additional reason behind the Russian mediation, besides their affinity to the Serbs, which was that NATO itself threatened Russia's position and influence since it was not a member.

[29] Security Council Resolution 824 (6 May 1993) declared Bihac, Goradzde, Sarajevo, Srebrenica, Tuzla, and Zepa to be 'safe areas'.

[30] Reports differ on numbers killed and range from 2,700 to 8,000. See, for example, Anthony Borden and Richard Caplan, 'The Former Yugoslavia: the War and the Peace Process', *SIPRI Yearbook 1996*, Stockholm, Stockholm International Peace Research Institute, pp. 217–18; or the *Washington Post*, 18 February 1997, p. A01.

[31] Warren P. Strobel, 'The Media and US Policies Toward Intervention: A Closer Look at the "CNN Effect"', in Chester Crocker and Fen Osler Hampson with Pamela Aall, eds., *Managing Global Chaos: Sources of and Responses to International Conflict*, Washington, DC, US Institute of Peace, 1996, p. 367.

safety.[32] The war in Bosnia would eventually be responsible for over 1 million IDPs, 1.1 million refugees who left Bosnia but moved to other parts of the former Yugoslavia, and 700,000 who left the region entirely.[33] It is unclear how many will return, although Germany, host to the largest number of Yugoslav refugees, started to repatriate them in March 1997.[34] International recognition of new states, sanctions, the peacekeeping operation, the media, large flows of refugees and continued defiance by Serb rulers all contributed to the use of force by the international community. There was an escalation of commitment despite initial failures at goal attainment, thereby ensuring entrapment. What was transpiring simultaneously at the negotiating tables?

The plethora of peace plans

To carve up Bosnia

Peace agreements occurred with regularity after the conflict began, yet until external efforts paired force with diplomacy, nothing compelled the parties to implement the agreements. To reiterate Clinton's remarks about Haiti, the final agreement worked because of 'the successful combination of the credible threat of force with diplomacy'. What were the major differences between the peace plans, and how did force finally coincide with diplomacy?

Europe's hour began in August 1991, just one month after imposing sanctions, when the European Community foreign ministers met in The Hague, and agreed to release loans to former Yugoslav republics that accepted mediation. At the second meeting in September of *The Hague Peace Conference*, chaired by Lord Carrington, a statement was issued declaring that internal borders could not be altered through the use of force[35], that rights of minorities must be guaranteed, and that intractable differences would be resolved through an arbitration commission.

[32] James Gow, 'Bosnia – A Safe Area: In the Twilight Zone of Policy', paper presented at the IPPR Seminars on the European Union and Former Yugoslavia, 24–28 November 1995.

[33] Thomas G. Weiss and Amir Pasic, 'Reinventing UNHCR: Enterprising Humanitarians in the Former Yugoslavia, 1991–1995', *Global Governance 3*, no. 1, January–April 1997, p. 44.

[34] The first 40 of 320,000 refugees were sent back in March, while the government planned to send a total of 80,000 back in 1997. Switzerland initiated a repatriation plan in early June 1997 for the 18,000 Bosnian refugees who have been living there.

[35] This meant that only the six former Yugoslav republics could receive independence, not areas within those republics, such as Kosovo in Serbia.

During these negotiations, an offer was made for special autonomous status within the larger state for the self-declared Serb region of Krajina (Croatia) and the Albanians living in Kosovo (Serbia). But, as Susan Woodward explained, 'the conference had no bargaining leverage with which to persuade the governments of Croatia or Serbia to accept this proposal', nor with the different ethnic communities that their rights would be protected.[36] Consequently, none of these conditions was observed, which was also understandable since the cease-fire that brought the parties to the negotiating table had broken down before the talks ended.

Carrington was desperate to stop the fighting between Serbia and Croatia from spreading into Bosnia, and although Cyrus Vance succeeded in stopping the Serbo-Croatian war, the latter task at that stage was beyond the capacity of the international community. In February 1992, just two months before Bosnian independence and one month before the war, Lord Carrington and the Portuguese diplomat, José Cutileiro (the Portuguese held the European presidency at the time), drew up the first international blueprint map for a new Bosnian state, the *Carrington–Cutileiro Plan*. This 'Statement of Principles', concluded on 18 March, intended to form the basis for further discussions in another attempt to thwart war in Bosnia. The plan transformed Bosnia into a confederation of three units, each with the right to self-determination, each divided into ethnically based cantons. One week later, President Izetbegovic, back in Sarajevo, reversed his position, as did the Bosnian Croat representative, Mate Boban. The Croats rejected it because they were not ceded enough territory, while Izetbegovic did not divulge his reasons for reneging.[37]

Carrington made his last attempt on 26–7 August 1992, before passing the baton of European Special Envoy to Lord David Owen at the *London Conference*, which was chaired by John Major (Britain now had the European presidency), but also sponsored by the United States and the UN. International representatives from twenty countries, including the P5 (permanent members of the Security Council), and the six republics of the former Yugoslavia, participated. The parties agreed that borders could not be changed through force, and that ethnic cleansing would stop. The international actors also specified the use of sanctions to isolate Serbia-Montenegro.

In addition, participants agreed to place heavy weapons under UN

---

[36] Susan Woodward, *Balkan Tragedy: Chaos and Dissolution after the Cold War*, Washington, DC, The Brookings Institution, 1995, p. 210.
[37] See Woodward, *Balkan Tragedy*, p. 281.

supervision at eleven sites. Typically, however, the international community did not provide the backing to implement this stipulation, which contributed to further agitation between Europe and the UN. The former had made an agreement on behalf of the UN, without involving the UN in the decision. Also established in London was the *International Conference on the Former Yugoslavia (ICFY)*, to be held in permanent session from September in Geneva, and run jointly by the European Community and the UN, the former in charge of mediation and the latter of operations on the ground.

In London, the US representative recommended the use of force, but this option was shelved due to Milan Panic, the Prime Minister of the FRY, who fully accepted the above-mentioned principles. Panic was soon to be replaced at the end of 1992 by the uncompromising Milosevic, after losing the Serbian presidential elections. The London Conference was not implemented, despite agreement by all parties, because, as Gow explained, 'the international community invested its hopes in what turned out to be the twin chimeras of the London Conference: that the presence of Panic made a difference and that strong words, urgent diplomacy and concerted international pressure, without a will to enforce compliance, might just be enough.'[38]

Next came the *Geneva Conference*, chaired by Cyrus Vance and David Owen, which embraced a comprehensive settlement, as in The Hague, and set up six working groups, one of which would soon produce the *Vance–Owen Peace Plan*, the first plan that had a real chance of succeeding. Vance–Owen resulted from tireless diplomatic shuffling by the titular representatives. The timing of the peace plan purposely coincided with the first release of images from the concentration camps, when the pressure to 'Do Something' was intense.

Vance–Owen attempted to shift away from the ethnic partitions envisaged in other plans and return to the idea of a multi-ethnic sovereign state, although the maps tended to resemble those drawn up in The Hague and in London. The constitutional arrangements envisaged in the plan were actually prepared by Finnish diplomat Martti Ahtisaari and his team, but it was called the Vance–Owen plan due to the two official negotiators directing the process.[39] At this time, Serbs controlled 70 per cent of Bosnia, up from a pre-war percentage of 32 per cent.

---

[38] Gow, *Triumph of the Lack of Will*, p. 231 (see pp. 228–32 for more information).

[39] Tihomir Loza, 'EU Contribution to the International Conference on Former Yugoslavia, 1992–1994: The Vance–Owen Plan', paper presented at the

The eventual agreement, concluded in January 1993, delineated a decentralised Bosnian state by proposing to maintain existing external borders and a central government with slight powers (essentially foreign policy), while it divided the territory into ten autonomous cantons. Three of these would be controlled predominantly by Muslims, three by Croats, three by Serbs, and one around Sarajevo would be mixed. The cantons would retain most of the power, and were designated Serb, Croat, or Muslim-majority, which effectively abandoned the principle of multi-ethnicity, with the Serbs to lose some, but not ail, of the territory gained during the war.

Vance–Owen placed Sarajevo under tripartite rule, to be governed on a consensual basis in the long term. In the short term, however, it would be administered by the UN. The consensual decision-making process ensured that each group had a veto, which appeased the Serbs. The three parties also agreed to a cease-fire on 27 March 1993, to come into effect the following day.

What went wrong with Vance–Owen?[40] The agreement did not specifically concoct ethnically pure regions, and so maintained the illusion of multi-ethnicity that had been advocated by the international community since the war began. Behind the façade, however, the agreement would have facilitated the establishment of homogenous cantons because they had ethnic tags on them. Further, Vance–Owen allowed the Bosnian Serbs and the Bosnian Croats to keep some of the land they had obtained through ethnic cleansing, which was opposed by the Bosnian Muslims. The plan also allowed power to remain in the hands of those who were not representative of the local populations, due to recent territorial conquest. Moreover, no one believed that the Bosnian Serbs would voluntarily abandon certain designated areas and allow displaced persons to return home.

The Bosnian Serbs did not favour Vance–Owen because it stipulated that they return some conquered land, leaving them with only 43 per cent of the territory, territory that was also not contiguous and therefore interfered with the idea of the creation of a mini-Serb statelet in the somewhat larger Bosnian entity. Early in May, Milosevic was pressured by Greek Prime Minister Constantine Mitsotakis in an emergency conference to approve Vance–Owen, which in turn meant he would apply

IPPR Seminars on the European Union and Former Yugoslavia, 24–28 November 1995.
[40] For a full discussion of Vance–Owen, see David Owen, *Balkan Odyssey*, London, Indigo, 1996; see also Gow, *Triumph of the Lack of Will*.

pressure on Karadzic to sign. The Bosnian Serb Assembly had already voted to reject the map on 2 April, and the Bosnian Serbs backed this decision in a referendum held in mid-May, thus overturning the ratification by Milosevic and Karadzic.

The plan was also destroyed by the US administration, which did not give it initial endorsement because US officials believed that Vance–Owen rewarded ethnic cleansing, and because they did not see how it would be enforced or implemented. The US government knew that the plan would be dead anyway without the concurrent deployment of foreign troops – 50,000 of them by US estimates – troops that the US government at the time was not willing to commit.

Vance–Owen attempted to maintain a multi-ethnic Bosnian state by carving Bosnia into ethnic statelets. Yet without sufficient inducements for the victors to relinquish conquered territory, or the threat of force if they did not, it was not a realistic possibility. As Owen remarked, 'Name me a time in history where anyone has been able to roll back a victorious army as much as we were advocating it.'[41]

The *Joint Action Programme* (JAP) on Bosnia, announced in Washington, DC in May 1993 by foreign ministers of Britain, France, Russia, Spain, and the United States, was a last-ditch attempt to cover the rifts that had developed among the international community over Bosnia – except of course it completely undermined the Vance–Owen Peace Plan. As Owen observed, 'It is ironic that the new US administration . . . [which] had been castigating the Vance–Owen plan for favouring the Serbs, for rewarding aggression and for accepting ethnic cleansing, had now gone through a 180-degree turn and was telling Dr Karadzic loud and clear that the pressure from every other country in the world, including the FRY, to withdraw was being relaxed.'[42] The JAP committed to protect militarily the 'safe areas' that had been established by the Security Council in April and May, and endorsed the War Crimes Tribunal. The plan on offer was also botched after a press report alleged that it endorsed Serb territorial gains in Bosnia. Izetbegovic rejected it on 23 May, claiming that the JAP 'would allow the Serbs to retain territory taken by force, prevent displaced populations from returning to their homes, and turn safe areas into reservations'.[43]

Meanwhile, the US government was trying to get the arms embargo lifted to assist the Bosnian Muslims, and also to conduct air strikes

---

[41] As cited in Loza, 'EU Contribution to the International Conference on Former Yugoslavia'.

[42] Owen, *Balkan Odyssey*, pp. 191–2.

[43] As cited in Owen, *Balkan Odyssey*, p. 184.

against the Bosnian Serbs, arguing that Security Council Resolution 770 sanctioned the use of force. From early 1993, this option was promoted as *Lift and Strike*. Secretary of State Warren Christopher tried to sell it to the Russians and Europeans, but both rejected it, the former possibly out of sympathy for the Serbs, and the latter, especially the British and the French, because they feared air attacks would provoke counter-attacks on their ground troops (no US troops participated in UNPROFOR).

In fact, it was only from the end of 1992, during the US presidential campaign, that Bush changed tack and offered to use air power if the Serbs harmed UN personnel, more to let the Serbs know that the UN would not be hostage to their threats than to intervene in the conflict, which up to then, he had judiciously avoided. This option was vetoed by the Europeans, as was the Lift and Strike option later, because of similar fears for their men on the ground. The US government then abandoned this option, refusing to act on its own.

Despite the demise of Vance–Owen, David Owen was not ready to concede defeat. Owen and the Norwegian Foreign Minister, Thorvald Stoltenberg, the new UN Special Envoy, convened another meeting in Geneva in June 1993. The agreement reached, dubbed the *Owen–Stoltenberg Plan* or the *HMS Invincible* package (the revised version was completed on the British naval vessel on 20 September), was also a retreat from earlier principles. It was based on a draft prepared by Croatian President Tudjman and approved by Serbia's Milosevic, demonstrating the international community's desperation to end the war.

The two negotiators of the plan, however, did claim that it maintained the two fundamental principles: Bosnia would remain a unitary state, and borders could not be changed by force. Again, self-controlling cantons that resembled a complex jigsaw puzzle were on the table, with a weak central government. Despite the desire of the negotiators to reinforce the message that forced territorial changes and ethnic cleansing were unacceptable, the new plan in reality abandoned both of these principles.

The map prepared by Owen and Stoltenberg divided Bosnia into three ethnic units that would belong to a confederal government based in Sarajevo. After two years, the constituent units could secede with the consent of the others, which implied that the Serbian and Croatian units could join their parent states if they so wished. This outcome was exactly what the international community had been endeavouring to avoid.[44] As in Lisbon, the plan was approved by the

---

[44] Economides and Taylor, 'Former Yugoslavia', in Mayall, ed., *The New Interventionism*, p. 84.

Bosnian Serbs and Croats, but not the Muslims. Izetbegovic rejected it because he believed the Serbs were not conceding enough territory (it left the Muslims with only 30 per cent of the country). He announced that the Bosnians would thereafter have to resort to arms in order to regain any territory. His parliament concurred, as did the Bosnian government on 30 August.

By the end of December 1993, members of the ICFY had relaxed the condition on sacrosanct borders, and began negotiating with the leaders of the republics over certain 'intractable issues', which resulted in a cease-fire that lasted until mid-January 1994 and a new agreement. At this time it appeared that territorial disagreements were going to be settled as the presidents of Serbia and Croatia issued a joint declaration to 'normalise relations' (meaning resolve the dispute in Krajina).[45] Izetbegovic vetoed this latest *EU Action Plan* as it left the Bosnian Muslims with only 33.5 per cent of the territory, and in this he was encouraged by the US government, who also wanted more territory for the Bosnian Muslims.

Four days after the 5 February 1994 mortar attack on a central market in Sarajevo, NATO issued an ultimatum to the Bosnian Serbs to end the siege of Sarajevo by withdrawing all heavy weapons from the exclusion zone.[46] In support of this move, Clinton cited four 'distinct interests: avoiding a broader European war, preserving NATO's credibility, stemming refugee flows, and a humanitarian stake in stopping the strangulation of Sarajevo and the slaughter of innocents in Bosnia'.[47] Towards the end of February, NATO aircraft destroyed four Bosnian Serb warplanes in the no-fly zone, which again challenged the assumption of impartiality.

Europe's hour had indeed come, and gone. The United States then brokered the Bosnian Muslim federation with the Bosnian Croats, called the *Washington Framework Agreement*, announced on 1 March – an alliance that could physically counter the Serbs, and thereby, hopefully, end the war in Bosnia. In March 1994 President Clinton hosted

---

[45] Woodward, *Balkan Tragedy*, p. 313.

[46] The zone created stipulated that no heavy artillery or mortars would be permitted within a 20 kilometre radius from the centre of Sarajevo. NATO was mandated by Security Council resolutions, acting under Chapter VII, to enforce the air exclusion zones and to attack weapons used against UN safe areas, and was the obvious choice to carry out such a task, although this was the first time NATO was contracted out in such a manner.

[47] As noted in Richard N. Haass, *Intervention: the Use of American Military force in the Post-Cold War World*, Washington, DC, Carnegie Endowment for International Peace, 1994, p. 41.

Izetbegovic and Tudjman, who signed the accord that created the Federation. This agreement put a stop to the hostilities that began in 1993 between Bosnian Muslims and Croats – some had even attributed the failure of the Vance–Owen plan to this war.

After two NATO air strikes in April to defend Gorazde (a 'safe area'), and another cease-fire, the *Contact Group*, set up by Owen and Stoltenberg to include Britain, France, Germany, Russia, and the United States, fashioned another peace plan in July 1994. In this, Bosnia was divided into two ethnic mini-states within a unitary state: the Croat-Bosniac Federation[48] would have 51 per cent of the territory and the Bosnian Serbs the remaining 49 per cent (the Bosnian Serbs controlled 70 per cent of Bosnia at this stage and therefore were being asked to relinquish 20 per cent of conquered territory). The decentralised theme remained – each unit would be relatively free to conduct its own affairs, with the option of eventual secession accepted.

The Contact Group warned the Bosnian Serbs that if they did not accept the plan, the arms embargo against the Bosnian Muslims would be lifted and more sanctions would be placed on Serbia. Milosevic also applied pressure – he was now willing to sacrifice the Bosnian Serbs in exchange for the removal of sanctions. Additionally, there was a credible threat of force from both NATO and the Federation. Karadzic nonetheless rejected the Contact Group plan, demanding other changes on 19 July, which resulted in the FRY announcing two weeks later the closure of its border with Bosnia to isolate further the Bosnian Serbs. This pressure, however, did not achieve the desired result. The Bosnian Serbs rejected the Contact Group plan on 28 August after another referendum.

Next into the fray was former President Jimmy Carter, flush from his successful last-minute negotiations in Haiti. Carter met the leaders of the warring parties in mid-December 1994, and they agreed, once again, on a 'total cessation of hostilities'.[49] The Bosnian Serbs settled on a four-month moratorium, which was finalised on 31 December and due to begin on 1 January 1995, called the *Cessation of Hostilities Agreement*. Signed by all parties to the conflict, the document stipulated that they would resume negotiations under the auspices of the Contact Group, control their weapons, allow for the free movement of human rights monitors, exchange prisoners and not obstruct relief convoys. The

---

[48] Bosniac is the term used to describe the Bosnian Muslims.
[49] Information provided here mostly from The Carter Center News, 'President Carter Helps Restart Peace Efforts in Bosnia-Herzegovina', Fall 1994, on the World Wide Web.

hostilities did not cease, especially in the Bihac area, and the parties to the agreement did not co-operate in implementing the other conditions.

All the above-mentioned peace plans foundered for one reason: there was never a proper enforcement method to ensure implementation. The parties had major differences over the various maps, but ironically, what would eventually be accepted at Dayton resembled the earlier agreements in many respects. Instead, compliance would be gained through rapid territorial gains by the Croats and the Bosnian Muslims, pressure from Milosevic, headstrong diplomacy, and extensive use of force by NATO.

NATO attacks

Another attack on a Sarajevo market led Lieutenant-General Rupert Smith, the NATO military commander, to request air strikes against Bosnian Serb positions on 8 May 1995. The Special Representative of the Secretary-General (SRSG) and head of UNPROFOR, Yasushi Akashi, turned down his request, even though Sarajevo was one of six 'safe areas' declared in Security Council Resolution 824 (May 1993). Akashi's decision was backed by the Secretary-General, who was also hesitant to use force. After this incident, UNPROFOR was reviewed by the UN, the Europeans, and the United States. The UN preferred scaling it down, the Europeans argued for a holding pattern, while the United States wanted to utilise more force. Even though no consensus was reached between the three, Lt.-Gen. Smith issued an ultimatum on 24 May to the Serbs to stop using their heavy weapons.

This warning was ignored. Over the next two days, the Bosnian Serbs again attacked Sarajevo. In response, six NATO jets duly bombed a Bosnian Serb Army ammunitions dump near Pale. The Bosnian Serbs counter-responded by more attacks on Sarajevo, Srebrenica, Tuzla, Gorazde, and Bihac (all 'safe areas'), and took several hundred peacekeepers hostage.[50] Milosevic soon intervened, and the hostages were released at the end of June. The British, French, and Dutch had meanwhile established a Rapid Reaction Force for Bosnia-Herzegovina with 14,000 troops on 3 June. These troops would operate under the auspices of the UN, but they could retaliate if UN forces were attacked. They were to support the enclaves in eastern

---

[50] See Borden and Caplan, 'The Former Yugoslavia', pp. 214–5, for more information.

Bosnia, resupply peacekeepers, and police the UN-declared weapons-free zones.[51]

After the massive slaughter in Srebrenica (July 1995), President Jacques Chirac declared that the French were willing to retake the enclave by force.[52] Then Zepa fell at the end of July, and 15,000 civilians were forced to leave, though this time they were not killed. The Bosnian Serbs next went for Bihac. Meanwhile, the international community had decided to revise its 'dual-key' policy of requiring NATO and the UN to approve air strikes, with the latter acquiescing to the authority of the former. NATO then threatened air strikes if the three remaining safe areas were attacked (Sarajevo, Tuzla, and Bihac).

On 26 July, the US Senate approved lifting the arms embargo on Bosnia-Herzegovina, to come into effect on 15 November. Clinton did not veto the legislation, which was in fact opposed by Izetbegovic, because there was enough support in Congress to over-ride any veto. The international community, and especially President Clinton, were suddenly faced with a self-imposed ultimatum, which if not met, could jeopardise the entire mission and further exacerbate the war.[53]

By early August, the direction of the war began to go against the Serbs: in Croatia, the Croatian Army beat the Serbs and recaptured the Krajina region, which had been lost at the beginning of the war – at the expense of 125,000–150,000 refugees and 50,000 soldiers who fled into neighbouring Serbia or Serbian-controlled Bosnia.[54] In Bosnia, a joint Muslim–Croat offensive, with support from the Croatian government, stopped the Serb attack on Bihac. These reversals altered the map to resemble the 51:49 territorial divisions proposed in the earlier Contact Group map, with more ethnically pure regions than before – changes that would facilitate US Special Envoy Richard Holbrooke's task.

The Bosnian Serbs persisted, despite these setbacks. On 28 August they shelled Sarajevo, killing thirty-six and wounding many more. Two days later, NATO launched *Operation Deliberate Force*, the largest military operation in NATO's history: by December 1995, approximately 100,000 bombing sorties had been flown by fighters and supporting

---

[51] Borden and Caplan, 'The Former Yugoslavia', p. 216.
[52] As cited in Borden and Caplan, 'The Former Yugoslavia', p. 218.
[53] The legislation was no longer relevant by the deadline due to the subsequent NATO bombing campaign.
[54] Figures obtained from Weiss, 'Collective Spinelessness', in Ullman, ed., *The World and Yugoslavia's Wars*, p. 70.

aircraft.[55] Throughout this bombing campaign, Holbrooke and his team were simultaneously working to persuade the Bosnian Serbs to sign the document lifting the Serbian siege on Sarajevo in exchange for a cessation of NATO bombing.

Holbrooke admitted intimidating Mladic and Karadzic into signing: 'they were headstrong, given to grandiose statements and theatre, but they were essentially bullies. Only force, or its credible threat, worked with them.'[56] This, along with another intervention by Milosevic, finally compelled the Bosnian Serbs to cease hostilities and withdraw weapons from Sarajevo. Additionally, Milosevic secured permission from the Bosnian Serbs to be Speaker for All Serbs in further negotiations. On 15 September humanitarian aid resumed.

What led the Serbs to continue their massacres in the 'safe areas' after a credible threat of force and UN troops on the ground? Serb defiance was most likely grounded in earlier empty warnings as well as conflicting messages from the international community, due to the squabbling between the United States and the European Union, the United States and the UN, the European Union and the UN, as well as between NATO and the UN. The Serbs had also learned from experience in Somalia and Haiti, especially after the US Army Rangers were killed in Somalia in October 1993. Again, there was a conspicuous retreat on the part of the Americans because of the Body Bag Syndrome, even though they were supposed to provide the leadership that the EU had been unable to. Karadzic and Mladic must have also assumed they could and should take as much territory as possible to enhance their position at the negotiating table.

Down to Dayton

On 5 October, Clinton declared a sixty-day cease-fire, which officially began on 12 October 1995. Meanwhile, talks moved from Geneva to Wright-Patterson Air Base in Dayton, Ohio on 1 November. After three weeks of quarantined negotiations, Clinton announced the *Dayton Peace Agreement* on Bosnia-Herzegovina on 21 November.

Dayton differed from earlier peace talks because the Bosnian Serb leadership (Karadzic and Mladic) was entirely excluded, while Bosnian Serb representatives only participated in the background. This removed

[55] Information provided by the NATO gopher site on the Web (www.nato.int), entitled 'NATO Basic Fact Sheet' No. 4, March 1997.
[56] Richard Holbrooke, 'The Road to Sarajevo', *The New Yorker*, 21 and 28 October 1996, p. 104.

some of Karadzic's and Mladic's legitimacy at home, and seemed to confirm what many had suspected all along, that Milosevic had been directing the war behind the scenes. Others argued that their exclusion demonstrated that the peace did not need to be made by those who perpetrated the war.[57]

What was contained in Dayton? Signed in Paris on 14 December 1995, Dayton incorporated 10 articles, 11 annexes, and 102 maps. It maintained the 51:49 division between the Croat-Bosniac Federation and the Republika Srpska within a unified state, with Sarajevo the unified capital of that state. The Bosnian Serbs retained the captured enclaves in Bosnia, while the Bosnian Muslims were given land around Sarajevo. For the Serbs, their take of the territory at 49 per cent approximated the *de facto* situation on the ground at the time, and also the average of their percentage pre-war (32 per cent) and their maximum occupied during the war (70 per cent). The Muslims lost nearly half their territory pre-war, when they held 44 per cent, to their final quota of 27 per cent, while the Croats gained slightly, from 17 per cent pre-war, to 24 per cent at Dayton.[58]

Dayton allowed special access for Bosnian Serbs and Croats to Serbia and Croatia respectively, and the maintenance of separate armies. It confirmed the right of return for refugees – or compensation in case they could not return – and their right to vote in their original place of residence. In another agreement, Croatians and Bosnians officially agreed to the Federation, and Bosnia-Herzegovina and the Federal Republic of Yugoslavia (FRY) exchanged formal recognition, with sanctions to be removed (enshrined in several Security Council resolutions).[59] Dayton also banned those accused of war crimes from holding office.

As for the organisation of the new government, Article III of Annex 4 (pertaining to the constitution) outlined the 'Responsibilities of and Relations between the Institutions of Bosnia and Herzegovina and the Entities'. The new central government in Bosnia was given responsibility for foreign, trade, and monetary policy (Article VII), including a central bank, with the governor appointed by the IMF for the next six years and a single currency tied to the D-mark; customs and immigration; the operation of common and international communications,

---

[57] Anthony Borden and Drago Hedl, 'How the Bosnians were Broken', *War Report*, February/March 1996, p. 41.

[58] Additional pre-war statistics include 5.5 per cent Yugoslavs and the balance others. See Leonard J. Cohen, *Broken Bonds*, Boulder, CO, Westview, 2nd edition, 1995, p. 139, for more information.

[59] Borden and Caplan, 'The Former Yugoslavia', pp. 222–3.

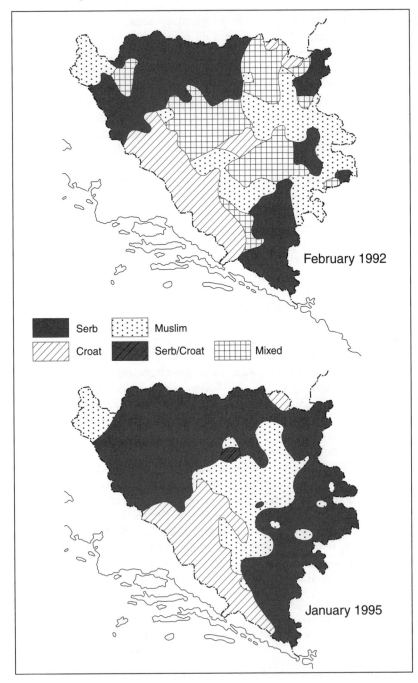

Map 5 The ethnic composition of Bosnia, February 1992 and January 1995

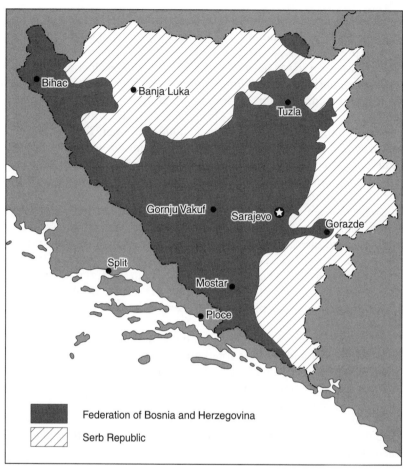

Map 6 The proposed division of Bosnia following the Dayton
Agreement

and air traffic control. The constitution guaranteed freedom of move-
ment throughout Bosnia-Herzegovina (Article I), a Constitutional
Court (Article VI), a Human Rights Commission (Article II), and a
Commission for Displaced Persons and Refugees (Annex 7, Article
VII).

Annex 4 delineated a three-person executive presidency (Article V),
with representation for each ethnic group. Decisions made by the presidency would require unanimity, but two votes could suffice unless the
third declared that her national interests were at stake, and then she

would need two-thirds of her constituency's parliament to support that decision. Article IV outlined the 15-person upper legislative chamber with representatives selected from the entities' respective assemblies, and a 42-person lower house directly elected from each entity.

The responsibility of the international community was also outlined in the document: UN forces were replaced by a 53,000-strong NATO implementation force (IFOR). Of this number, the United States provided 20,000, Britain 13,000, France 8,000, and even Germany participated with 4,000 troops, with the remaining troops provided by non-NATO countries. The troops were tasked to perform standard peace enforcement functions that UNPROFOR was unable to do, including monitoring the withdrawal and disarmament.

Significantly, the commander was authorised to use force to protect troops and carry out responsibilities. The NATO forces were also mandated to arrest indicted war criminals, though not to pursue them. In December 1996, responsibility was then transferred to SFOR (Stabilization Force), with more than half the strength of IFOR at 33,000. SFOR is expected to remain in Bosnia for some time, and will lower deployment levels when conditions appear to be suitable.

The combination of force, changed dynamics on the ground, pressure from Milosevic, and resolute international diplomacy finally ended the war. None of these alone had accomplished the task. NATO commander Lt.-Gen. Smith admitted that the bombing was not achieving what it was supposed to, since few targets remained. One of Smith's aides said, 'We would have failed without the Holbrooke initiative.'[60] The formal peace accomplished, what does the future hold for the Bosnian state?

Conclusions

Dayton in practice

One year after Dayton, the Peace Implementation Council, composed of the Contact Group and principal donor countries, met in Paris in mid-November 1996, and set thirteen priorities for further implementation of Dayton for 1997–8:

1   regional stabilisation (arms control)
2   security (law and order)

---

[60] As cited in *The Economist*, 13 January 1996, p. 42.

3   human rights
4   democratisation
5   elections (municipal in 1997 and general in 1998)
6   freedom of movement
7   repatriation of refugees and displaced persons
8   arrest of war criminals
9   reconstruction
10 a market economy
11 reconciliation
12 education and
13 mine removal.[61]

A conference was also held in Dayton the same month, where Holbrooke, John Kornblum (Holbrooke's successor), and Assistant Secretary of State Strobe Talbott endorsed a reintegrated Bosnia-Herzegovina.[62] Are these priorities achievable? Does Dayton provide a practical/working solution to a seemingly intractable conflict. The possible pitfalls of Dayton are discussed below.

Dayton is overly ambitious. As in Somalia, the goals and priorities listed above are numerous, and probably impossible for the international community to reach in a limited time frame with limited funds. The lesson from the Haiti operation, which aspired to realisable aims, was not absorbed. Yet at the same time, the complexities of the war and the aspirations of the different groups precluded a Haitian-style agreement. And although Dayton was written by expatriates, the agreement was an attempt to incorporate the demands of the parties with those of the international community.

Dayton is fuzzy on end-product. Dayton is faulted for not making the shape of the future Bosnian state more explicit. In other words, it is unclear whether the fundamental principles backed by the international community – that Bosnia remain a unitary state and that its borders not change as a result of force – will hold. Three possible scenarios are therefore conceivable:

1   Bosnia could be partitioned. Although the right to secession was not confirmed, Bosnia could split into two or three entities. Alternatively, the Serb and Croat parts could eventually attach themselves to Serbia and Croatia since Dayton allows 'parallel spe-

[61] Jane M.O. Sharp and Michael Clarke, 'Making Dayton Work: The Future of the Bosnian Peace Process', Centre for Defence Studies, 4 December 1996, p. 1.
[62] From Sharp and Clarke, 'Making Dayton Work', p. 2.

cial relationships'. This possibility would leave a very small, rump Bosnian state.

2   Bosnia could remain as described in Dayton. The two entities could continue to co-exist, with reconciliation occurring at a later stage in the process as trust is gradually rebuilt.

3   Bosnia could be reintegrated, once again forming a truly multi-ethnic state.[63]

This latter outcome will have the best chance of occurring if the international community maintains a firm commitment to implementing the agreement.

The counter-argument to the lack of clarity in Dayton would be that it is impossible to tell what the end-product will be, even if it were laid out in detail, and by leaving the future vague, Bosnians may fashion their own compromise that works best for them. Thus if the state breaks up and all that is left is a Bosniac or Muslim micro-state, this would not necessarily create an international precedent. Many micro-states, in Europe, Asia, Africa, and the Pacific, already exist, and some are very successful (such as Singapore or Luxembourg).

Dayton does not integrate the military with the civilian mission. UNHCR was the lead co-ordinating agent for both the military and civilian side during UNPROFOR, but this role was discontinued and the civilian and military parts have since operated separately. Carl Bildt, the former Swedish Prime Minister, was appointed High Representative at Dayton, and then was replaced by Carlos Westendorp, former Spanish Foreign Minister. The High Representative is mandated to co-ordinate and monitor the civil aspects of implementation, including rehabilitation and the return of refugees, the holding of elections, the monitoring of human rights, demobilisation, the facilitation of dialogue between contending parties, and reporting on progress to the UN, other international organisations, and governments. The High Representative is also responsible for overseeing the new UN civilian International Police Task Force.

Yet, as specified in Dayton, 'The High Representative has no authority over the IFOR', a provision that has thus far yielded difficulties, since he has no formal authority to make the organisations responsible for the above-mentioned tasks do anything. He can only make suggestions from his base in Sarajevo, a base that has no organisational affiliation. Holbrooke insisted that this be a stipulation, although it is unclear why the civilian side of Dayton was separated from the

---

[63] Jane M.O. Sharp, 'Recommitting to Dayton', *War Report*, November/ December 1996, p. 8.

military, especially after the success experienced in Haiti through the integration of the two, and the failure in Somalia due to their separation.

Bildt later admitted to the need to integrate the two sides of Dayton once he was replaced. After NATO forces captured one indicted criminal and killed another in early July 1997, Bildt remarked, 'By design or by default, the Dayton peace agreements have entered a new phase. This phase will require a far more co-ordinated effort from the political and military sides... And this effort will not be completed by June 1998, when President Bill Clinton has said that US troops should leave.'[64]

Co-ordination of Bosnian policy did occur within US government circles in Washington, DC, where State Department, National Security Council, and USAID officials, who formed the Executive Committee (ExComm) similar to the one for Haiti, were meeting three times a week to discuss the progress on implementation of Dayton. Issues of importance to the committee included stabilisation measures, the political settlement, economic reconstruction, police reform, humanitarian concerns, such as return of refugees and IDPs, de-mining, and elections (the United States donated one-sixth of the cost of the OSCE's bill).[65] Recently as well, the former Transitional Administrator for UNTAES, Jacques Paul Klein, was appointed number two for the overall operation of SFOR. He may provide the right mix in a leadership position since he is a former military officer in a civilian post, with a successful record of civil–military integration in the former Yugoslavia (in UNTAES, discussed on page 166–7).

Dayton reinforces ethnic divisions. The war in Bosnia transformed the territory from an ethnically mixed republic into three essentially homogenous territorial units (although officially there are only two), with small minorities, each with its own army. Few heterogeneous towns remain, such as Mostar and Tuzla, and even in these, the ethnic groups have been separated, as in Mostar where the Croats and Muslims now live on different sides of the Neretva river. A formal split seems likely. As Borden and Caplan explained, Dayton 'entrenches the ethnic divisions that gave rise to the conflict in the first place'.[66] By separating the groups, it may be difficult, if not impossible, to convince all three

---

[64] Carl Bildt, 'In the Balkans, NATO Must Go After the Masterminds', editorial, *International Herald Tribune*, 14 July 1997.

[65] Tara Magner, 'Beltway Bureaucrats for Bosnia', *War Report*, February/March 1996, p. 20.

[66] Borden and Caplan, 'The Former Yugoslavia', p. 231.

parties that they can live in a multi-ethnic (con)federation after four years fighting against such an outcome, albeit within their self-made boundaries.[67]

The political leaders in all the new states are pro-segregation, while the presidency is composed of representatives of the three major groups, which excludes minorities, those with a 'mixed' background or those who do not wish to be labelled in these categories. This also means that a member of one ethnic group can only represent that group, e.g., a Serb could not represent the Federation. Moreover, those politicians who supported a multi-ethnic state, such as Milan Panic in the FRY, were marginalised and out-voted, although they may be in fashion again in the future if reconciliation occurs as intended.

The counter-point to the argument that Dayton magnifies the ethnic divide is equally persuasive. It is not possible to force people to live together who do not wish to, and a 'separate but equal' system may in the long run be the best way to promote trust between groups. As trust grows, the dividing lines would disappear.

This is in fact what happens in most confederations, which either disintegrate (as the Senegambian Confederation did in 1989), or integrate further if enough trust develops in the central authority, and the constituent units believe that their interests would be better served by transferring more sovereignty to the centre. The Swiss Confederation, which was forged after years of civil war and coups in various cantons, along with outside intervention, became a federation. Very diverse groups of people, speaking different languages and belonging to different religions, came together to create one of the most successful federations.[68] The United States was also a confederation that later became a federation.

Other factors could contribute to the development of trust, such as the single currency envisaged in Dayton, or closer trading links and other economic activity. International pressure could also assist. Already in the United States, congressional legislation prevents funding going to projects that do not promote multi-ethnic co-operation.[69]

---

[67] Although the new state is referred to as a federation, it may also be a confederation as the arrangement between the three communities, though legally two, with minimal central government responsibility is a confederal one. See conclusion for more information about the differences between these governmental arrangements.

[68] Although the Swiss Confederation is called a confederation, it is in fact a federation.

[69] Susan Woodward, 'Bosnia after Dayton: Year Two', *Current History*, 96, 608, March 1997, p. 100.

Dayton endorses ethnic cleansing. The ethnic make-up of Croatia, Serbia and Bosnia has changed, probably permanently due to the ethnic cleansing of which all parties were guilty during the war. For example, Croatia had a pre-war Serb population of 600,000, which was reduced to between 100,000 and 150,000 after Dayton, down from 12 per cent pre-war to 3 per cent, and this number could be reduced further.[70] In Bosnia, the Republika Srpska was created primarily through genocide and ethnic cleansing. Dayton sanctified these changes, but only in Bosnia, while it effectively overlooked similar problems in Croatia.

A perilous peace?

In addition to the possible problems manifest in the Dayton Agreement, other concerns threaten the precarious peace.

The Croat-Bosniac Federation is fragile. The Federation may collapse, especially if Mostar represents the future. Many Croats have blocked the return of Muslims to their homes in east/west Mostar, even though Dayton designated this as a right. Other Bosnian Croats (and indeed some Bosniacs) cannot understand why officially they do not have their own mini-state, as the Bosnian Serbs do.

In practice, some say that the Croat Republic of Herzeg-Bosna already exists. Those who claim this point to the Croatian elections in October 1995, in which Bosnian Croats were allowed to vote, even though this directly countered the Croat-Bosniac Federation Constitution. In fact, many Croats want to be affiliated with Croatia proper. Some Muslims in the federation argue that the Croats could be allowed greater autonomy in terms of culture, religion and national identity, as well as control over the Bosnian Croat army, while others claim that more autonomy would lead to separate states. Additional problems include the exclusion from the federal institutions of Serbs and non-nationalists who live in the territory because only Muslims and Croats are allowed representation.

The economies of the former republics are weak. As in the other cases discussed in this book, sanctions and the war have had disastrous effects on the economies of all the republics of former Yugoslavia, excepting Slovenia. At the time Dayton was initialled, over 40 per cent of the population of Serbia-Montenegro lived below the poverty line.[71] By early 1997, Serbia's unemployment rate reached 50 per cent, and the country had a $2

---

[70] Borden and Caplan, 'The Former Yugoslavia', p. 209.
[71] Bojicic et al., 'Post-War Reconstruction in the Balkans', p. 8.

billion trade deficit.[72] In the Republic of Srpska component of Bosnia, unemployment reached 90 per cent after the war.[73]

In Bosnia, according to one study, per capita GDP fell from $2,719 to $250 between 1991 and 1994. Rail tracks, roads, electricity and gas systems, telecommunications, healthcare, schools, housing, historical and cultural sites have been severely impaired, if not entirely demolished, and 45 per cent of all industrial plants destroyed. This study estimated that the costs of reconstruction would total $10.8 billion.[74]

The World Bank estimated a $5 billion figure for rehabilitation, while Bosnian government projections ran to $43 billion.[75] In January 1996, the World Bank and the European Commission opened offices in Sarajevo to initiate projects aimed at kick-starting the economy. Economic concerns need full redress so that they cannot become the excuse to return to war. In the meantime, the Bosnian Serbs have not been complying with Dayton, which is why they have not received the aid they need. They have blocked the establishment of a central bank, have failed to comply with demobilisation, and have signed an economic and military co-operation agreement with Yugoslavia.[76]

Police reform is slow. The 2,000 members of the International Police Task Force (IPTF), a civilian police-training force mandated by Security Council Resolution 1035 (December 1995), have encountered difficulties in retraining the Bosnian police force.[77] The primary problems relate to minority returns and general respect for human rights. Security Council Resolution 1088 (December 1996) expanded the power of the IPTF to include the right to investigate abuses by the local police, yet thus far the execution of this mandate has not been satisfactory because international trainers did not anticipate the degree of corruption and gross abuses of human rights in the local police force. With-

---

[72] *The Economist*, 8 February 1997, p. 45.
[73] *International Herald Tribune*, 8 July 1997.
[74] Bojicic et al., 'Post-War Reconstruction in the Balkans', pp. 5–7.
[75] *The Economist*, 16 December 1995, p. 50.
[76] 'As NATO Patrols, Karadzic Hides in Plain Sight', *International Herald Tribune*, 10 July 1997.
[77] See 'Bosnia and Hercegovina: Beyond Restraint, Politics and the Policing Agenda of the UN International Police Task Force', *Human Rights Watch Report*, Vol. 10, No.5, June 1998, for more information. See also the UN Web page on peacekeeping in Bosnia–Herzegovina, http://www.un.org/Depts/dpko/. Together the United Nations Police Task Force (IPTF) and UN Civilian Office operations became known as the United Nations Mission in Bosnia and Herzegovina (UNMIBH).

out a functioning police force, which gains the trust of the community, Dayton will not be successful.

Security Council Resolutions 1088 and 1107 (May 1997) established a Human Rights Office, which began operations in November 1997, to carry out these investigations. They have been hampered, however, by the inability of the international force itself to establish clear guidelines as to what constitutes a human rights abuse. Moreover, many of the trainers come from parts of the world where their own police force does not have such a distinguished record. The UN is attempting to redress these problems in its hiring practice. The international trainers are attempting to reduce the local police force, from both the Federation and the Republika, by half, and have implemented a rigorous process to realise this goal. This task has been complicated by the Republika's obstruction of Dayton in general, and because Karadzic still controls much of the day-to-day life in the region, despite being barred from holding office. The restructuring of the forces requires that candidates reapply for their jobs, which means they then go through an intensive vetting process to ensure their backgrounds are not tainted and that they are not under indictment at the Tribunal. They then take a series of intelligence and psychological tests.

The names of those who complete this process successfully go on a list that is published in the local newspaper, so that if any member of the local population has a complaint, they can register it with the IPTF for investigation. Those candidates that survive this whole process receive a new identification card and uniform and begin a one-year probation period, during which time they also receive training by the international monitors. By June 1998, the process had been completed in the Federation, except for two cantons, and in the Republika it had only recently begun.[78] The transparency of the process should ensure that those who do make it through the qualification period gain the trust of their communities.

The right of return exists only on paper. Although Dayton stipulates that all refugees have the right to return to their homes to live and/or vote, very little returning has occurred for either purpose.[79] If there is no cooperation on this front, more trouble could ensue. In March 1996, UNHCR hoped to assist 870,000 returnees by the end of the year; by

[78] This information has been provided by the report, 'Bosnia and Hercegovina: Beyond Restraint', *Human Rights Watch Report*.
[79] See, for example, 'As NATO Patrols, Karadzic Hides in Plain Sight', *International Herald Tribune*, 10 July 1997.

September it had revised its target down to 135,000.[80] In 1997, UNHCR reported 108,500 returnees to Bosnia–Herzegovinia, primarily from Germany, Switzerland and Austria, with 816,000 IDPs still of concern to the organisation.[81] Moreover, the time frames introduced have not been realistic; for example, in Croatia, Serbs were given three months to return and reclaim property, which would be given to IDPs and refugees if they did not get back in time. In December 1995, the Security Council issued a resolution calling on the Croats to lift the time restriction.[82]

All three groups have been intimidating refugees and IDPs. For example, in Sarajevo, many Bosnian Serbs have left, even though Dayton pledged that they could stay (except the Bosnian Serb army, which was supposed to leave). President Izetbegovic said that their women and children would be safe if they stayed, and his Foreign Minister had to add 'so would the men', demonstrating the lack of support on all sides for the protection of minorities.[83] The new government had hoped to resettle Muslim refugees in emptied homes. Meanwhile many Serbs were burning down their homes before leaving, while all three groups have been accused of small-scale violence.

International involvement initially threatened to be short-term. Initially, Clinton made an election promise to have all US troops out by December 1996, but then extended the deadline, just two weeks after the elections, until June 1998. The deadline was again extended until June 21, 1999, and is likely to be extended again. According to David Scanlon, SFOR spokesperson, indicating a recent shift in policy, 'SFOR is now working toward an "end state", not an "end date". Deadlines no longer apply to the mission here . . . what is left is to ensure a stable and secure environment so that the less concrete civil aspects of Dayton can be implemented and a lasting peace established.'[84] The US government has been asked to pay 30 per cent of the bill of the entire operation (with the other two-thirds from Europe,[85] Japan and some Muslim countries), although the United States paid fully for the 'train-and-

---

[80] Sharp and Clarke, 'Making Dayton Work', p. 10.
[81] See http://www.unhcr.ch/un&ref/numbers/numbers/htm for more information.
[82] UN document S/PRST/1995/63, 22 December 1995, Press Release.
[83] *The Economist*, 2 December 1995, p. 46.
[84] From correspondence with Lt.-Cmdr. David Scanlon, SFOR spokesperson, April 1999.
[85] By early 1996, EU member states had already contributed 67 per cent of the total humanitarian assistance given by the international community, and of that, 70 per cent went to Bosnia-Herzegovina (1.7 billion ECU).

equip' programme, and have been contributing approximately $2.5 billion annually thus far.

The US government has been sponsoring the 'train-and-equip' programme for the Croat-Bosniac Federation, supposedly to deter further conflict by making the playing field more even. The commitment to rearm the Muslims had been given as a verbal agreement, without which Izetbegovic would not have agreed to Dayton.[86] The Americans also preferred to train soldiers instead of having Iran continue to do so (Iran had been supporting the Muslims for several years). If the Federation was properly equipped and trained to defend itself, this would supposedly hasten the exit of foreign troops.

The Europeans have been wavering in their military commitment to stay in Bosnia for the long term, claiming they would leave with the Americans (as occurred in Somalia), though this could be the perfect opportunity to demonstrate a common foreign and security policy, and give the WEU a *raison d'être*. A long-term and firm commitment needs to be evident to build confidence in the peace process, and to dissuade those who may think they just need to wait until foreign troops leave before embarking on another war of aggression to reclaim 'lost' territory. The EU has, however, set realistic time frames for the accomplishment of the different objectives of Dayton. According to Mario Zucconi, 'DG1A estimate the time required for ... military stabilisation, 1–2 years; reconstruction, 10 years; reconciliation, more than a generation.'[87] If the international community can participate through support for economic and political reforms over the next ten years, these objectives could be achievable.[88]

---

[86] Jane M.O. Sharp, 'Dayton Report Card', *International Security*, 22, 3, Winter 1997/98, p. 116.

[87] Mario Zucconi, 'Brussels Aid', *War Report*, February/March 1996, p. 21.

[88] Economic inducements, and the threat of withholding them, have been used by western countries, especially the United States at the World Bank, to armtwist the Serbs and Croats to comply with Dayton. For example, in early July 1997, the World Bank postponed indefinitely a vote on a $30 million loan to Croatia, in order to pressure Croatia into allowing Serb refugees to return to their homes and to assist the International War Crimes Tribunal to apprehend those indicted for war crimes. As reported in the *International Herald Tribune*, 'there is a growing sentiment [in the US Congress] that the administration should condition its support of loans and other assistance to the Balkans on co-operation with Dayton, particularly on the issue of war criminals': 3 July 1997. Over $800 million worth of reconstruction loans for the Serbs have also been held up due to non-compliance with Dayton (*International Herald Tribune*, 8 July 1997). America was vetoing Serb borrowing from both the World Bank and the IMF until Milosevic helped to arrest war criminals,

Implications

As mentioned in Chapter 1, the international community has only recently encountered the collapsed state phenomenon, and thus its bumbling tactics as it attempted to resolve the crisis in Bosnia (and in Panama, Haiti, and Somalia) must also be seen in this light. Further, international disagreements that impeded a co-ordinated response – between the United States and the EU, the EU and the UN, and the UN and NATO, as well as between individual states – can also be attributed to the adaptation of these states and organisations to distinct post-Cold War concerns, particularly humanitarian-based. Disputes in the Security Council between the permanent members, notably the United States, Britain, and France, also impeded the smooth functioning of that organisation. Richard Holbrooke's remark that 'the damage that Bosnia did to the UN was incalculable' may be an exaggeration as the UN managed to handle the crisis in Haiti in a more efficient manner.[89]

As in Somalia and Albania, the initial excuse for involvement was the protection of humanitarian assistance. And also as in Somalia, Bosnia soon became a wholesale security operation. The international commitment escalated because of recognition of new states, sanctions, the peacekeeping operation, the media, increased numbers of refugees, and continued defiance by Serb leaders. Yet it is also unlikely that an alternative to the use of force existed, and this escalated commitment did serve to end the war.

Similar to Haiti, once the military intervention transpired – or the large-scale bombing campaign in this case – the post-conflict operation operated fairly efficiently, in sharp contrast to the run-up to the use of force. Civil Affairs (CA) units, which were indispensable in Panama, Haiti, early on in Somalia, and even in Kuwait after its 'liberation', have been fundamental to the reconstruction of Bosnia-Herzegovina thus far. These troops (along with their European counterparts) have been performing basic but necessary tasks, such as repairing roads and utilities, rehabilitating public health, improving trade, assisting with elections, and training police.

US PSYOPS troops have been keeping the local populations

democratise Serbia, and give Albanians in Kosovo some autonomy (*The Economist*, 28 June 1997, p. 32).

[89] Alison Mitchell, 'Clinton's About-Face', *New York Times*, 24 September 1996, A8, as cited in Amir Pasic and Thomas G. Weiss, 'The Politics of Rescue: Yugoslavia's Wars and the Humanitarian Impulse', *Ethics and International Affairs*, 11, 1997, p. 4.

informed about these projects and the mine removal programmes, as well as updating them on the implementation of Dayton. By the end of 1996, there were approximately 500 CA and PSYOPS troops present, the majority of whom were reservists.[90] And significantly, they have also been able to assist the High Representative to provide the co-ordinating capacity for the civil reconstruction and relief efforts of 500 UN, multilateral and governmental agencies, and NGOs, including a plethora of acronyms – UNHCR, UNICEF, UNESCO, OSCE, ICRC, USAID, and the World Bank.

The biggest hurdle will be for the different communities to learn how to live together again after such a bitter and protracted war. At least 250,000 civilians were killed in Bosnia-Herzegovina, 200,000 were wounded, and 2.8 million internally displaced or refugees (60 per cent of the pre-war population). The task will be further exacerbated by the scale of the infrastructure destruction already mentioned and the estimated number of remaining land mines at 1.5–4 million.[91]

The War Crimes Tribunal should help heal some wounds, if only through giving victims a chance to air their story, although most indicted criminals, especially Karadzic and Mladic, remain at large, which also hinders reconciliation. As of July 1997, it appeared that NATO was about to change its policy of not actively pursuing the two men, and instead attempt a special forces operation to capture them both and bring them to The Hague to stand trial.[92] If this does occur, it may put western troops at risk, which has been the main reason why NATO troops have not already brought them both in. The success of the court is necessary for the public perception that justice is served, and therefore that the peace will hold.

In September 1996, the new Bosnian state held its first elections, with Izetbegovic winning the majority of votes, placing him in the chair of the three-person presidency, and making him Bosnia's head of state internationally. Two-thirds of the electorate voted, although only

[90] Glenn W. Goodman, Jr., 'Rebuilding Bosnia: Army Civil Affairs and PSYOP Personnel Play Critical Nonmilitary Role in Operation Joint Endeavor', *Armed Forces Journal International*, February 1997, p. 22–3.

[91] Information supplied on the World Wide Web from the World Bank Group.

[92] A signal of this change took place in mid-July 1997, when British NATO troops killed Simo Drljaca, the former police chief in Prijedor (as he was resisting arrest) and captured Milan 'Mico' Kovacevic. Both men had been charged by the court with complicity in genocide against Muslims and Croats during the Serb takeover of Prijedor, which began in April 1992. 'NATO Is Jeopardizing Peace, Bosnian Serb Leaders Warn', *International Herald Tribune*, 12–13 July 1997.

14,700 of the eligible 150,000 Muslim voters chose to return to their former residences to vote, and most voted along ethnic lines.[93] While implementation of the Dayton accords has not yet proved to be entirely satisfactory to any party, the fulfilment of the agreement hinges on a commitment of the parties concerned and of the international community.

Interestingly, the United Nations Transitional Authority in Eastern Slavonia, Baranja and Western Sirmium (UNTAES), mandated in January 1996 to reintegrate 'the territory and people of Eastern Slavonia into the sovereign institutions of Croatia', accomplished its mandate before shutting down in January 1998, and succeeded where Dayton has not.[94] As the UNTAES report noted just before terminating:

Within the UNTAES area, there has been no large outflow of new refugees from the region and reintegration has been peaceful. Demilitarization was completed on 20 June 1996. A Transitional Police Force was established on 1 July 1996. Local and regional elections were conducted successfully on 13 and 14 April 1997. In the latter part of 1997, some 6,000 Croats and 9,000 Serbs returned to their original homes. Close co-operation with the International Tribunal for the former Yugoslavia resulted in the successful exhumation of the Ovcara mass grave site and the arrest of an indicted war criminal.[95]

The Transitional Administrator for UNTAES, Jacques Paul Klein, indicated several key points, including a 'Do-able Mandate'. UNTAES had a 'clearly defined . . . mandate embodied in the Basic Agreement and in Security Council Resolution 1037'.[96] The region remained multi-ethnic, the police force re-integrated, elections were held (albeit in a somewhat disorganised manner), the region was demilitarised and paramilitaries have left. A significant factor accounting for the success of this mission has been that UNTAES has been backed by force, with troops not afraid to use it when necessary.[97] Moreover, the civilian and military parts of

---

[93] *The Economist*, 21 September 1996, p. 50.

[94] The region is populated by a significant number of Croatian Serbs, Serb IDPs, and minorities, such as Hungarians, Slovaks, and Ruthenians. Jacques Paul Klein, 'The Prospects for Eastern Croatia: The Significance of the UN's Undiscovered Mission', *RUSI Journal*, April 1997, p. 20.

[95] United Nations Transitional Administration for Eastern Slavonia, Baranja and Western Sirmium, Recent Developments, Prepared by the Department of Public Information, United Nations, 22 December 1997.

[96] For more information, see Klein, 'The Prospects for Eastern Croatia', pp. 19–24.

[97] Troop numbers in fact increased from 1,600 at the end of UNCRO in January 1996 to 5,000 combat troops and support units by mid-1997. Klein, 'The Prospects for Eastern Croatia', p. 22.

the mission were joined and both were under the authority of the civilian head, Klein.

Dayton may have been the most complicated nation-building mission since World War II that has not (thus far) gone awry, although its impact on the 1999 Kosovo campaign will be discussed in Chapter 6. What then are the comprehensive lessons learned from the recent experience in nation-building, initiated by the international community with significant prodding and backing from the United States? The final chapter examines how attempts at nation-building after military intervention have evolved, primarily in a positive manner, since the invasion of Panama in December 1989.

6   Hubris or progress: can democracy be forced?

The titular evolution in the four cases examined in this book – from *Operation Just Cause* in Panama to *Operation Joint Endeavour* in Bosnia – signifies America's increased understanding of its role as international caretaker since the end of the Cold War. The former name implies insecurity through self-justification, and an attempt to forge ahead alone – irrespective of the wishes of international partners – while the latter denotes a more humble personification, and a shared purpose. The nation-building efforts analysed in this book have also progressed along these lines, as this final chapter explains in three parts. First, it examines the common threads linking and leading to the Panama, Somalia, Haiti, and Bosnia interventions; second, it points to the lessons learned and applied within the military, in civil–military relations, and in peace support operations; while third, it concludes by discussing the overall developments in nation-building, areas of continued concern and how future operations might achieve greater success.

This study examines three issues critical to western policy makers: (1) military intervention and the use of force, which often lead to (2) peace support operations, which in turn can lead to (3) nation-building attempts. The success or failure of each component directly impacts the others. For example, if the military component proceeds smoothly but the peace support operation or nation-building efforts do not, as in Somalia, the chances of overall mission success are reduced considerably. Moreover, a failure in one of these areas will drastically affect future decisions on the use of force in similar scenarios, as indeed occurred when the international community was silent during the Rwanda genocide. Likewise, relatively successful peace support operations, as in Haiti and Bosnia during IFOR and SFOR, paved the way for the Albania and Kosovo operations.

Common considerations: what factors preceded the interventions?

The similarities in the cases studied therefore merit mention, if only to serve as early warning signals for future crises that may lead the US government or other powers on the path to choosing the military option. Such knowledge could contribute to the decision by the possible intervener to continue and, if so, to plan accordingly, as transpired in Haiti. Alternatively, attention to these factors could allow that government to step back and go in an altogether different policy direction.

In all these cases, the period leading up to the intervention was marked by inconsistent policy, public waffling, and empty threats – by the US government in Panama and Haiti, the international community in Somalia, and Europe and then the United States in Bosnia. It is perhaps impossible for democratic states to eschew such behaviour because, as Bruce Russett explained, 'In the absence of direct attack, institutionalised checks and balances make democracies' decisions to go to war slow and very public.'[1] Other common issues that drive democratic states to intervene, however, can be considered, particularly large refugee flows to developed states, the media spotlight on humanitarian suffering, continued defiance by nasty rulers, and increased sanctions.

These factors have not been as prominent in other civil crises, and consequently can partially account for the absence of a threat to intervene, in Burundi, Algeria, or Sudan, for example, where the conflicts may be as horrific – if not worse – than the cases examined in this book. Additionally, the decision to intervene is also based on the relative power and size of the country concerned, and likelihood of a successful outcome. For example, it is extremely unlikely that the US government would ever threaten China or Nigeria with intervention.

The presence of the above-mentioned factors, compounded by time, therefore, produces the *Do Something Effect*, and pushes the US government and other western countries into choosing the military option. Joe Klein remarked that President Clinton 'acted militarily only after marathon hand-wringing and when he had no choice'.[2] It would be difficult to overcome the effect these factors have on government policy-making, yet their influence can at least be mitigated.

Large increases in refugee flows, especially to a powerful neighbouring

---

[1] Letter to the editor, *The Economist*, 29 April 1995.
[2] Joe Klein, 'Diplomacy Without Tears: Will the Secretary of State's Tough Talk Make Peace?', *The New Yorker*, 13 October 1997, p. 47.

country, are one indicator. In Panama and Somalia, this was not a factor, but it was to a significant degree in Haiti and Bosnia. Later, refugees from Albania going to Italy and Greece, and from Liberia and Sierra Leone to Nigeria and other West African states, as well as within Central Africa, also played a significant role in the decisions by their neighbours to intervene in those countries. Most governments cannot easily prevent refugees from arriving, not only because it is difficult and expensive to police borders, but also for human rights reasons. And this tool is often wielded by developing countries.

Aristide used the threat of increased refugee flows from Haiti to the United States to receive more foreign aid, while King Hassan of Morocco has also issued similar warnings over the years in negotiations with Spain. Even without such threats, aid to developing countries, especially those located in the sphere of influence of the major powers, is partially driven by the desire to improve the situation at home so that the inhabitants will not want to leave. Development aid to strengthen governance and the local economy should be a priority, as this may be the only way to stop such large flows.

Media coverage of all these crises has also had a significant impact and forced policy makers to react because of the ensuing public outcry, albeit in an inconsistent manner in these cases. Although it also fuelled the initial military response in Panama, the 'CNN Effect' became a factor after the Gulf War when safe-havens for the Kurds were established. Public opinion, stirred up by CNN footage of Kurds encamped in barren mountains, briefly forced western governments to take action.

By the time of Somalia, the media not only helped push the US government into intervening because images of starving children were viewed with discomfort by most Americans, but significantly, this time it was also partly responsible for the abrupt termination of the UN operation as those same Americans witnessed their boys being killed in a brutal fashion by the very people they had gone to help. In Somalia, the US government reacted too impulsively to the media, instead of utilising it to debate the merits of continued action and how to rectify the mistakes already made, which, arguably, might have been more effective.

In Haiti, the opposite occurred. Significant coverage of events during the period leading up to the intervention spurred a healthier debate in the United States about a possible intervention, and gave those organisations that would be involved ample time to plan. The refugee crisis, however, was exacerbated by the US media, even though at its height, Cuban refugees were also arriving in large numbers without any corresponding threat to the Cuban government. Notably, during the lead up to the intervention, articles on Haiti were soon listed in the 'domestic' pages of the US press.

In Bosnia, televised Serb atrocities promoted a serious international dialogue, which in turn belatedly helped convince wavering US and European publics of the need for NATO bombing campaigns.[3] This coverage was also responsible for the establishment of the International War Crimes Tribunal. If the US government is going to continue to intervene, it has to utilise the media better than it currently does to explain in detail the purpose of the intervention, and what it hopes to achieve before, during, and after, instead of allowing the media to push policy.[4]

The increase in refugee flows and media coverage in these cases forced the US and European governments, with the support of the United Nations Security Council, to threaten action against the *errant rulers*. As these threats mounted, it exposed all three to charges that their warnings were being ignored and not ameliorating the deteriorating situations in Panama, Somalia, Haiti, and Bosnia. Indeed, Noriega, several Somali war-lords, Cedras and company, and the Bosnian Serb leadership continued to defy international pressure, because, as mentioned, international policy pre-intervention was confused, did not follow a hard line, and wavered enough to give the impression to the wayward rulers that they could continue their activity unabated, particularly when they endangered the lives of foreign soldiers.

Defiance was all the more beguiling because several of these leaders had previously been supported by the US government before becoming troublesome – including, but not limited to, Noriega, Siad Barre, Cedras, and even Saddam Hussein. This non-compliance eventually compelled the US government to choose force in order to demonstrate that the sole Superpower could not and would not be pushed around by nasty, tin-pot, small-time, thug dictators and war-lords. The United

[3] Pressure to intervene militarily began at the beginning of the conflict. See, for example, Jane M.O. Sharp and Vladimir Baranovsky, 'For a NATO–Russian Intervention in the Balkans', *International Herald Tribune*, 26 February 1993, Jane M.O Sharp, 'Intervention in Bosnia: The Case For', *The World Today*, February 1993, and Jane M.O. Sharp, 'If not NATO, Who?', *The Bulletin of the Atomic Scientists*, October 1992.

[4] For more information on how the media help to set public opinion and policy, see Frank R. Baumgartner and Bryan D. Jones, *Agendas and Instability in American Politics*, Chicago, Chicago University Press, 1993, and John W. Kingdon, *Agendas, Alternatives and Public Policies*, New York, Harper Collins College Publishers, 1995.

Nations Security Council also needed to demonstrate that its resolutions were intended to be observed, not ignored, and thus approved of the military option in Somalia, Haiti, and Bosnia.

In all these situations, the common assumption was that if the rulers were removed, democracy would neatly fall in place; what Thomas Carothers has referred to as the 'Evil Man' complex.[5] This simplistic analysis on the part of the US government overlooks the obvious fact that the entire system needs to be rebuilt because it is completely rotten, and that these Evil Men survive and prosper precisely because there is no democratic foundation, as was evident in Panama directly after troops arrived when a power vacuum caused massive looting. The removal of one Evil Man in such a situation only guarantees that another one will quickly fill his place. For example, in Somalia, after Siad Barre was removed, war-lords such as General Aideed filled the power vacuum. Aideed, in turn, was replaced by one of his sons, Hussein Aideed, who assumed control over his father's faction after he was killed in August 1996. Since then, Hussein has been pursuing the same agenda as his father.

Sanctions also accompany large refugee flows, pressure applied through the media, and defiance by nasty rulers. Yet sanctions do not usually achieve their desired aim of reversing or ending the crisis, as was blatantly evident in Panama, Iraq, Somalia, and Haiti. In some cases, however, such as in the former Yugoslavia and possibly South Africa, they do work to some degree. One study conducted in 1991 demonstrated that in 115 cases, sanctions only worked in 34 per cent of them.[6] Sanctions can also promote nationalist solidarity amongst the targeted population in defiance against the major powers, rather than causing the public to rise against their leader as the policy intends. John Galtung remarked that the 'collective nature of economic sanctions makes them hit the innocent along with the guilty', which is why an 'attack from outside is seen as an attack on the group as a whole, not only on a fraction of it'.[7]

---

[5] From personal discussions with Thomas Carothers, Senior Analyst at the Carnegie Endowment for International Peace.

[6] Gary Hufbauer, Jeffrey Schott, and Kimberly Elliott, *Economic Sanctions Reconsidered*, Washington, DC, Institute for International Economics, 1991, pp. 93–4, as quoted in Vojin Dimitrijevic and Jelena Pejic, 'UN Sanctions Against Yugoslavia: Two Years Later', in Dimitris Bourantonis and Jarrod Wiener, eds., *The United Nations in the New World Order: The World Organisation at Fifty*, Basingstoke, Macmillan, 1995, p. 126.

[7] Johan Galtung, 'On the Effects of International Economic Sanctions', *World Politics*, 3, 1967, pp. 389–90, as quoted in Vojin Dimitrijevic and Jelena Pejic,

Even in the rare event that the public does react and go against the government, leaders normally take the necessary precautions to remain in power. Thomas Carothers explained,

Confronted with a choice between accepting the economic deprivation of the citizenry or a total loss of power, a stubborn dictator will inevitably choose the former. And he will step up repression to ensure that those countrymen do not react to their deteriorating economic situation by trying to throw him out.[8]

Moreover, sanctions are almost always by-passed by those with money and power, sometimes by import substitution, but mostly by smuggling.

Additionally, the policy of applying sanctions is inherently short-sighted and frequently (and ironically) leads to the collapse of the domestic economy. For example, the Haitian embargo, which endured for several years without accomplishing its stated purpose of removing the Cedras regime, affected long-term recovery in the country because essential medical, food, and financial supplies were drastically reduced, while most jobs in the basic industries were lost. This caused more refugees to attempt the journey to the United States, and greater economic instability. In all the cases discussed in this book, the sanctions imposed by the UN only served to make the post-conflict renewal period more difficult (except for Somalia which has not yet reached this stage). More research needs to be conducted to decide which sanctions work best – and when.

The inability to cope with each of these factors, as summarised in Table 6.1, to varying degrees and through lack of alternatives, soon entrapped the US government into choosing the most extreme option – that of force. In justifying the decision to intervene in Haiti, the US Ambassador to the UN Madeleine Albright explained,

Together, we – the international community – have tried condemnation, persuasion, isolation and negotiation. At Governors Island, we helped broker an agreement that the military's leader signed but refused to implement. We have imposed sanctions, suspended them and strengthened them. We have provided every opportunity for the de facto leaders in Haiti to meet their obligations. But patience is an exhaustible commodity. . . The status quo in Haiti is neither tenable nor acceptable.[9]

'UN Sanctions Against Yugoslavia: Two Years Later', in Dimitris Bourantonis and Jarrod Wiener, eds., *The United Nations in the New World Order: The World Organisation at Fifty*, Basingstoke, Macmillan, 1995, p. 125.

[8] Thomas Carothers, 'Lessons for Policymakers', p. 120, in Georges Fauriol, ed., *Haitian Frustrations: Dilemmas for US Policy*, A Report of CSIS American Program, Washington, DC, 1995.

[9] UN Document S/PV.3413, 31 July 1994, p. 12.

Table 6.1 *Summary of factors common to the cases*

Table 6.1	Panama	Somalia	Haiti	Bosnia
	December 1989	*December 1992*	*September 1994*	*August 1995*
Time until the US reacted with force	43 months	24 months	38 months	51 months
Justification for intervention	Democracy denied	Humanitarian crisis (famine)	Democracy denied	Humanitarian crisis
Situation prior to intervention	Nasty dictatorship	Civil war leading to state collapse	Nasty dictatorship	Civil war leading to state collapse
Electoral status	Results overturned	No election held	Results over-turned by coup	Referendum boycotted by Serbs
International setting	US sphere of influence	Exacerbated by end of Cold War	US sphere of influence	Exacerbated by end of Cold War
Refugee crisis affecting West	No	No	Yes (US)	Yes (Europe)
Extensive media coverage	Yes	Yes!	Yes!	Yes!
Increased sanctions	Yes	Yes	Yes	Yes
Nation-building successful?	Qualified Yes	Resounding No	Qualified Yes	Qualified Yes

Lawrence Freedman remarked that in Bosnia, the Security Council had 'experimented with almost every available form of coercion short of war'.[10] Only after the fact – in all these cases – did the United States government add the public rationale (e.g., 'to defend democracy' or 'to maintain our reliability') to the list of when the United States can use force (see Shalikashvili, Christopher, and Lake guidelines in chapter 1).

Diplomacy alone did not resolve these crises (though it has for many others), but combined with force, this pairing proved successful in paving the way for the implementation of the peace support operations. And once the decision to intervene had been made, further entrapment

---

[10] Lawrence Freedman, 'Why the West Failed', *Foreign Policy*, 97, Winter 1994–95, p. 59. In Bosnia, the unsuccessful peacekeeping operation (UNPROFOR) only pushed the international community deeper into the quagmire, also contributing to the decision to use force.

ensued as it became clear that a hasty withdrawal would only ensure that the situation on the ground reverted to that which caused the intervention in the first place. The peace support operation and the nation-building component thus entered into play.

Lessons learned and applied

The rules of disengagement

The likelihood that America and its allies will continue to become entangled in military interventions followed by nation-building missions is high based on past behaviour, the relative success of some of the endeavours and the increase in the number of civil conflicts since the end of the Cold War. In order that future operations achieve greater coherence, clarification of the 'rules of engagement' is necessary, not just for the military, but also for civil–military relations, and for peace support operations. This can best be addressed through an examination of the lessons learned in these areas in Panama, Somalia, Haiti, and Bosnia.

One of the most important concerns the *role of the US military in political reconstruction*. A conspicuous change in US behaviour has been the gradual reduction in US military control over nation-building activities, with Germany and Japan representing the peak. Both operations were directed entirely by the military (the US and European militaries in Germany and the US military alone in Japan), even though civilian agencies, such as the US Treasury, worked together with the military to implement reforms.

Panama was the last operation in which the military overtly directed political reconstruction, although here at least, the US military has had extensive experience and relations with Panamanians.[11] Somalia was the last in which the military made important behind-the-scenes decisions

[11] Most US military personnel in Panama also spoke Spanish, which contributed to their integration in the society, whereas in the subsequent operations, the language ability has not been so extensive, and hence has obstructed better relations with the domestic population. In Haiti, however, the US military has been deploying Creole-speaking US soldiers, and other troops contributing countries have emphasised French language skills when employing personnel, which has contributed to the good relations. Some Serbo-Croatian speaking soldiers were also sent to Bosnia as well, but not to the same degree as the other two. The Somali language is perhaps the one least spoken by foreigners, and this factor may have also accounted for some of the problems encountered.

(such as the preparation of the nation-building resolutions for the Security Council). By the time of Haiti and Bosnia, the military's task remained primarily confined to security, although it did participate in political reconstruction discussions at the senior level, while US Civil Affairs, Special Forces, and PSYOPS troops supported political activity in both campaigns.

After the Panama invasion, the US military began reviewing its role in 'smaller-scale contingency operations', due to the mistakes made there, and because the US military establishment anyway prefers to focus on straight military matters and to leave political reform to civilian agencies. This is, of course, perfectly logical and complies with western education, which ensures that both soldiers and civilians understand the importance of keeping the military subservient to civilian rule. Problems arise, however, when the military is requested to participate in political activity, as in Panama when the secrecy of the operation excluded civilians from political planning. As a result, civilian agencies with much more experience in democratisation work, especially in Central America, were brought in only after the invasion had occurred.

In addition to political involvement, Somalia forced a rethink of the overall role of the US military in peace support operations, which it does not like because they are difficult to train for as they are considered unpredictable (or 'grey'). Moreover, these operations are not viewed as high priority because they do not directly affect the security of the United States. The US military leadership also believes that troops involved in peacekeeping lose some of their combat-ready sharpness, and that those units need three to six months of retraining to recover their war-fighting edge.[12]

Whether they like it or not, the US and European militaries have an important role to play, and will be requested to participate in future peace support operations. The military is much better than civilian agencies at co-ordination and logistics, as well as their traditional tasks of enforcement and security. Significantly, there is a clear chain of command in the military, which is conspicuously lacking in many international organisations, and these are fundamental components for the smooth running of an operation. Additionally, in early stages, when the situation on the ground is too dangerous for most civilian agencies, the military can prepare the ground-work for

---

[12] This discussion was informed by correspondence with Walter Clarke, Adjunct Professor, US Army Peacekeeping Institute, US Army War College.

political reconstruction, such as enforcing a curfew, demobilising militias, demining, or providing security for elections, and in some cases, even running them.

The US military will remain involved in peace support operations because future threats to international security will most likely take the form of situations such as those discussed in this book, as opposed to a direct attack on US soil. As William S. Cohen, US Secretary of Defense, admitted,

the demand for smaller-scale contingency operations is expected to remain high over the next 15 to 20 years. US participation . . . must be selective, depending largely on the interests at stake and the risk of major aggression elsewhere. However, these operations will still likely pose the most frequent challenge for US forces through 2015 and may require significant commitments of forces, both active and Reserve.[13]

Continued cuts in the US defence budget have also forced the US military to adapt, primarily for reasons of survival. Since Somalia, for example, military training in peacekeeping has expanded in the US Army at the Army's Joint Readiness Training Center in Louisiana and at the Combat Maneuver Training Center in Germany. A Peacekeeping Institute has been established at the Army War College, and peacekeeping training for Marine Corps takes place at Quantico.[14] Soon, the acronym MOOTWA (Military Operations Other Than War, also known as OOTW) may carry greater weight at the Pentagon than the Cold War term, MAD (Mutually Assured Destruction).

If the US military establishment persists in its isolationist policy and antipathy for peace support operations, however, irrespective of what the Secretary of Defense may claim, European and other international militaries will have to play a more significant role. This was already becoming evident in Bosnia, where the US Congress in late 1997 was threatening to withdraw entirely from SFOR if European militaries did not take on an even larger burden (they already provide the bulk of troops). European militaries do not view peace support operations as suspiciously as their US counterpart because of their historical experience in 'grey' military operations during the colonial period, while the British military has more recent experience in Northern Ireland as well. The only other alternative will be an increase in the use of private security firms, what some people call 'mercenaries', which raises questions of

---

[13] Report of the Quadrennial Defense Review, May 1997 (Section III, Defense Strategy).
[14] The Army even conducts some joint training exercises with NGOs.

accountability. These firms and 'soldiers' fulfil a role that US and European governments, which are afraid to commit ground troops to insecure regions, have increasingly eschewed.

Co-ordination compels compliance

Although the role of the US military remains rather vague as it is under review, the acceptance that it should play a subservient role in political reconstruction activities – by both the military and civilian leadership – has enhanced co-operation between the two.[15] Civil–military relations have indeed improved, from the lack of co-operation in Panama due to the need to maintain secrecy, to Haiti and Bosnia where both were involved in the planning and implementation of political reconstruction. Secretary Cohen remarked, 'Smaller-scale contingency operations will also put a premium on the ability of the US military to work effectively with other US government agencies, nongovernmental organizations, private voluntary organizations, and a variety of coalition partners.'[16] Yet when it works, co-ordination depends too much on the personalities involved rather than on a prior agreement on standard operating procedures.

In Panama, even after civilians participated in the political reconstruction process, distrust between military and civilian agencies, such as between ICITAP and the military police trainers, hindered smooth running. In Somalia, the operation with the worst management problems, there was a conspicuous lack of co-operation on all sides and turf wars: between New York and Mogadishu, between civilian and military operators in Mogadishu, and even between US and foreign militaries. Additionally, while preparing for the intervention, similar to Panama, there was no joint planning between the military and the heads of relief organisations, even though the military was originally deployed to provide protection for these organisations. In such a climate, it was hardly surprising that it became extremely difficult to carry out the mandate.

In sharp contrast, the operation that experienced the fewest difficulties in implementation was Haiti, where *military, civilian, and development agencies were melded in a tight partnership*. The development role was integral from the beginning, civilian and military actors were trained together before deployment, and a civilian directed the entire operation.

---

[15] Additionally, even though civilian agencies within the government now want more military participation, today fewer civilians working for the government have military experience than in the past, which therefore might lead civilians to place unrealistic expectations on the military in planning for these types of operations.

[16] Report of the Quadrennial Defense Review, May 1997 (Section III, Defense Strategy).

This does not guarantee that Haiti will develop a stable democracy, but at least a well-co-ordinated initial phase has allowed for the best possible environment in which democratic reforms may take root.

In Bosnia, co-ordination improved after Carl Bildt's period as High Representative during IFOR, when he was not given any authority over the military and therefore had no means to enforce the Dayton Accords. The military and civilian roles were not linked at all. Meanwhile, UNTAES[17] in Croatia, which integrated the two, achieved more success in executing its mandate. Recently, the former Transitional Administrator for UNTAES, Jacques Paul Klein, was appointed deputy to Carlos Westendorp, the subsequent High Representative. As mentioned, Klein has thus far provided efficient leadership since he is a former military officer in a civilian post, with a successful record of civil–military integration in the former Yugoslavia.

Of future concern are strategies for melding civilian and military operations more fully on the ground, and reducing the distrust between the two. Joint training, as occurred prior to deployment in Haiti, and ongoing information sharing exercises, as in the CMOC or CIMIC,[18] should be a requirement for all operations. Greater co-ordination will not necessarily rid these operations of problems because bureaucratic politics are inevitable, but it should improve them. Institutionalising these mechanisms, however, will be no easy task. As Thomas Weiss commented, '"Co-ordination" is probably the most overused and least understood term in international parlance. Everyone is for it, but no one wishes to be co-ordinated.'[19]

Peace support operations

Today the international community has a greater understanding of the complexities of peace support operations, and has successfully applied lessons learned from expensive failures, as in Somalia, to subsequent operations, as in Haiti.[20] For example, UNMIH did not simultaneously

[17] United Nations Transitional Authority for Eastern Slavonia, Baranja and Western Sirmium.
[18] Civil–Military Operations Center (the US version) or Civil–Military Coordination (UK version).
[19] Thomas G. Weiss, 'Rekindling Hope in UN Humanitarian Intervention,' in Walter Clarke and Jeffrey Herbst, eds., *Learning From Somalia*, Boulder, CO, Westview, February 1997, p. 217.
[20] See Clinton Administration Policy on Reforming Multilateral Peace Operations (PDD 25), US Department of State, 22 February, 1996, for more information about US recommended changes to UN peace support operations.

incorporate Chapter VI and VII operations, due to the misunderstanding and obstruction of the mandate caused by both functioning at the same time in Somalia. As the UN Secretary-General later remarked, the UN 'has come to realize that a mix of peacekeeping and enforcement is not the answer to a lack of consent and co-operation by the parties to the conflict'. Another important lesson learned from Haiti was that the goals set by the international community must be limited and realistic, again in contrast to Somalia and earlier in Bosnia during UNPROFOR, when the Security Council Resolutions were overly ambitious, too numerous to be implemented and therefore destined to fail. This does not mean that the overall operation will succeed or that the country will develop into a stable democracy, but at least the international community is not asking itself to do more than it can realistically achieve.

The protection of aid workers, humanitarian relief, relief supplies, and foreign troops in what is now known as 'humanitarian space' has also become a significant factor that has interfered with the realisation of the mandates in all the operations barring Panama. As Thomas Weiss noted, 'The protection of relief workers had been the rationale for committing troops to Bosnia in the first place, and the fear of reprisals against troops and aid personnel had deterred the application of greater military force against the Serbs all along.'[21] This sentence could apply equally to Somalia, and more recently, in Albania as well.

Even in Panama, ironically, one of the justifications for the invasion was the threat to American lives, yet only one US citizen had been killed prior to the invasion, while twenty-three US troops were killed during *Operation Just Cause*. By the time of Somalia, US soldiers were no longer allowed to die, at least not on a humanitarian mission (US military deaths were more acceptable during the Gulf War). The fear of 'body bags' thus far is mainly an American preoccupation, although in Bosnia, anxiety about Serb reprisals on British, Dutch, and French peacekeepers put a stop to NATO bombing sorties for some time, and later during IFOR and SFOR, impeded the active apprehension of indicted war criminals, particularly Karadzic and Mladic, by NATO troops.[22] As a

---

[21] Weiss, 'Collective Spinelessness', in Ullman, ed., *The World and Yugoslavia's Wars*, p. 72.

[22] The British military conducted a poll in 1997 to see how many deaths of British soldiers the public would tolerate, and found the numbers quite high (*circa* fifteen per month). Respondents remarked that soldiers joined on a voluntary basis and should therefore be well-aware of the risks they might encounter. Indeed, the British, French, and Dutch all lost more soldiers than

senior US Commander remarked, 'We tried this in Somalia . . . and it didn't work. We don't want to get into a conflict with the Bosnian Serbs. It is not worth the risk to our troops.'[23]

If the US government continues to allow its decisions to be dominated by what Thomas Weiss refers to as 'a zero-casualty foreign policy',[24] then the Americans will be unable to provide the necessary leadership in these missions, and relations with allies will also suffer. It is indeed absurd that an American life abroad is valued more than it is at home, especially considering that the US military is a *voluntary* service.[25] Future soldiers are fully aware of the risks they are embarking upon, as are those who work for NGOs and IGOs, such as the Red Cross or Medicins Sans Frontiers, or journalists in war zones. In fact, more Red Cross workers have been killed working in the field in recent years than have US soldiers abroad.[26]

This is not to argue that the lives of US soldiers are dispensable, but rather that their security will be enhanced by clearer and more robust rules of engagement. If strong signals are sent out to errant leaders that mistreatment of foreign personnel will be met with serious reprisals, aid workers and soldiers will operate in a more secure environment. The planned international criminal court could provide the forum to punish those guilty of mistreatment of international personnel, as has been suggested by various scholars and practitioners.

It could also be argued that the US government is now capable of avoiding 'sunk-cost traps'[27] by pulling out when things appear to be going badly, instead of drowning itself in another Vietnam. The hasty withdrawal from Somalia, however, was not based on a careful cost–benefit analysis, especially if it is true that the US public actually

the Americans did in the four cases discussed in this book combined, while the Pakistanis suffered grave losses in Somalia without withdrawing.

[23] 'As NATO Patrols, Karadzic Hides in Plain Sight', *International Herald Tribune*, 10 July 1997.

[24] Weiss, 'Collective Spinelessness', in Ullman, ed., *The World and Yugoslavia's Wars*, p. 91.

[25] Considering that thirty Americans were killed in Somalia, nineteen in Grenada and twenty-three in Panama, being a soldier is a safer occupation than a police officer, foreign correspondent, aid worker, or even a taxi driver in most major US cities.

[26] European Commission Humanitarian Office Working Paper, 'Security of Relief Workers', Draft 8.1 – 11.2.98, European Commission, p. 1.

[27] For more information on sunk-cost traps, see Karin von Hippel, 'Sunk in the Sahara: the Applicability of the Sunk Cost Effect to Irredentist Disputes', *Journal of North African Studies*, 1, 1, Summer 1996, pp. 95–116.

supported a maintenance of the operation.[28] Moreover, faction leaders can and have utilised this American fear to great effect, as in Haiti with the *USS Harlan County* incident.

Length of involvement is also critical. US policy makers frequently refer to the Vietnam-induced fear of 'mission creep', as occurred while planning for IFOR, when the original strategy called for troops to be out by December 1996. Perhaps calls for early withdrawal are merely a diversion for the US Congress, since inevitably most continuations have been granted. In Bosnia, SFOR was extended until June 1997, then June 1999, and presumably will be again due to the 1999 Kosovo operation. In Haiti, extensions occurred with much greater frequency. A public, lengthy commitment is critical for allowing confidence-building measures sufficient time to be adopted.

The pattern that has emerged in these operations – a major power or regional organisation leading the intervention, with the support of a dozen or so other international states and UN Security Council backing – bestows an added legitimacy on the operation that unilateral interventions do not have, and allows for more burden sharing. Except for Panama, all subsequent operations have fallen into this pattern: Iraq, Somalia, Haiti, Georgia, Rwanda, Liberia, Bosnia, Albania, Sierra Leone, and Kosovo. Most regional organisations, barring NATO, do not have the financial wherewithal, nor the organisational strength and military capacity, to undertake such a responsibility for very long without additional support from the major powers.

ECOMOG, which has been intervening in Liberia and Sierra Leone, has lasted because it is largely backed by Nigeria. Even so, the 1998 intervention in Sierra Leone was accomplished with the help of the British private security firm, Sandline, while earlier interventions were riddled with difficulties.[29] The regional organisations, when they are unable to intervene, typically endorse the intervention when it is in their sphere of influence, as the OAU did in Somalia, the OAS eventually did in Haiti (though not in Panama), and the EU and the OSCE did in Bosnia.

---

[28] See Steven Kull, I. M. Destler, and Clay Ramsay, *The Foreign Policy Gap: How Policy Makers Misread the Public*, College Park, MD, Center for International and Security Studies at Maryland, 1997, for more information.

[29] See 'Funmi Olonisakin, 'African "Home-Made" Peacekeeping Initiatives', *Armed Forces and Society*, 23, 3, Spring 1997; 'Funmi Olonisakin, 'UN Cooperation with Regional Organizations in Peacekeeping: EOMOG and UNOMIL in Liberia', *International Peacekeeping*, 3, 3, 1996; and Abiodun Alao, *The Burden of Collective Goodwill: International Involvement in the Liberian Civil War*, Ashgate, Aldershot, 1998, for more information.

A return to the non-interventionary norm?

The post-Cold War interventions have given rise to a thorny debate about the future of the principle of non-intervention in international law and politics. Some have criticised these interventions as being contrary to the spirit and the objectives of the well-established non-interventionary norm, thereby contributing to the erosion of the principle itself. Others, meanwhile, argue that the post-Cold War interventions have given the Security Council the opportunity to activate the mechanisms for collective security originally intended in the UN Charter, but which had been hindered as a result of Superpower competition.

The latter group would further argue that these interventions have contributed to the reaffirmation of the original objective of the UN Charter of establishing a global police force, backed by the Security Council.[30] Some in this camp have, however, also registered concern about the selective and seemingly arbitrary criteria employed to justify intervention. The post-Cold War experience indicates that collective intervention authorised by the UN Security Council appears to have reflected more the foreign policy considerations of the major powers, particularly the United States, rather than a consensus over normative criteria compelling the international community into action.[31]

The Panamanian crisis perhaps first reared its ugly head in June 1986 when the *New York Times* published Seymour Hersh's article, bringing Noriega's drug and arms dealing to international attention. Yet the intervention did not occur for another three and a half years (forty-three months, see Table 6.1).[32] The Somali state collapsed in January 1991, and two years later, US troops landed in large numbers – the lack of an authority on the ground facilitated a quicker

---

[30] This was the meaning of President Roosevelt's notorious statement to his allies towards the end of World War II when he referred to the need to establish 'four policemen' (i.e., the United States, the United Kingdon, the USSR, and China; France had not yet been elevated to the status of a major ally).

[31] For more information, see Helmut Frenderschub, 'Between Universalism and Collective Security: Authorisation of Use of Force by the UN Security Council', *European Journal of International Law*, 5, 1994, pp. 492–531, and Alexandros Yannis, 'State Collapse and the United Nations: Universality at Risk', in Claire Spencer, ed., *Brassey's Defence Yearbook 1999*, London, Brassey's, 1999.

[32] Although it is difficult to pinpoint the start date of any crisis because factors that lead to its genesis often appear years in advance, the following comments reflect when these crises first entered the international consciousness.

response in this case. The Somali conflict had also erroneously been viewed as a purely humanitarian mission to feed starving women and children, while the extremely intractable Somali civil war that precipitated the humanitarian crisis was largely overlooked.

In Haiti, meanwhile, the UN Security Council waited twenty-one months after Aristide's overthrow to pass the first resolution (841) applying sanctions, due to fears of violating the non-interventionary norm, although the first of many OAS resolutions condemning the coup was passed days after it took place. The intervention itself transpired over three years (thirty-eight months) after the coup, primarily because it had garnered approval – and was requested – by the 'legitimate' government (Aristide). The US government argued that the junta had not been empowered by the people, and that the majority of Haiti's citizens were supportive of the intervention. These arguments resembled those used after Panama, but then they were not considered acceptable by the international community.

Reaction to events in Bosnia took even longer than in Haiti, with the major bombing campaign that led to the introduction of NATO troops occurring over four years after the state disintegrated (fifty-one months), although the peacekeeping operation was initiated early in February 1992, just one month before the war started. Even though the Yugoslav state had also collapsed (like Somalia), the wars engendered by this collapse appeared far more complicated. Intervention in Bosnia therefore did not crystallise until human rights abuses reached a horrific stage. International reluctance to become embroiled in the Kosovo conflict in mid-1998 was also based on the norm of non-intervention, especially because the Kosovo region, inhabited in the main by ethnic Albanians, remained under the jurisdiction of the FRY. Kosovo was a region of Serbia, and not at that time considered a territory that could legally receive independence (unlike Bosnia or Serbia, or even Montenegro, if it so chooses), although legal precedents may be set in the aftermath of the March–June 1999 NATO bombing campaign, undertaken – as in Bosnia – for humanitarian purposes. Here, again, refugees, media coverage, defiance by Milosevic and sanctions preceeded the use of force.

Although the Italian-led intervention in Albania in March 1997 and the Nigerian intervention in Sierra Leone in June 1997 occurred very soon after those conflicts erupted, again, both states had effectively collapsed. Further, large numbers of refugees were inundating their powerful neighbours, thus muting international opposition. The non-interventionary norm has evolved in a significant fashion, especially when crises, such as those in Haiti and Somalia, can be termed 'threats to international peace and security', but it has not disappeared entirely.[33]

Many civil conflicts thus continue unabated, with no threat of intervention, even though they may appear similar to the cases discussed in this book. Examples include democracy denied in Algeria, Burma (Myanmar), and Nigeria; threat of refugees from Cuba and Algeria; humanitarian crises in Burundi and Sudan; not to mention cases such as Afghanistan, Chechnya, and others embroiled in severe civil wars. There has also been no corresponding entrapment in these cases caused by the combination of increased refugees, the media spotlight, confrontational rogue leaders, and sanctions, nor is it feasible that these could co-exist in all cases.

Conclusions

Advances in nation-building?

Evaluations of lessons learned by researchers, western militaries, the UN, the major powers and NGOs have contributed to improvements in the effectiveness of peace support operations and initial democratisation activities, yet what marked changes have there been in nation-building efforts overall? If we return to the Allied occupation after World War II, it appears at first sight that little has been learned – today's democratic Germany and Japan can be sharply contrasted to the four cases analysed in this book. Yet it is also important to reiterate that Allied success in implementing democratic reforms was enhanced by respect for education and high literacy rates, advanced levels of industrialisation and, of course, the unconditional surrender – factors conspicuously lacking in these cases.

The United States, Britain and France also had a significant interest in preventing the re-emergence of Germany and Japan as powerful and aggressive nations. Stable and democratic German and Japanese states were hence viewed as vital for international security. Panama, Somalia, Haiti, and Bosnia have not been considered as critical. Further,

---

[33] As Charles William Maynes wrote regarding the use of force, 'Earlier, the purpose was deterrence and ensuring acceptable external behavior. Now, it is increasingly becoming compellence and appropriate internal behavior.' Charles William Maynes, 'Relearning Intervention', *Foreign Policy*, Spring 1995, p. 97. He also mentioned that Presidential Decision Directive 25, outlining the use of force by the US in UN endeavours, allows for the dispatch of UN or other peacekeeping troops for the restoration of democracy, p. 107.

intervention in the one European case transpired more to preserve the North Atlantic Alliance than to bring peace to the Balkans.

Some might argue here that Vietnam was also given the full weight of US attention, yet it did not develop into a stable democracy. In Vietnam, however, the US government never reached the stage where it had the opportunity to rebuild the state. Had the United States won the war, similar aplomb in democratising Vietnam might have been on display. In any case, the US government was more concerned with installing an anti-communist government, rather than promoting democratic reforms.

Success in Germany and Japan, moreover, was achieved by policies that focused on sweeping economic, political and educational reforms that affected the entire population for many years. Again, external interest and support for the same in these post-Cold War cases have not been nearly as significant, although it could also be argued that the first of these interventions only took place after 1989, and *democratic reforms need a solid and lengthy commitment before they take root*. In Germany, the Allies remained fully involved for six years after the writing of the constitution, a total of ten years from the end of the war – although the full-scale, intensive democratisation component lasted four years until mid-1949, when the formal occupation ended. After the Allies left, the US government continued to support German political and economic reforms for years until Germany became a stable, democratic state. As Richard Merritt explained of US success in democratising Germany, 'Its accomplishment require[d] clarity of goals, complete co-operation among the occupying powers, and withal persistence in the face of inner doubts, resistance to external criticism, and acceptance of the glacial pace inherent to the process.'[34] Of the cases examined Bosnia (and possibly Kosovo) will receive a greater commitment because of its location in Europe. Recall the comment in chapter 5 by the SFOR spokesperson that SFOR was working towards an 'end state' not an 'end date'.

Germany and Japan also differed from the cases discussed in this book (and Vietnam) because in the latter five, the United States essentially interfered in (un)civil, intra-state conflicts, while Germany and Japan fought against the Allies in inter-state wars of aggression. The US military prefers engagement in conventional conflicts and has more experience in this realm, even though civil conflicts now occur with much greater frequency. The conflicts in Panama, Somalia, Haiti, and Bosnia were caused by deep-rooted domestic problems, while Germany and

---

[34] Richard L. Merritt, *Democracy Imposed; US Occupation Policy and the German Public, 1945–1949,* New Haven, Yale University Press, 1995, p. xiii.

Japan lacked similar cleavages. In these four cases, sharp rifts and enormous disparities in wealth and education defined relations between the elite and the masses.

More international aid targeted directly at reducing poverty and illiteracy could obviously make a difference, but interest here is slight, particularly in the United States Congress, where government representatives want to spend less money and exert less energy, not more, abroad. Interestingly, studies have demonstrated that the US public in general supports spending on foreign affairs. In 1995, for example, the average American believed that the US government was spending at least five times more than the amount actually allocated. When told what the real figures were, the majority endorsed maintaining or increasing that amount, not reducing it.[35] Yet influential representatives in the US Congress continue to push for reductions in foreign assistance funding. And they have been successful in their campaign. *In 1997, less than 0.5 per cent of the total US budget went on foreign economic and humanitarian assistance.*[36]

This amount is not remotely comparable to that which enabled Germany and Japan to become stable democracies, to the benefit of the United States as well as its allies in terms of security, trade and political relations not to mention the benefits for the Germans and Japanese. For example, in 1948, the first year of the Marshall Plan (1948 to 1952), aid distributed to sixteen European states comprised 13 per cent of the entire US budget, and this total did not include all the costs incurred during the German occupation, and included none of the costs in Japan.[37] The equivalent for fiscal year 1997 would be $208 billion, in sharp contrast to the actual appropriation of $18.25 billion.[38] Although many Americans might claim that foreign assistance is no longer the priority it was after World War II, it is also true that the threat posed by recent conflicts to international peace and security is serious, and

[35] See, for example, 'Americans and Foreign Aid', Program on International Policy Attitudes, A joint program of the Center for the Study of Policy Attitudes and the Center for International and Security Studies of the University of Maryland, 23 January, 1995; or Kull, Destler and Ramsay, *The Foreign Policy Gap*.
[36] From the USAID home page on the Web (www.info.usaid.gov), December 1997.
[37] Curt Tarnoff, 'The Marshall Plan: Design, Accomplishments, and Relevance to the Present', Congressional Research Service, Report For Congress, First Published 6 January 1997.
[38] Author's calculation. Budget information provided by US State Department home page on the Web (www.state.gov).

could be mitigated if developing countries were given more targeted aid. As Paul Hoffman articulated back in 1967,

Today, the United States, its former partners in the Marshall Plan and – in fact – all other advanced industrialized countries . . . are being offered an even bigger bargain: the chance to form an effective partnership for world-wide economic and social progress with the earth's hundred and more low-income nations. The potential profits in terms of expanded prosperity and a more secure peace could dwarf those won through the European Recovery Program. Yet the danger that this bargain will be rejected out of apathy, indifference, and discouragement over the relatively slow progress toward self-sufficiency made by the developing countries thus far is perhaps even greater than was the case with the Marshall Plan. For the whole broad-scale effort of development assistance to the world's poorer nations . . . has never received the full support it merits and is now showing signs of further slippage in both popular and governmental backing.[39]

Development assistance thirty years on shows signs of slipping even further.

Money alone is not the answer, and in many cases foreign assistance comprises too large a percentage of the GDP of poor states, and often even enables non-democratic rulers to stay in power. In the Gambia before the 1994 coup, for example, foreign aid comprised 10 per cent of national income, while in Somalia before its collapse, foreign aid reached 70 per cent of the national budget. It is also possible that many of these states would have been far better off without the aid in the first place, as it tends to enrich only the elite at the expense of the masses.

Whenever the public-foreign-aid to private-foreign-investment ratio is disproportionately in favour of the former, the economies in question are less likely to grow, while aid dependency soon thereafter becomes the *modus vivendi*. Financial assistance that encourages states to be responsible for their economic and political development does work, as occurred in Germany and Japan. Ian Davis commented, 'The need here is to see recovery as a vital therapeutic process that provides much needed work for a traumatised community and possibly also provides them with a much needed income that can assist them to recover.'[40]

[39] Paul G. Hoffman was the head of Economic Cooperation Administration of the US Congress appointed by President Truman. The quote comes from 'Peace Building – Its Price and Its Profits', *Foreign Service Journal*, June 1967, p. 19.

[40] Ian Davis, 'Defining Roles for Military and Civilian Authorities in Disasters linked to Development Planning', paper presented at *Defence, Disaster, Development: Security in the Third Millennium*, 15–16 December 1997, Prague, Czech Republic. Although he was referring to disaster relief, the same could be applied to post-conflict reconstruction.

State collapse and reconstruction

Reconstruction of states – and this does not simply mean a restoration of the *status quo ante* – requires a comprehensive strategy, tailored to the level of state disintegration. This final section discusses why states collapse, and what possibilities exist for successful political reconstruction.[41]

State collapse and international security   The dissolution of the Soviet empire led to the largest wave of state creation since the end of World War II; since 1989, membership of the United Nations has grown by 16 per cent. Ironically, this recent increase has also largely upheld the tenuous compromise reached after 1945, namely, that new states could only be created by decolonisation, and then only within existing national boundaries. All other attempts at secession were proscribed, with the formation of Bangladesh in 1971 the only clear-cut exception to this rule. The new generation of states recognised after the demise of the Soviet empire in fact corresponds to the three earlier waves of state creation: in the nineteenth century after the withdrawal of the Spanish and Portuguese from their Latin American empires, in 1918 after the fall of the European dynastic empires, and in 1945 after the collapse of the European overseas empires in Asia, Africa, the Caribbean, and the Pacific.

In contrast to the post-World War II period, however, a new phenomenon now also accompanies the end of empire: a sharp increase in the number of imploded (or imploding) states. Indeed, the process by which the latter takes place could be considered a microcosm of the former. If a collapsing empire resembles a tree with dense branches, then a collapsing state would similarly correspond to the repetitive pattern on one particular branch of the tree viewed from up close (which in turn is akin to the pattern on one twig). While empires disintegrate because of over-extension and over-expenditure on defence (to greatly simplify Paul Kennedy's thesis), which in turn causes centralised controls to disband, states collapse for similar reasons.

A state collapses when public institutions, legitimate authority, law and political order (including the police and judiciary) disintegrate, and

---

[41] Although reference to *failed states* has become routine in recent years, this author endorses the terms *collapsed* or *imploded*, as the former word implies that there are standards of success to which all states aspire, which is not the case. The term also suggests that if an unruly dictator had maintained control over the mechanisms of the state, it would therefore not have failed.

most state assets are either destroyed or stolen.[42] This happens when states are unable to contain the disruptive forces that contribute to the deterioration of central authority, such as corruption, ethnic and territorial disputes, humanitarian disasters, international interference, too much spending on defence, and refugee flows. The majority of collapsed and collapsing states are in Africa, where 34 per cent of the total number of states have done one or the other.

Burundi, Central African Republic, Congo-Brazzaville, Liberia, Mozambique, Rwanda, Sierra Leone, Somalia, and the former Zaire have imploded at least once in the past decade (although several are attempting to rebuild and have already reinstated fragile governments), while Algeria, Chad, the Comoros, Guinea-Bissau, Mali, Nigeria, Sudan, and Zambia have been at risk during the same period. The only major difference between a collapsed and a collapsing state is that in the latter, the government still controls the capital city, and therefore maintains some control over the economy and security.[43] When the state collapses, chaos engulfs the capital city as well, and aid agencies and foreign embassies withdraw.

As mentioned, ethnic, religious and boundary disputes partially account for the collapse of these states, which is hardly surprising in Africa considering that African borders were drawn by Europeans without regard to ethnic groups, religion or physical territorial markers.[44]

[42] See Karin von Hippel, 'The Proliferation of Collapsed States in the Post-Cold War World', in Michael Clarke, ed., *Brassey's Defence Yearbook 1997*, London, Centre for Defence Studies, 1997, pp. 193–209, for more information.

[43] The governments in both Nigeria and Sudan still control territory outside the capital, with networks that extend throughout the state. These two cases thus have not reached the stage that the others listed in the group have. By mid-1999, with the election of General Obasanjo, Nigeria looks the most promising of the aforementioned areas.

[44] In most African states, borders cut across ethnic groups, in fact, a total of 191 ethnic groups are split by boundaries between states. This means that every African state has at least one ethnic group that is divided by an international boundary. Thirteen of these are shared by Cameroon and Nigeria, ten between Kenya and Uganda, twenty-one by Burkina Faso's territorial limits, while the Berbers and the Swazis are ethnic groups that are separated by eleven and three boundaries respectively. The diversity of ethnic groups within Africa's fifty-three states is even more impressive than is suggested by the number of groups that bestride more than one border because Africa is home to 2,000 (or 25 per cent) of the total number of ethnic groups in the world, and this also partially accounts for the high number of intra-state conflicts in Africa. While the former Somali Republic was ethnically as homogenous as conceivable and one of the few real nations in Africa (in addition to Botswana, Lesotho, and Swaziland), and Rwanda and Burundi are predomi-

Similar conflicts pervade other parts of the world where states are at risk, such as in Afghanistan, the Balkans, and parts of the former Soviet Union, where borders also did not result from consensus. The resurgence of nationalism in the past ten years has indeed touched most parts of the world, and undermined many burgeoning democracies.[45]

In addition to internal pressures, international factors and actors have also abetted the process of state collapse. The Superpowers supported many non-democratic rulers during the Cold War through the provision of arms and economic assistance, but withdrew the majority of this 'aid' after 1989. Since then, the imposition of sanctions and pressure applied by multilateral lending agencies for political reforms have also stymied the cash flow. This fairly sudden withdrawal of financial and political support, in turn, unleashed forces that contributed to the implosion or partial implosion of these states, which were mostly governed in an overly centralised fashion. This is particularly true in matters pertaining to ethnic minorities, which in most cases have not been allowed to manage their own affairs.

Additionally, as mentioned in chapter 4, the multilateral lending agencies, along with major western powers, now push most rogue regimes to hold elections without providing concomitant political development assistance. These electoral demands have also contributed to state collapse, or partial collapse, in several instances. For example, after international pressure, elections were held in Algeria in 1991, only to be cancelled by the military government before the next round because it appeared probable that the Islamic party (FIS) would win. This action added fuel to the already burgeoning civil conflict in the country, while the feeble outcry by the western powers demonstrated their hypocrisy because they did not want to see a fundamentalist party ruling an already unstable region.

nantly bi-ethnic states (the majority Hutus and minority Tutsis), Zambia is home to 72 ethnic groups, Nigeria has possibly 395 (although three major ethnic groups – the Hausa, Yoruba and Ibo – control most of the state), and the Sudan has 19 major ethnic groups and 597 'distinct sub-groups' plus a Muslim/Christian divide just in case things weren't bad enough. Ieuan L. Griffiths, *The African Inheritance*, London, Routledge, 1995, pp. 91–2, 131.

[45] See Karin von Hippel, 'The Resurgence of Nationalism and its International Implications', in Brad Roberts, ed., *Order and Disorder after the Cold War*, Cambridge, MA, CSIS, MIT Press, 1995, for more information. This is not to say that during the Cold War these conflicts did not exist, but rather that they were not given the attention they now receive due to the overarching policy of containment. For more information, see James Mayall, 'Sovereignty, Nationalism and Self-Determination', *Political Studies*, 47, 1999, pp. 474–502.

In Rwanda, international pressure for elections probably played a role in the 1994 genocide. The hastily assembled constitution included guarantees to safeguard minority rights, but it was forced on a public already embroiled in a civil war without adequate preparation, participation or explanation of its purpose. Rwanda, in turn, adversely affected the situations in Burundi, the former Zaire, Congo-Brazzaville, Central African Republic, and even Zambia, contributing to the collapse or partial collapse of these states due to the spill-over effect from the enormous refugee flows, and the desire for revenge that ignored boundaries.[46]

Despite their contribution to these crises, wealthier states are no longer interested in the African emergencies (except in parts of North Africa, because of its proximity to southern Europe), primarily because of the Somalia débâcle, but also because they do not directly affect their security interests. Emergency migratory flows typically go to neighbouring states, while the region is non-nuclear. In today's zero-sum game of international assistance, the attention lens focuses on the complex emergencies that are in the vicinity of the wealthier nations. Even the few 'success' stories on the continent are considered high risks for foreign investment, while African organisations and states have neither the financial nor political wherewithal to cope on their own.

Whereas most other crises attract more international attention – be it in Bosnia and therefore part of Europe, Indonesia and therefore important for East Asian security, Afghanistan and therefore sandwiched between fundamentalist Iran, nuclear Pakistan, and unstable Central Asian republics – the crises in Africa also affect international security and pose a great risk to an already unstable international order. Imploding states interfere with international trade, create large numbers of refugees and IDPs, have the potential to destabilise neighbouring states and even regions, and in several instances have contributed to their collapse, as occurred in the Balkans, East Africa, and the Great Lakes region, and much of West Africa. Robert Kaplan explained with reference to the hundreds of thousands of Liberian and Sierra Leonian refugees and IDPs that have fled into each other's territories, and into neighbouring Guinea and Ivory Coast, 'the borders dividing these four countries have become largely meaningless'.[47]

---

[46] This point does not downplay the significant involvement and pressure exerted by neighbouring countries in all these conflicts, but the international pressure to democratise played a role as well.

[47] Robert Kaplan, 'The Coming Anarchy', *The Atlantic Monthly*, February 1994.

The ultimate option of the West, military intervention, will always be a last resort to be used in extreme cases, yet there are other types of pressure to apply. Inhabitants of collapsed states have an incentive to rehabilitate their public institutions as most multilateral aid agencies, especially the World Bank and the IMF, are prevented by their articles of agreement from granting loans to non-state entities. Yet these same organisations need to understand their contribution to the crisis in the first place before reinvesting, as do major international powers, who are often content to have semi-strong-men in power so that the seat at the UN is filled and some semblance of order reappears. When that strong-man later misbehaves, these powers try to remove him through many of the means already mentioned, leading once again to state collapse and further attempts by the West to rebuild the state. Accordingly, it is of utmost importance to attend to the means of countering state collapse.

The trilateral approach to rebuilding collapsed states: an old approach to a new problem   A strategy for rebuilding and democratising states *after* intervention needs to consider three fundamental elements: re-establishing security, empowering civil society and strengthening democratic institutions, and co-ordinating international efforts. The three are necessarily linked and cannot be fully implemented without the others. For example, strengthened democratic institutions will not endure unless the state maintains the legal monopoly on force.

This strategy can be utilised in situations of state collapse, as well as in those where states are at risk; it just needs to be adapted to the level of state disintegration. In Panama and Haiti, the elected leaders could at least be reinstated, and thus democratisation efforts built on the shaky democratic foundations, while Somalia and Yugoslavia were hampered by other considerations that impeded them from reaching this stage, particularly how to cope with war-lords. Elements of this approach were indeed applied in the cases discussed in this book, but not in a holistic fashion, which can also account for the problems encountered. The trilateral strategy is in fact nothing new: it resembles that adopted successfully by the Allies in Germany and Japan. Can it be applied to a new and different type of crisis?

Re-establishing security.   Prior to implementing democratic reforms and as a necessary step in upholding them, the state needs to re-establish a sufficient degree of security. In most developing states, governments are unable to do this. Instead, they are forced to share protection with a number of non-state actors, who may be called war-lords, the Mafia, rebels, guerrillas, terrorists, or paramilitaries. The restoration and maintenance of governmental control over security is contingent upon military, police, and judicial reforms.

Some states choose to abolish the *armed forces* entirely and maintain only the police, as in Costa Rica, Haiti, or Panama. An alternative could be to retrain the military for domestic concerns, such as border patrols for trafficking in drugs, arms and/or nuclear materials, anti-terrorism, coastal/environmental protection, disaster management, and rebuilding infrastructure (e.g., an engineer corps). Military reforms should also include a reduction in defence expenditure. The UN in 1995 proposed a 20:20 contract, for developed countries to spend at least 20 per cent of their overseas aid, and less developed states to spend 20 per cent of their budgets, on basic needs, instead of weapons.

Police reform is also vital, and has been a major component of the cases in this book. In most situations, an entirely new force is necessary, one that could ensure public safety and gain the confidence of the local population. The goal is to achieve a comprehensive change in mindset of the local police and of the public, as previously the police (and military) had only served to terrify civilians through extortion and torture, instead of providing protection.[48]

Thus far, the newly trained forces have inevitably included some members of the old force due to the lack of experienced personnel, and the belief that it would take longer to train an entire corps of new officers than to retrain some of the old. Such a policy has not been without controversy, although the method applied in Haiti appears to have garnered more domestic support (i.e., phasing out the old force in increments, while simultaneously recruiting and training new troops). The model used in Bosnia also displays the advances in promoting accountability by international police trainers.

Judicial reforms are also necessary and linked to other security sector reforms. Many excellent training organisations already exist, such as ICITAP, while watch-dog organisations, such as Human Rights Watch, ensure that the training bodies maintain high standards. Without accountable criminal investigative procedures, trained judges and lawyers, and prisons that adhere to fundamental human rights standards, police reform would be redundant.

The soon-to-be established international criminal court could also send the appropriate message to would-be criminals to adhere to

---

[48] See, for example, William Stanley and Charles T. Call, 'Building a New Civilian Police Force in El Salvador', in Krishna Kumar, ed., *Rebuilding Societies After Civil War: Critical Roles for International Assistance*, Lynne Rienner, Boulder, 1997, pp. 107–34.

international law, especially when the state has broken down. This court may take the pressure off countries emerging from civil war, such as Rwanda and Bosnia, with scarce resources and overwhelming demands to bring perpetrators to justice. If a war-lord is aware that he may be called to task for massive human rights abuses, irrespective of the existence of a central authority, he may be less likely to commit such crimes. The attention paid by a number of Somali war-lords to the Pinochet affair, after he was arrested in London in October 1998, testifies to this point.[49] And even if the court did not deter crimes, at least it would prevent the international community from negotiating with particular war-lords if they have been indicted.[50] This, in turn, could allow members of civil society to resume positions of authority.

Demilitarisation is also a priority, albeit extremely difficult to achieve, especially in heavily armed societies, such as Somalia (or the United States). This would include disarmament, demobilisation, and demining as integral components, with the aim of reintegrating militia and soldiers into civil society.[51] Germany and Japan were thoroughly demilitarised by the Allies, as well as re-educated about the need for this. This also included a purge of the nasty elements in both societies who had contributed to the war. Purging the guilty helps to rebuild trust, which in turn leads to greater individual responsibility, as people are made aware of the direct consequences of their actions, and hopefully will thus not attempt to violate humanitarian law.

Little political will currently exists to become so extensively involved in demilitarisation due to the fear of casualties. An alternative model may be to extend new forms of community-based security, which recognise the right to bear arms, but impose effective discipline through the authority of local councils and elders. Modelled on Switzerland, this could form the basis of a citizen's army if one is required. In north-west Somalia (or Somaliland), major disarmament has occurred in such a fashion, and those who carry guns are members of the police, not the militia. This has been accomplished primarily without foreign assistance.

[49] Author discussions in Kenya and Somalia, 1999.
[50] This point was informed by discussions with Mohamed Abshir 'Waldo', who has assisted in the formation of a regional government in north-east Somalia, called Puntland.
[51] For more information about different ways of disarming, see Joanna Spear, 'Arms Limitations, Confidence Building Measures, and Internal Conflict', in Michael Brown, ed., *The International Dimensions of Internal Conflict*, Cambridge, MA, MIT Press, 1996.

Undertaking reparations to those who lost their homes or property during the conflict, or a restoration of the property if possible, also helps to build trust, and was again successfully accomplished in Germany. Germany and Japan also taught us that the domestic population needs to be convinced of the mission. Public relations in the post-Cold War cases have indeed improved since Panama and Somalia through intensive public information activities by civilians and the military.

Security sector reform need not be an overwhelming task, but it does need to be adapted depending on the particularities of each case. In some instances, it may be possible for external powers to control the reform process, while in others, it may need to be domestically-dominated. Development aid in the United Kingdom, for example, is increasingly concerned with these reforms, while expertise exists in many countries. A permanent security sector reform unit could be established at UN headquarters, perhaps in conjunction with UNSECOORD, to co-ordinate all police, military and judicial reform activities, and manage scarce resources to help prevent overlap, in situations of state collapse or for states at risk. Such a centre could operate in a similar fashion to the Electoral Assistance Division of the Department of Political Affairs at the UN, with an expert consultant database continuously updated.

Empowering civil society.   Linked to the question of security is the need to consider the influence of non-state actors, especially warlords, particularly when the state collapses. When a state collapses, pathological short-termism and fear prevail, while power devolves to villages and streets, where war-lords thrive exactly because there is no state. Because war-lords contributed to the collapse, they are then in a position to consolidate their power by controlling strategic resources (e.g., diamond mines) and valuable real estate (e.g., ports and airports), for use of which they charge heavy access fees.

The intervening power's choice of 'authority' in any negotiations, therefore, can have serious repercussions, as in Somalia during UNOSOM II when Aideed was empowered at home and abroad by being branded Enemy Number One by the US government. At the time, and indeed today, there has in fact been a plethora of war-lords operating throughout Somalia, with no one war-lord controlling the entire territory – an important point that the international community misread and continues to. As Kenneth Allard remarked, 'During operations where a government does not exist, peacekeepers must avoid actions that would effectively confer legitimacy on one individual or organisation at the expense of another.'[52]

Moreover, because internationally sponsored 'reconciliation' meetings held since the start of that conflict have been composed primarily of war-lords, and therefore not inclusive of Somali clans, traditional leaders and other members of civil society, they always fail: the most recent example was the 1997 Cairo initiative.[53] Although faction leaders may claim control over large chunks of territory, they are incapable of delivering their promised constituencies since their rule is fluid and dependent on their military strength. Once they lose control of a port or airport, for example, which is inevitable due to the intense competition over pieces of the ever-diminishing rubble that is erroneously viewed as pie, they can no longer pay their militias, who subsequently move on to the next highest bidder.

Parts of Bosnia are similarly controlled by war-lords; descriptions of the regions now incorporate the term 'feudalism' with frequency. When Biljana Plavsic became President of the Republika Srpska in 1996, with backing from the US government, she started to denounce the corruption, claiming on Pale television that in the Republika, 'police are involved in smuggling and stealing from their own state . . . where a majority of the population is living in abject poverty'. She also asserted that bribery was the norm, while the government was not paying teachers or doctors.[54] Fortunately for her in this case, she was backed by NATO troops and western policy makers in her opposition to Karadjic, who has the support of the Serbian police and state television. Yet she still faces an uphill struggle, and her replacement may not continue her policy.

When more attention is paid to the war-lords, this usually occurs at the expense of traditional leaders from civil society. Ignoring the faction leaders entirely is arguably ineffective, since they control the situation on the ground and will need to relinquish their hold if peace is to be realised, as eventually occurred in Haiti. In Bosnia, however, Karadzic

---

[52] Kenneth Allard, *Somalia Operations: Lessons Learned*, Fort McNair, Washington, DC, Institute for National Strategic Studies, National Defense University Press, 1995, pp. 8–9. See also Alexandros Yannis, 'State Collapse and Prospects for Political Reconstruction and Democratic Governance in Somalia', *African Yearbook of International Law*, 5, 1997, pp. 23–47.

[53] See, for example, 'Somali Warlord Denies Blocking Peace Process', Agence France Press (AFP), 24 February 1998; or 'Baidoa Conference Off, 26 Factions Say', AFP, 9 February 1998.

[54] Lawrence Weschler, 'High Noon at Twin Peaks', Letter from the Republika Srpska, *The New Yorker*, 18 August 1997, p. 33.

and Mladic's exclusion from Dayton and subsequent exclusion from political participation (because of their indictment by the International War Crimes Tribunal) has allowed other leaders to emerge and participate, although the two still wield enormous influence because they have not been completely ostracised or arrested, and many other politicians who have assumed office in the FRY as well as in the Republika Srpska are equally hard-line nationalists.[55]

Even though Karadzic and Mladic did not participate in Dayton, the international community still negotiated with Milosevic, who was also accused by some of crimes against humanity, if not of starting the entire war in the former Yugoslavia. This issue resurfaced in the crisis in Kosovo that erupted in summer 1998 and again in early 1999, when Milosevic was finally made international pariah during the NATO bombing campaign. Had he been excluded from Dayton and called to task for his responsibility in the wars in Yugoslavia, perhaps the subsequent humanitarian crisis that led to the bombing campaign might not have reached such a dire state. *Leaders from civil society should be included in all negotiations.* They still maintain respect in their communities, and could be capable of convincing those with weapons to disarm and negotiate, if sufficiently empowered.

The final and perhaps the most important reason to focus on leaders from civil society, rather than those with guns, is that democracy is not a priority for the latter, who are mainly concerned with sustaining and aggrandising their real estate. When war-lords discuss the composition of a future state, the debate tends to focus on who will fill which post in the next government – particularly the positions of president, prime minister and minister of finance – not what type of government should be established. Further, the normal assumption is that the new state will be unitary, because this type of state is easier to dominate.

In direct contrast, members of civil society have a vested interest in promoting democratic reforms that include power-sharing mechanisms and decentralisation of power that could help to ensure that war-lords (or another dictator) cannot maintain control. For example, during meetings with Somali civil society leaders in 1996 and 1997, sponsored by the European Commission, the majority of participants converged on their decision to establish the most decentralised state possible, with very strong power-sharing mechanisms to prevent one person usurping

---

[55] As mentioned in more detail in chapter 5, it was unclear if Karadzic and Mladic's exclusion from Dayton signified that Milosevic indeed wielded the power, or if their exclusion caused them to lose power.

power at the centre.[56] Throughout this period, the war-lords continued to meet in different venues, normally outside Somalia, sponsored at great cost by different regional powers, where the discussion never broached what kind of state Somalia would be, but only who would fill which position in the next *unitary* state.

Special emphasis should also be placed on the inclusion of women as their role is often enhanced during civil conflicts because traditional male-dominated structures break down. Pressure and attention from the international community and NGOs can help to empower members of civil society in these negotiations. The alternative, which is always the easiest option to choose, is to allow these war-lords to be the ones responsible for establishing a state, which is how most European states developed. Charles Tilly argued that European states were formed by the very same war-lords who eventually became weary of the day-to-day insecurity that they themselves created. In order to ward off other marauders, they therefore legitimated their position by establishing a strong central authority that assured continued control.[57]

This attitude is based on the erroneous assumption by many members of the international community that *any* state is better than no state. As Sigurd Illing, EC Special Envoy to Somalia, argued, 'No one can convince me that Hitler Germany was better than no German government, or that the Pol Pot government was better than no Cambodian government.'[58] Since Siad Barre's downfall in 1991, Somalis are determined

---

[56] The author, who worked as a consultant to the European Commission, organised meetings in Kenya in 1996 and in different parts of Somalia in 1997 with leaders from civil society, where these preferences were voiced. See also, for example, Letter to the Somali National Salvation Council from George B. Moose, US Assistant Secretary of State, 30 July 1997, regarding one such meeting with war-lords. The Americans stressed that the meeting should be inclusive of all groups and members of civil society, and reflecting the policy promoted by the EC, he noted, 'A second factor which the United States regards as crucial to the success of the anticipated conference is that participants address structural issues of governance, not merely the composition of a future government. Formation of a nationally representative cabinet is only one of the tasks that challenge Somalis. More fundamental to the needs of the people is the creation of a national vision and a specific plan to achieve it.'

[57] Charles Tilly, 'War Making and State Making as Organized Crime', in Peter Evans, ed., *Bringing the State Back In*, Cambridge, Cambridge University Press, 1985, pp. 169–191.

[58] Interview with the author, EC Somalia Unit, Nairobi, Kenya, 22 September 1997.

to avoid another dictator, and they have demonstrated time and again that any authority that is not viewed as legitimate will not be accepted, which is why they have been without a central government for so long.

Somalia is viewed by many as an anarchic society, yet in many respects, Somalia has more accountability than many so-called 'intact' states. For example, today in some parts of Somalia, electricity lights up the streets at night (a service sadly lacking in most of neighbouring Kenya). Somalis are willing to pay for local services that directly affect their lives, but not to some nebulous 'central authority'.[59] In some regions of the country, such as the north-west/Somaliland and the north-east/Puntland, trade flourishes with export revenues exceeding pre-collapse rates, and local and regional administrations function with traditional and religious authorities acting as legislative and constitutional assemblies that legitimise their authority. Thus it could be argued that Somalia without a government is better off than a centralised, non-representative Somali government, which counters Alexander Hamilton's famous remark: 'A NATION without a NATIONAL GOVERNMENT is, in my view, an awful spectacle.'[60]

It is also possible that the international community's rigid adherence to the Montevideo Convention of 1933 exacerbates conflict. To gain recognition under international law, a state needs to have a defined territory, a population, effective government, and the capacity to enter into international relations. Fulfilment of these conditions is necessary for recognition, yet their erosion or disappearance later in time does not mandate that it should thereafter be withdrawn. The application of such a principle would decertify a large number of states, mostly in Africa, and in some parts of the former Soviet Union and former Yugoslavia, where borders are largely insignificant and porous, disputes rampant, and governments systemically corrupt and unable to control much territory outside the capital, if that. In fact, only the fourth stipulation is still met by some collapsing states, and while having a 'population' merely signifies that the territory is not *terra nullius*, in many of these states several borders are straddled by populations of which the members often hold more allegiance to their ethnic group than the state.

In some instances, war-lords only need to grab the centre, because

---

[59] Another example of a free and non-regulated market comes from Mogadishu. Currently there are three mobile telephone companies competing for business in the city. One company now offers a free phone and free local calls as an inducement to use its service. Again, in nearby Kenya, a mobile phone and local calls are prohibitively expensive.

[60] Alexander Hamilton, *The Federalist Papers*, edited by Isaac Kramnick, Harmondsworth, Penguin, 1987, p. 487.

they then fulfil the convention, which in turn allows them to receive foreign aid and all the other goodies that come with state recognition. This is also why fighting during civil wars is heavily concentrated in the capital city. If the international community could instead institute a mechanism for removing recognition until such time that the state demonstrated a commitment to establish a representative government that respected fundamental human rights, perhaps this might reduce the scramble by war-lords for control of the state.

Strengthening democratic institutions. The international community, led by the United States and Europe, can also help to buttress the power base of members of civil society through fortifying (or establishing) democratic and transparent institutions. This can be accomplished through programmes that strengthen the rule of law, enhance respect for human rights, support international electoral observers, improve financial management and accountability, promote decentralisation, expand civilian control of the military, and improve electoral processes, legislatures, political parties, the media, and education at all levels of society. Additionally, the development and implementation of democratic constitutional arrangements with power-sharing mechanisms is also a priority. The military purges in Germany and Japan were accompanied by a thorough democratisation programme, which also included security guarantees for the region. A modern version would not be as all-encompassing due to financial and political constraints, but the expertise certainly exists and could be pooled.

It is also true, however, that the international community may have to accept that the Westphalian state-based system may not endure for much longer in all parts of the world, especially in Africa.[61] Something entirely new may need to replace the old order so that the state will not revert to the situation that caused the intervention in the first place, as occurred in Somalia after UNOSOM left. In Haiti, this worry has caused the Security Council to renew the mandate of the peace support operation numerous times, and in Bosnia, SFOR was extended past its June 1998 deadline for similar reasons. Yet this 'something' may have to take the shape of a 'government' that stretches beyond the state's external frontiers – democracy should be flexible enough to be adapted to entities without central governments.

One approach may be greater decentralisation, at least for the African

---

[61] See Jeffrey Herbst, 'Alternatives to the Current Nation-States in Africa', *International Security*, 21, 3, Winter 1996/7, for more information.

crises, where traditional culture and levels of command and authority operated at the local level before colonial powers interfered in the continent. Power could be devolved to villages and communities, even including those that cut across international borders. This example could also apply to many of the crises in the former Soviet Union, the former Yugoslavia, Afghanistan, Albania, or in terms of Russian relations with its 'near abroad'.

Consociational principles could also be used to realign loyalties within a larger regional grouping. Consociational arrangements provide options for power sharing between different groups, with jobs and public moneys distributed according to group sizes. They are based on the concept of separate but equal, and are feasible options for deeply divided societies. Each group administers its own community needs, such as education, and minorities are given the right to veto legislation. These principles apply irrespective of where members of a particular group live, and thus they are often referred to as non-territorial arrangements. Consociational principles can be used in any type of political system, from a unitary state to a loose confederation.

For example, in Africa, individuals could choose to associate with others of the same ethnic group (or preferred ethnic group in the case of mixed ethnic offspring), or even with others who share religious or political beliefs, or who speak the same language, regardless of where they live. All groupings of a certain size would then have a specified number of seats allocated within a larger unit, such as a confederation (see below). Smaller groups could choose to join with others to increase their strength.

If greater decentralisation is therefore needed, and consociational principles applied, then confederations could assist in loosening the state structure and reorganising the system. A confederation is a union of separate but equal states linked by international treaties. Confederations are created for specified purposes, such as for common defence or free trade, and the centre acts as a co-ordinating body only. Member states are given the right to veto or opt out of decisions that they feel damage their interests.

To take this example to its extreme – albeit unlikely – conclusion, loose confederations could be created in Africa, with membership drawn from these new associations in a manner that would assure loyalty to the confederation. Social psychologists have found that conflicts tend to be lessened if individuals feel that they belong to a particular group, while simultaneously perceiving that they are distinguishable from other groups – when the 'need for assimilation and inclusion' is combined with the 'need for differentiation'.[62] A confederation, if it is not too large, could enable individuals to belong to their state or association, within a regional confederation, satisfying the needs for inclusion and separation.[63] Thus there could be a North African Confederation, a West African Confederation, an East African Confederation, and a Southern African Confederation. The separate confederations could then have representation in the OAU.

The resulting overlap in loyalties, as attempted at Dayton, may also help to ameliorate crises caused by ethnic disputes. As mentioned in the previous chapter, this is indeed what transpired with the Swiss Confederation, which was forged after years of civil war and coups in various cantons, as well as outside intervention. Very diverse groups of people, speaking different languages and belonging to different religions, came together to create one of the most successful confederations, which later evolved into a federation as enough trust grew between the constituent members to allow for a greater transfer of sovereignty to the centre.[64]

Not only would it be difficult to convince those in power to relinquish their hold to allow for greater decentralisation, but major systemic changes normally only occur after a complete breakdown, such as the formation of the League of Nations and the United Nations after two world wars. In South Africa, the recent all-embracing political and societal upheavals were made possible by the holding of elections in which the entire population participated for the first time. Even at the micro-level, in business, for example, the best time to restructure a big

---

[62] Marilynn B. Brewer, 'When Contact is Not Enough: Social Identity and Intergroup Cooperation', *International Journal of Intercultural Relations* 20, 1996, p. 296.

[63] One of the reasons the former Soviet Union collapsed was that the union was far too grand to subsume the loyalties of so many different groups.

[64] Although the Swiss Confederation is called a confederation, it is in fact a federation. A federation is a grouping of free and independent states, which transfer limited amounts of sovereignty to federal institutions. The centre and the provinces share power, and the centre is unable, on its own authority, to change the constitution. Confederations might be a more viable option for most of Africa, especially when considering the history of failed federations in Africa. Of the attempted federations, or confederations between only two states in Africa, only that between Tanganyika and Zanzibar (1964) survives today, and even that union is currently under threat. All others, such as the Senegambian Confederation (1982–9), disintegrated. Confederations only need to meet common goals between the member states, such as for trade or defence purposes.

bureaucracy is when a major operational change takes place that jars the normal day-to-day running of the company, such as the installation of a new computer system or a take-over by another company.

Despite the crises subsuming many states today, they are occurring in small waves rather than all at once. Any significant reorganisation of states, therefore, is surely a pipe-dream, but the principles described above can work on smaller levels, which in turn could lead to greater changes on a step-by-step basis. The European Union may provide the proper inspiration as it has been evolving in a slow, yet consistent, fashion since the European Coal and Steel Community came into force in 1952. For example, regional free trade agreements could pave the way for pan-African (or Asian or Russian) economic integration. Further, if the international community finds itself in another Somalia-type situation, it would have more leeway to endorse a radical option.

Finally, in any political arrangement, safeguards can be instituted to protect minorities, but they will also need external support to ensure their implementation, which again means *prolonging the international presence until trust can be rebuilt.* Christopher's insistence on exit strategies should be disregarded – it is impossible to predict in advance when the moment will be right to disengage. The intervening powers should not therefore leave after elections have been held, as many in the US Congress would prefer, but instead should remain to support the domestic political and economic institutions as they grow, as indeed appears to be the case in Bosnia with SFOR.

If such programmes are not sustained, the only other way to prevent a recurrence of war is to carve the state into smaller, more ethnically pure pieces. This option sanctifies ethnic cleansing, but is unfortunately the one most likely to be chosen because it is less expensive and the time commitment is shorter. Consociational arrangements, in contrast, do not force populations to move because they are allowed to associate with others – no matter where they live.

Finally, as mentioned earlier concerning foreign assistance, *the composition of the post-conflict state must largely be decided by the inhabitants of those states to ensure ownership of the peace process, and in turn, success in its implementation.* As Christopher Dandeker noted, this is particularly the case when considering 'strategic peacekeeping' in complex emergencies where the solution may only come about through negotiations by the parties on the ground – and not by the third-party intervenor.[65] The best will in the world on behalf of the international community cannot

---

[65] From a lecture given by Professor Dandeker entitled, 'Military Culture and Peace Support Operations', King's College London, 10 December 1997.

replace local endorsement of democratisation. Political reconstruction needs to be managed and implemented by local actors, albeit with external pressure, advice (e.g., how to institute consociational practices) and some funding.

International co-ordination. Just as co-ordination is important during a peace support operation, so too is it vital during reconstruction. Due to the volatility of crisis environments and the multiplicity of external actors engaged in mediation and assistance efforts, international co-ordination has been increasingly considered a crucial element of involvement in conflict prevention, management and resolution. This is especially the case when dealing with a collapsed state, since there are no official counterparts on the ground with legitimate negotiating status.

The Afghanistan Programming Board, the Monitoring and Steering Group in Liberia and the Somalia Aid Co-ordination Body, which were all established on an *ad hoc* basis, are the best examples of such international co-ordinating mechanisms in situations of state collapse. In May 1997, the Organisation for Economic Co-operation and Development (OECD) issued a policy paper entitled 'Guidelines on Conflict, Peace and Development Cooperation', in which international co-ordination was considered a key principle for successful international involvement in crisis management. Although agreement has been reached that co-ordination is necessary, attempts to develop common objectives and principles on an international level are cursory at best. The five international communities that need to be co-ordinated are non-governmental organisations, donors/governments, multilateral organisations, militaries, and, significantly, the private sector.

The role of the private sector has largely been overlooked, even though foreign corporations also play an indirect – and sometimes direct – role in complex emergencies. Multi-national corporations can exacerbate conflicts, but they can also help in their resolution. Many mining and oil companies, for example, have a large stake in unstable regions and often wield enormous influence with whatever remnant of a government exists, and even in some cases, with rebel groups. They also offer employment essential during rehabilitation, and provide the most efficient means of tying post-conflict reconstruction requirements – such as communications, transport, water, sanitation, and housing – with other necessities such as employment creation and government income through tax returns.[66] Their inclusion in co-ordination efforts should be a priority.

[66] Informed from discussions with Nick Harvey.

Co-ordination of international efforts in reconstruction is particularly vital for the following reasons:

- to facilitate the adoption of common policies and responses,
- to prevent overlap of programmes,
- to maximise the effective use of available resources, and
- to promote a secure operational environment for aid activities (e.g., against hostage-taking, harassment, or extortion).

Although the UN already tasks certain agencies with the lead co-ordinating role, and others have been created in situations of state collapse, an effort should be made to institutionalise and expand the terms of reference of these bodies for all conflicts, as soon as they erupt.

The three components discussed in this section, security, democratisation and co-ordination, already exist at some level in most peace support and nation-building operations, yet they have not been regulated to the degree necessary to ensure wider coherence internationally. Each also needs to be augmented and strengthened. Only when they form part of the same overall strategic package can we hope to achieve greater synergy in future missions.

Former National Security Adviser Anthony Lake, who outlined the cautious-engagement approach adopted by the US government mentioned in chapter 1, concluded, 'Neither we nor the international community has either the responsibility or the means to do whatever it takes for as long as it takes to rebuild nations.'[67] Although this point is valid, he also admits their failure to comprehend the overall dilemma by his remark, 'whatever it takes'. This inability to conceptualise what it takes to rebuild states is associated with the recent increase in seemingly intractable conflicts, but it also signifies the lack of interest in addressing these crises in a comprehensive manner. Today's strong democracies in Germany and Japan reflect the value of such a commitment. More attention paid to resolving prevailing complex crises can thus ensure that future operations achieve similar success.

---

[67] Anthony Lake, Assistant to the President for National Security Afffairs, Remarks at George Washington University, 'Defining Missions, Setting Deadlines: Meeting New Security Challenges in the Post-Cold War World', 6 March, 1996.

Bibliography

BOOKS AND REPORTS

Alao, Abiodun, *The Burden of Collective Goodwill: International Involvement in the Liberian Civil War*, Ashgate, Aldershot, 1998.

Allard, Kenneth, *Somalia Operations: Lessons Learned*, Fort McNair, Washington, DC, Institute for National Strategic Studies, National Defense University Press, 1995.

Andreopoulos, George J. and Selesky, Harold E., eds., *The Aftermath of Defeat: Societies, Armed Forces, and the Challenge of Recovery*, New Haven, Yale University Press, 1994.

Appleman Williams, W., McCormick, T., Gardner, L., and LaFeber, W., eds., *America in Vietnam: A Documentary History*, New York, WW Norton and Co., 1989.

Bailey, Paul J., *Postwar Japan: 1945 to the Present*, Oxford, Blackwell, 1996.

Barker, J., Brett, E.A. Dawson, P. Lewis, I.M. McAuslan, P. Mayall, J. O'Leary, B, and von Hippel, K., *A Study of Decentralised Political Structures for Somalia: A Menu of Options*, London School of Economics and the European Union, commissioned by the European Union, EC Somalia Unit, with the Assistance of the United Nations Development Office for Somalia, August 1995.

Baumgartner, Frank R. and Jones, Bryan D., *Agendas and Instability in American Politics*, Chicago, Chicago University Press, 1993.

Bourantonis, Dimitris and Wiener, Jarrod, eds., *The United Nations in the New World Order: The World Organisation at Fifty*, Basingstoke, Macmillan, 1995.

Brown, Michael, ed., *The International Dimensions of Internal Conflict*, Cambridge, MA, MIT Press, 1996.

Brown, T. Louise, *War and Aftermath in Vietnam*, London, Routledge, 1991.

Bull, Hedley, ed., *Intervention in World Politics*, Oxford, Clarendon Press, 1985.

Carothers, Thomas, *In the Name of Democracy: US Policy Towards Latin America in the Reagan Years*, Berkeley, University of California Press, 1991.

Clarke, Michael, ed., *Brassey's Defence Yearbook 1997*, London, Centre for Defence Studies, 1997.

Clarke, Walter and Herbst, Jeffrey, eds., *Learning From Somalia*, Boulder, CO, Westview, February 1997.

Clarke, Walter and Herbst, Jeffrey, 'Somalia and the Future of Humanitarian Intervention', Center of International Studies, Monograph Series, No. 9, Princeton University, 1995.

Clay, Lucius D., *Decision in Germany*, New York, Doubleday, 1950.

Cohen, Leonard J., *Broken Bonds*, Boulder, CO, Westview, 2nd edition, 1995.

Crocker, Chester, and Hampson, Fen Osler with Aall, Pamela, eds., *Managing Global Chaos: Sources of and Responses to International Conflict*, Washington, DC, US Institute of Peace, 1996.

Drysdale, John, *Whatever Happened to Somalia? A Tale of Tragic Blunders*, London, Haan Associates, 1994.

Ermarth, Michael, ed., *America and the Shaping of German Society, 1945–1955*, Oxford, Berg, 1993.

Evans, Peter, ed., *Bringing the State Back In*, Cambridge, Cambridge University Press, 1985.

Fauriol, Georges A., ed., *Haitian Frustrations: Dilemmas for US Policy*, A Report of the CSIS Americas Program, CSIS, Washington, DC, 1995.

Fearey, Robert A., *The Occupation of Japan, Second Phase: 1948–50*, Westport, CT, Greenwood Press, 1950.

Fishel, John T., *The Fog of Peace: Planning and Executing the Restoration of Panama*, Carlisle, Pennsylvania, Strategic Studies Institute, US Army War College, 15 April 1992.

Friedmann, W., *The Allied Military Government of Germany*, London, Stevens & Sons, 1947.

Gimbel, John, *The American Occupation of Germany: Politics and the Military, 1945–1949*, Stanford, Stanford University Press, 1968.

Gow, James, *Triumph of the Lack of Will: International Diplomacy and the Yugoslav War*, London, Hurst and Company, 1997.

Griffiths, Ieuan L., *The African Inheritance*, London, Routledge, 1995.

Haass, Richard N., *Intervention: the Use of American Military Force in the Post-Cold War World*, Washington, DC, Carnegie Endowment for International Peace, 1994.

Hamilton, Alexander, *The Federalist Papers*, edited by Isaac Kramnick, Harmondsworth, Penguin Books, 1987.

Hayes, Richard E., 'Interagency and Political-Military Dimensions of Peace Operations: Haiti – A Case Study', edited by Dr Margaret Daly Hays and RAdm. Gary F. Weatley, USN (Ret.), Directorate of Advanced Concepts, Technologies, and Information Strategies, Institute for National Strategic Studies, National Defense University, NDU Press Book, February 1996.

Henkin, Louis, Hoffman, Stanley, and Kirkpatrick, Jeanne, eds., *Right vs. Might: International Law and the Use of Force*, 2nd edition, New York, Council on Foreign Relations, 1991.

Herring, George C., *America's Longest War: The United States and Vietnam, 1950–1975*, 2nd edition, New York, Alfred A. Knopf, 1986.

von Hippel, Karin, *Report on the First Seminar on Decentralised Political Structures for Somalia*, European Union, Lake Naivasha, Kenya, June 1996.

Report on the Second Seminar on Decentralised Political Structures for Somalia, European Union, Lake Nakuru, Kenya, November 1996.

Hirsch, John L. and Oakley, Robert B., *Somalia and Operation Restore Hope:*

Reflections on Peacemaking and Peacekeeping, Washington, DC, US Institute of Peace, 1995.

Hunter et al., 'White Paper: An Analysis of the Application of the Principles of Military Operations Other Than War (MOOTW) in Somalia', The Army–Air Force Center for Low Intensity Conflict, February 1994.

Huntington, Samuel P., *The Third Wave: Democratization in the Late Twentieth Century*, Norman, OK, University of Oklahoma Press, 1991.

Information and Pocket Guide to Germany, US Army Service Forces, 1944.

Jøergensen, Knud Erik, ed., *European Approaches to Crisis Management*, The Hauge, Kluwer International Press, 1997.

Karnow, Stanley, *Vietnam: A History*, London, Century Publishing, 1983.

Kingdon, John W., *Agendas, Alternatives and Public Policies*, New York, Harper Collins College Publishers, 1995.

Kull, Steven, Destler, I.M. and Ramsay, Clay, *The Foreign Policy Gap: How Policymakers Misread the Public*, College Park, MD., Center for International and Security Studies at Maryland, 1997.

Kumar, Krishna, ed., *Rebuilding Societies After Civil War: Critical Roles for International Assistance*, Boulder, CO, Lynne Rienner, 1997.

Lewis, I.M., *Blood and Bone*, New Jersey, The Red Sea Press, 1993.

A Modern History of Somalia: Nation and State in the Horn of Africa, Boulder, CO, Westview Press, 1988.

A Pastoral Democracy, New York, Africana Press, 1982.

Loser, Eva, ed., *Conflict Resolution and Democratization in Panama: Implications for US Policy*, Washington, DC, The Center for Strategic and International Studies, Significant Issues Series, Vol. XIV, No. 2, 1992.

Malcolm, Noel, *Bosnia: A Short History*, London, Macmillan, 1994.

Maren, Michael, *The Road to Hell: The Ravaging Effects of Foreign Aid and International Charity*, Amazon Press, 1997.

Martin, Edward M., *The Allied Occupation of Japan*, Westport, CT, Greenwood Press Publishers, 1972.

The May 7, 1989 Panamanian Elections, Washington, DC, National Democratic Institute for International Affairs and National Republican Institute for International Affairs, 1989.

Mayall, James, ed., *The New Interventionism, 1991–1994: United Nations Experience in Cambodia, former Yugoslavia and Somalia*, Cambridge, Cambridge University Press, 1996.

Menkhaus, Ken and Prendergast, John, 'The Political Economy of Post-Intervention Somalia', *Somalia Task Force Issue Paper 3* (published on the Internet), April 1995.

Merritt, Richard L., *Democracy Imposed: US Occupation Policy and the German Public, 1945–1949*, New Haven, Yale University Press, 1995.

The Military Balance, London, International Institute of Strategic Studies, 1996/97.

Mitrany, David, *A Working Peace System*, Chicago, Quadrangle Books, 1966.

Nishi, Toshio, *Unconditional Democracy: Education and Politics in Occupied Japan, 1945–1952*, Stanford, Hoover Institution Press, 1982.

Owen, David, *Balkan Odyssey*, London, Indigo, 1996.

Peterson, Edward N., *The American Occupation of Germany: Retreat to Victory*, Detroit, Wayne State University Press, 1977.
Prunier, Gérard, *The Rwanda Crisis: History of a Genocide, 1959–1994*, Kampala, Fountain Publishers, 1995.
Roberts, Brad, ed., *Order and Disorder After the Cold War*, Cambridge, MA, CSIS, MIT Press, 1995.
Sahnoun, Mohamed, *Somalia: the Missed Opportunities*, Washington, DC, US Institute of Peace, 1994.
Shultz, Richard H., Jr., *In the Aftermath of War: US Support for Reconstruction and Nation-Building in Panama Following Just Cause*, Maxwell Air Force Base, AL, Air University Press, 1993.
Silber, Laura and Little, Allan, *The Death of Yugoslavia*, London, Penguin Books/BBC Books, 1995.
SIPRI Yearbook 1996, Stockholm, Stockholm International Peace Research Institute, 1996.
Soler Torrijos, Giancarlo, *La Invasion a Panama: Estrategia y Tacticas para el Nuevo Orden Mundial*, Panama, CELA, 1993.
Spencer, Claire, ed., *Brassey's Defence Yearbook 1999*, London, Brassey's, 1999.
Turner, Ian D., ed., *Reconstruction in Post-War Germany: British Occupation Policy and the Western Zones, 1945–1955*, Oxford, Berg, 1989.
Ullman, Richard H., ed., *The World and Yugoslavia's Wars*, New York, The Council on Foreign Relations, 1996.
UNHCR, *The State of the World's Refugees*, Oxford, Oxford University Press, 1995.
Volden, Ketil and Smith, Dan, eds., *Causes of Conflict in the Third World*, Oslo, North/South Coalition and International Peace Research Institute, 1997.
Willis, F. Roy, *The French in Germany, 1945–1949*, Stanford, Stanford University Press, 1962.
Woodward, Bob, *The Commanders*, London, Simon and Schuster, 1991.
Woodward, Susan, *Balkan Tragedy: Chaos and Dissolution after the Cold War*, Washington, DC, The Brookings Institution, 1995.
Zartman, I. William, ed., *Collapsed States: The Disintegration and Restoration of Legitimate Authority*, Boulder and London, Lynne Rienner, 1995.

JOURNAL ARTICLES AND SHORT PAPERS

The American Society of International Law, Proceedings of the 84th Annual Meeting, Washington, DC, 28–31 March 1990.
Berdal, Mats, 'The United Nations in International Relations', *Review of International Studies*, 22, 1996.
'Bosnia and Hercegovina: Beyond Restraint, Politics and the Policing Agenda of the UN International Police Task Force', *Human Rights Watch Report*, 10, 5, June 1998.
Brewer, Marilynn B., 'When Contact is Not Enough: Social Identity and Intergroup Cooperation', *International Journal of Intercultural Research* 20, 1996.
Bryden, Matt, 'Strategy and Programme of Action in Support of Local and

Regional Administrations in Somalia in the Field of Institution-Building', A Draft Proposal to the EC Somalia Unit (unpublished), October 1996.

Carothers, Thomas, 'The Democracy Nostrum', *World Policy Journal*, 11, 3, Fall 1994.

Chopra, Jarat and Weiss, Thomas G., 'Sovereignty is no Longer Sacrosanct: Codifying Humanitarian Intervention', *Ethics and International Affairs*, 6, 1992.

'Civil Affairs in *Operation Just Cause*', *Special Warfare*, 4, Winter 1991.

Fish, John T. and Downie, Richard D., 'Taking Responsibility for Our Actions: Establishing Order and Stability in Panama', *Military Review*, April 1992.

Franck, Thomas, 'The Emerging Right to Democratic Governance', *The American Journal of International Law*, 86, 46, 1992.

Freedman, Lawrence, 'Why the West Failed', *Foreign Policy*, 97, Winter 1994–95.

Frenderschub, Helmut, 'Between Universalism and Collective Security: Authorisation of Use of Force by the UN Security Council', *European Journal of International Law*, 5, 1994, pp. 492–531.

Gilboa, Eytan, 'The Panama Invasion Revisited: Lessons for the Use of Force in the Post Cold War Era', *Political Science Quarterly*, 110, 4, 1995–96.

Goodman, Glenn W., Jr., 'Rebuilding Bosnia: Army Civil Affairs and PSYOP Personnel Play Critical Nonmilitary Role in Operation Joint Endeavor', *Armed Forces Journal International*, February 1997.

Herbst, Jeffrey, 'Alternatives to the Current Nation-States in Africa', *International Security*, 21, 3, Winter 1996/7.

von Hippel, Karin, 'Sunk in the Sahara: the Applicability of the Sunk Cost Effect to Irredentist Disputes', *Journal of North African Studies*, 1, 1, Summer 1996.

'The Resurgence of Nationalism and its International Implications', in Brad Roberts, ed., *Order and Disorder After the Cold War*, Cambridge, MA, CSIS, MIT Press, 1995 (previously published in *The Washington Quarterly*, 17, 4, Autumn 1994).

Hoffman, Stanley, 'The Politics and Ethics of Military Intervention', *Survival*, 37, 4, Winter 1995–96.

Huntington, Samuel P. 'The Clash of Civilizations?', *Foreign Affairs*, Summer 1993.

Jan, Ameen, 'Peacebuilding in Somalia', IPA Policy Briefing Series, New York, International Peace Academy, July 1996.

Klein, Jacques Paul, 'The Prospects for Eastern Croatia: the Significance of the UN's Undiscovered Mission', *RUSI Journal*, April 1997.

Maren, Michael, 'Feeding a Famine', Forbes MediaCritic, Fall 1994.

Mayall, James, 'Nationalism and International Security After the Cold War', *Survival*, Spring 1992.

'Sovereignty, Nationalism and Self-Determination', *Political Studies*, 47, 1999.

Maynes, Charles William, 'Relearning Intervention', *Foreign Policy*, Spring 1995.

Menkhaus, Ken, 'International Peacebuilding and the Dynamics of Local and

National Reconciliation in Somalia', *International Peacekeeping*, 3, 1, Spring 1996.

Olonisakin, 'Funmi, 'African "Home-Made" Peacekeeping Initiatives', *Armed Forces and Society*, 23, 3, Spring 1997.

'UN Co-operation with Regional Organizations in Peacekeeping: EOMOG and UNOMIL in Liberia', *International Peacekeeping*, 3, 3, 1996.

Pasic, Amir and Weiss, Thomas G., 'The Politics of Rescue: Yugoslavia's Wars and the Humanitarian Impulse', *Ethics and International Affairs*, 11, 1997.

'Peace Building – Its Price and Its Profits', *Foreign Service Journal*, June 1967.

Powell, Colin L., 'US Forces: Challenges Ahead', *Foreign Affairs*, 72, 5, Winter 1992–93.

Roberts, Adam, 'From San Francisco to Sarajevo: The UN and the Use of Force', *Survival*, 37, 4, Winter 1995–96.

Sharp, Jane M.O., 'Dayton Report Card', *International Security*, 22, 3, Winter 1997/98.

'Intervention in Bosnia: The Case For', *The World Today*, February 1993.

'If not NATO, Who?', *The Bulletin of the Atomic Scientists*, October 1992.

Sommer, John G., 'Hope Restored? Humanitarian Aid in Somalia, 1990–1994', Refugee Policy Group, November 1994.

Weiss, Thomas G. and Pasic, Amir, 'Reinventing UNHCR: Enterprising Humanitarians in the Former Yugoslavia, 1991–1995', *Global Governance*, 3, 1, January–April 1997.

Woodward, Susan, 'Bosnia after Dayton: Year Two', *Current History*, 96, 608, March 1997.

Yannis, Alexandros, 'State Collapse and Prospects for Political Reconstruction and Democratic Governance in Somalia', *African Yearbook of International Law*, 5, 1997.

NEWSPAPERS, MAGAZINES AND WIRE SERVICES CONSULTED

Agence Haïtienne de Presse (AHP)
Associated Press
The Atlantic Monthly
The Carter Center News
The Courier
The Economist
Foreign Broadcast Information Service (FBIS)
The International Herald Tribune
The Times
The Miami Herald
The New Yorker
Reuters
Voice of America
War Report
The Washington Post

OFFICIAL DOCUMENTS

UN documents (including UNOSOM documents, Security Council reports and resolutions, General Assembly reports and resolutions, and Secretary General reports, and other information released by the UN).

United Nations Mission in Haiti (UNMIH), Mid-Mission Assessment Report, April 1995–February 1996, The Lessons-Learned Unit, DPKO, New York, March 1996.

Managing Arms in Peace Processes: Haiti, United Nations Institute for Disarmament Research, Disarmament and Conflict Resolution Project, UN, Geneva, 1996.

Adibe, Clement, *Managing Arms in Peace Processes: Somalia,* United Nations Institute for Disarmament Research, Geneva, 1995.

The United Nations and Somalia (1992–1996), The United Nations, Blue Books Series, Volume VIII, Department of Public Information of the United Nations, New York, 1996.

Comprehensive Report on Lessons-Learned from United Nations Operation in Somalia, April 1992–March 1995, Friedrich Ebert Stiftung, Germany; Life and Peace Institute, Sweden; Norwegian Institute of International Affairs; in Cooperation with the Lessons-Learned Unit of the Department of Peacekeeping Operations, UN, New York, December 1995.

European Commission documents.

United States government press releases, speeches and other official documents.

Shalikashvili, John M., Chairman of the Joint Chiefs of Staff, 'National Military Strategy, Shape, Respond, Prepare Now – A Military Strategy for a New Era', 1997.

Tarnoff, Curt, 'The Marshall Plan: Design, Accomplishments, and Relevance to the Present', Congressional Research Service, Report For Congress, First Published 6 January 1997.

Letter to the Somali National Salvation Council from George B. Moose, US Assistant Secretary of State, 30 July 1997.

Anthony Lake, Assistant to the President for National Security Affairs, Remarks at George Washington University, 'Defining Missions, Setting Deadlines: Meeting New Security Challenges in the Post-Cold War World', 6 March 1996.

OAS documents and resolutions.

Addis Ababa Agreement of the First Session of the Conference on National Reconciliation in Somalia, 27 March 1993.

Draft Transitional Charter of Somalia, Mogadishu, 1 November 1993.

CONFERENCE PAPERS

Bojicic, Vesna, Kaldor, Mary, and Vejvoda, Ivan, 'Post-War Reconstruction in the Balkans', Sussex European Institute Working Paper No. 14, November 1995.

Caplan, Richard, 'The EU's Recognition Policy Towards Republics of Former

Yugoslavia', paper presented at the IPPR Seminars on the European Union and Former Yugoslavia, 24–28 November 1995.

Davis, Ian, 'Defining Roles for Military and Civilian Authorities in Disasters linked to Development Planning', paper presented at *Defence, Disaster, Development: Security in the Third Millennium*, 15–16 December 1997, Prague, Czech Republic.

Gow, James, 'Bosnia – A Safe Area: In the Twilight Zone of Policy', paper presented at the IPPR Seminars on the European Union and Former Yugoslavia, 24–28 November 1995.

Licklider, Roy, 'State Building After Invasion: Somalia and Panama', Presented at the International Studies Association annual convention, San Diego, CA, April 1996.

Loza, Tihomir, 'EU Contribution to the International Conference on Former Yugoslavia, 1992–1994: The Vance–Owen Plan', paper presented at the IPPR Seminars on the European Union and Former Yugoslavia, 24–28 November 1995.

Sharp, Jane M.O. and Clarke, Michael, 'Making Dayton Work: The Future of the Bosnian Peace Process', London, Centre for Defence Studies, 4 December 1996.

Yannis, Alexandros, 'Perspectives for Democratic Governance in Somalia', paper presented at the 6th International Congress of Somali Studies, Berlin, Germany, 6–9 December 1996.

Index